'I must now turne the course of my journey another way, unto the rest of the BRIGANTES, who were planted on the further side of the Hilles toward the Irish Sea: and first unto LANCA-SHIRE, which I goe unto (God speede mee well) after a sort somewhat against my will: For I feare me that I shall not satisfie my selfe, and much lesse the Reader. For very few things fell out to my desire, when I travailed over the greatest part thereof, the old names in every place have beene so worne out by the continuall assault of Time. But least I might bee thought to neglect the hearty good *Lanca-shire* men, I will proceed, in hope that Gods assistance, which hitherto hath been favourable unto me, will not now faile me.'

The opening of William Camden's description of Lancashire in his *Britannia*, from the first English translation by Philemon Holland (London, 1610).

'It is a Country replenished with all necessaries for the use of man, yeelding without any great labour the commodity of corne, flax, grasse, coales, and such like. The Sea also adding her blessing to the Land, that the people of that Province want nothing that serves either for the sustenance of nature, or the satietie of appetite. They are plentifully furnished with all sorts of fish, flesh and fowles. Their principall fuell is Coale and Turfe, which they have in greate abundance; the Gentlemen reserving their woods very carefully, as a beauty and principall ornament to their Manors and Houses. And though it be far from *London* (the capitall Citie of this Kingdom) yet doth it every yeere furnish her and many other parts of the Land besides, with many thousands of cattell (bred in this Country) giving thereby and otherwaies a firme testimony to the world, of the blessed abundance it hath pleased God to inrich this noble Dukedome withall.'

Part of the description of Lancashire in 1612 by John Speed on the verso of the Lancashire map in *The Theatre of the Empire of Great Britaine* (London, 1612).

'The air of this county in general is more serene than that of any other maritime county in England, so that the inhabitants are strong and healthy, except near the fens and sea shore, where sulphurous and saline effluvia, which on the approach of storms are extremely fetid, produce fever, scurvies, consumptions, rheumatisms, and dropsies. There are also certain tracts in the more inland parts of the county, which the inhabitants call mosses, that are moist and unwholesome.'

From the article on Lancashire in the anonymous text for *England Illustrated* printed by Robert and James Dodsley (London, 1764).

AUTHOR'S PREFACE

This section contains some background information and notes likely to be helpful to all readers. The literature of cartography is vast and there is an abundance of further reading, as indicated in the Bibliography at the end, where the general reference works are only a small recommended selection from the huge number available. It would have made this book unbearably pedantic if I had attempted to give the origin of all my information on the maps and to justify every detail included here. So references and footnotes have been kept to a minimum and in particular relate to points which are not discussed elsewhere in the literature in any great detail. Although the main text should be self-explanatory, some special topics have been treated separately, in boxes scattered through the text, as listed in the Contents.

Almost all authors of books on maps feel obliged to quote at least part of an apt passage from John Speed, '... it may be objected that I have put my sickle into other men's corn, and have laid my building on other men's foundations (as indeed who can do otherwise, especially in a subject of this nature ...)'.[1] Like them I freely confess that much information here was first planted and nurtured by others and has been taken from secondary sources, such as the volumes on *County Atlases of the British Isles* by R.A. Skelton and D. Hodson, *British County Maps* by Y. Beresiner, and many other reference compilations consulted (some listed in the Bibliography) right back to William Harrison in 1907. When doubt arose I have sought out the original sources to check the statements of those compilers and in this way many errors and false assumptions have been detected and corrected. For information supplied privately I am grateful in particular to Philip Burden, Doreen Green, Stephen Luck and Bill Shannon. Much was gained recently from the great store of new detail in *British Map Engravers* by Laurence Worms and Ashley Baynton-Williams. Corrections of any surviving inaccuracies from knowledgeable and alert readers will be most welcome. Of course I accept full personal responsibility for all such faults.

'Geography is about maps, but Biography is about chaps' is another frequently found quotation.[2] This book covers both aspects by discussing not only the maps, but also the chaps who made the maps. Hopefully this will add to the interest of the text, even if for some it will be totally irrelevant that John Speed had eighteen children or that Jan Jansson was the son-in-law of Jodocus Hondius. The sequence followed in the text is basically chronological, in the order of first publication of the map in almost all cases, but all later reprinting (and some of the copying by others) is discussed along with each map described, making a simple linear time thread impossible. The Speed map, for example, has a history extending over nearly 200 years and when presenting that story in chapter 3 it is necessary to cross-reference with maps and chaps treated both earlier and later in the text sequence. Occasional obscurities at such points may be resolved via the index. It is a much less satisfactory alternative to split the story of each map into separate instalments on every printing, scattered throughout the chapters in strict date order. I have also deviated from exact chronology where strong logical links suggest maps would be better discussed together in the text. Such exceptions are clearly seen in the chronological table given as Appendix 1 and indicated also in Appendix 2, which shows those links between the maps.

Lengths and weights are usually quoted in both metric and old Imperial units. Map sizes are quoted as width followed by height (as normally viewed), and are the dimensions of the mapped area itself, not including any decorative borders or additions in margins, such as imprints and titles. Sizes have been measured across the centre of each map because some maps are not exactly rectangular; in particular the Saxton map width is 5mm less across the foot than at the top, presumably due to an error when cutting the copper sheet accepted by the engraver. Dimensions are quoted to the nearest millimetre, but it must be remembered that after printing the wet paper could shrink or stretch to make sizes vary somewhat between specimens. Map scales are given in miles per inch, and in Appendix 3 there is a conversion list for those who prefer a different measure for that.

In various places estimates are included of the costs of making maps and atlases, and prices charged for them by the publishers are sometimes quoted. Here shillings and pence as originally specified (at twenty shillings to the pound and twelve pence to the shilling) are converted into anachronistic decimal currency. Equivalent cost estimates suggested for today are only approximate. There is no way to be exact in such conversion, as over the centuries each commodity has had price inflation to different degrees. Even recently the changes vary in this way. An inflation factor of seventeen over the past 50 years is given by the official calculation.[3] This is true enough for motor cars and clothes, but from my own experience I note that a Hallé Orchestra concert ticket costs about 50 times as much as in 1964 and a paperback book is 30 times as expensive, as is a pint of beer. However, the price of a bottle of ordinary wine is only a factor of four higher and a small TV costs the same in cash as it did fifty years ago, despite being improved beyond any comparison. Hence there is no way to make easy conversions based on, say, Falstaff's bar bill.

International comparison of prices is even more suspect.[4] Our credit-based cashless economy is not new, but is a reversion to early practices before reliable money was in circulation. In records from the sixteenth or seventeenth century the costs and prices are stated in purely notional 'florins', used for accountancy and transfer payments across the various European Countries. Though nothing was constant, for those two

PRINTED MAPS OF LANCASHIRE:

the first two hundred years

by Ian Saunders

Centre for North-West Regional Studies
Lancaster University
2013
Series Editor: Sam Riches

Printed Maps of Lancashire: the first two hundred years

This volume is Number 6 in the New Series of Resource Papers published by
the Centre for North-West Regional Studies at Lancaster University

Designed, typeset, printed and bound by
Badger Press Ltd., Bowness-on-Windermere, Cumbria

British Library Cataloguing-in-Publication Data
A CIP catalogue record for this book is available from the British Library

ISBN 978-1-86220-307-5

Cover: detail of Fig.22, Map 3H: 'Lancastria Palatinatus, Anglis Lancaster et
Lancas shire' (1645) by Johan Blaeu, from *Theatrum Orbis Terrarum, sive Atlas
Novus* (perhaps 1648), reproduced at near original scale on the back with
cartouches from (top) Fig.58, Map 5R: 'The County Palatine of Lancaster,
surveyed by Willm Yates' (1786); (foot) Fig.23, Map 3J: 'Comitatus
Lancastrensis, The Countie Palatine of Lancaster' by Jan Jansson II, from
Appendix Atlantis to the Mercator-Hondius Atlas (1636).

Cartouche on title page: detail of Fig.24, Map 3K: 'Lancastria Palatinatus,
Anglis Lancaster & Lancas shire' second state (1646) by Jan Jansson II,
from *Novus Atlas, sive Theatrum Orbis Terrarum* (1652).

The author and publishers gratefully acknowledge the financial support of
Dr Philip Welch and Lancaster University Friends Programme.

centuries the florin was equivalent to around 10g of silver, while an English pound was 115.1g of silver before 1600 and 111.4g afterwards (until 1717). So an English pound corresponded to about ten florins.

The name 'florin' was attached to a real English coin only when the two shilling piece was created in 1849, as the initial step towards the British decimal currency achieved about 120 years later. (It is now the 10p bit and contains no silver.) The actual coins used for cash transactions in the 1500s and 1600s were diverse. Money in circulation was worn and clipped, if not actually debased by the addition of impurities, and the real value of any coin was always subject to negotiation during transactions. It was common practice to melt down any new coins occasionally received to extract the bullion value, usually greater than the face value.

Nominally a rijksdaalder or a ducat with around 25g of silver was worth two and a half florins, while a 15g carolus guilder or gulden was one and a half florins. Thus seven carolus guilders corresponded to an English pound. In 1647 a new house with garden was built in Haarlem for 150 carolus guilders, about £20. Galileo had an annual salary of 180 florins as a new professor of mathematics at the University of Padua in 1592 (increased to 1000 florins by 1609, after he had used his telescope to achieve international renown). From such meagre facts an estimate of inflation from those days till now can be attempted. As noted later, the 1570 Ortelius first world atlas was priced at 16 florins if bound and coloured, about one and a half English pounds, which was a month's income for a Tudor country parson. Hence the suggestion is made that this atlas would cost over a thousand pounds today (when country parsons have less status and wealth than in 1570). Other comparisons have been made giving equivalents for this price in the range from about £500 to £5,000. There is much uncertainty.

Some problems are completely intractable, such as the style of illustration possible for maps originally much larger than A4. These can be printed in a book of this size only in a very reduced form or as a section illustrative of the whole map. Here both methods are used for all large maps, a reduced overall view to give an impression of the whole map plus a section from it (usually small) at close to actual size to convey an impression of the quality of detail included. For convenience in making comparisons the area chosen is consistently from Lancaster southwards. To all of you with a base elsewhere in Lancashire I proffer my apologies for this choice, but one can please only some of the people, some of the time.

Where more than one date is given in figure captions, the first is when the map was first issued and any others are the dates of publication for examples shown. Most of the illustrations are from items in my own collection, built up over thirty years of obsession with the antique maps of my adopted county, but for a few other rare specimens I must very

gratefully acknowledge the assistance of Philip Burden, Chris Abram, Brian Kentish, Bill Shannon and Lancaster University Library, who provided access to items for copying and gave permission for image use in this publication. I must also record my very sincere thanks to Bill Shannon for his detailed advice and help in producing the text, to Sam Riches for her patience and aid with publication, in particular her scrupulous removal of errors and inclusion of extra details, and above all to my wife for her support and toleration of the many, many months I have spent with the maps, books and computer while writing this, and not on doing the diverse things on her long list of urgent matters needing my attention.

Old and New Dates

The Gregorian calendar was introduced in 1582 by Pope Gregory XIII, but England and many other Protestant countries continued to use the old Julian calendar, which was several days out of step and started the New Year on 25 March not 1 January. Although Scotland had adopted a 1 January New Year day in 1600, the British change to the Gregorian calendar took place in 1752, when the New Year began everywhere in the Kingdom on 1 January and Wednesday 2 September was followed by Thursday 14 September, cutting out 11 days.

Thus in the years before 1752 an event between 1 January and 24 March has an ambiguous date, sometimes indicated by the form 9 February 1713/4. This book adopts the usual practice of using the day recorded at the time, and the year as given by 'new style' starting in January. For example, the fire which destroyed Blaeu's printing business is recorded as happening on 23 February 1672 (as stated in Amsterdam by local Gregorian reckoning) rather than on 13 February 1671 (or perhaps 1671/2), as it would have been recorded in a contemporary English account using the Julian calendar, while for an event on the same day in England the date would be written here as 13 February 1672.[5]

NOTES

1. From the Preface to *The Theatre of the Empire of Great Britaine*, by John Speed (Sudbury & Humble, London, 1612).

2. Introductory Remarks in *Biography for Beginners* by G.K. Chesterton and E.Clerihew Bentley (T.W. Laurie, London, 1905)

3. Inflation estimates since 1750 can be found from the composite price index, J.O'Donoghue, L.Goulding and G.Allen, *Consumer Price Inflation Since 1750*, Economics Trends 604, Office for National Statistics (London, 2004), in particular via the Bank of England inflation calculator http://www.bankofengland.co.uk/education/Pages/inflation/calculator/how.aspx (accessed December 2012 and before).

4. For an indication of the complexities, see Rodney Edvinsson, *Foreign exchange rates in Sweden 1658-1803,* Stockholm Papers in Economic History, No. 8 (Stockholm University, 2009). http://swopec.hhs.se/suekhi (accessed December 2012).

5. The Blaeu fire is sometimes wrongly described as starting on 22 February, but actually began at 3.30am on 23 February. For a description of the fire and the financial losses involved see J. Goss, *Blaeu's The Grand Atlas...* (Studio Editions, London, 1990), p.9.

Contents

1   The Era of Gestation (up to 1550)   1
    Box 1 The Orientation of Maps   6
    Box 2 The Use of Copper Plates for Printing   7

2   The Era of Invention (1550–1600)   8
    Box 3 The First Atlases and Their Makers   8
    Box 4 The Pioneer of County Mapping   13

3   The Era of Decoration (1600–1690)   23
    Box 5 The Blaeu Amsterdam Atlases   33
    Box 6 The First English Road Mapping   43

4   The Era of Imitation (1690–1750)   47
    Box 7 The Problems of Magnetic North   49

5   The Era of Innovation (1750–1788)   64
    Box 8 The New National Mapping by Kitchin   70

APPENDIX 1
– *Tables of map details*   92

APPENDIX 2
– *The 'Family Tree' of all Lancashire maps which
descend from the Saxton survey*   101

APPENDIX 3
– *Scales for Lancashire maps*   102

PICTURE CREDITS   103

BIBLIOGRAPHY   104

INDEX   106

1   The Era of Gestation (up to 1550)

Diagrams serving as maps have been made ever since people started to draw, and surviving examples go back to rock paintings about 8000 years old. This book covers only a very small part of the great story of cartography, a single example of the county by county mapping system virtually unique to our nation as we explore the origins and evolution of printed maps of the 'County Palatine of Lancaster'. This old title reflects the direct rule of the county by the monarch as Duke of Lancaster (since 1399) and defines the historic area which is our subject, namely Lancashire in pre-1974 extent including Merseyside, Greater Manchester and Furness Fells in Cumbria (formerly Lonsdale-over-Sands). However, maps of estates, towns, or any other sub-divisions of the county are not discussed and the inclusion of Lancashire on general maps of England is not considered, apart from a few important early examples. Map printing started just after 1470 with Lancashire appearing on its own from 1577. The description here ends around 1788 with the appearance of the first map showing Lancashire at a large scale and its later history, including the first copying, leaving a large part of the story of the mapping of the county to be told in another place.

There are fascinations in any early map beyond the geographical and historical information it contains. The content selected for inclusion indicates the interests of the society when it was created, the design shows the nature of prevailing artistic tastes and the accuracy of mapping reflects the contemporary state of science. Maps reflect what is actually on the earth's surface. Surveying is performed, but with varying degrees of reliability. The selection of what to include or omit begins with the survey. Maybe at a particular scale a town would be included, but not a farmhouse. Where in between is the cut-off? In practice this is undefined and inconsistent.

Early maps were drawn on an arbitrary scale, usually chosen to suit the size of the paper (or parchment) available. One inch represented about five statute miles (around 1:330,000 scale) on the largest maps of Lancashire before 1750, allowing the inclusion of little detail. As the quality of mapping gradually improved scales became larger. By 1900 all of England was mapped at six inches per mile and almost all at 1:2500 (about 25 inches per mile), while many towns and cities had been surveyed in almost complete detail at 1:500 (nearly 11 feet per mile), requiring 304 sheets for Liverpool alone.

Methods of displaying the details selected for inclusion evolved slowly over many centuries. Today we expect north to be at the top of the map, appropriate roads to be shown and a mile to be exactly 1760 yards, but all these conventions were established slowly and are not found on the earliest maps, where the top can be east, west, north or even south, and miles are a very variable length averaging about 2400 yards. Roads and a familiar mile length began to appear on Lancashire maps only from 1676. We have learned to interpret contour lines as the clearest way to show hills and valleys, but that is a relatively recent idea for use by the public, long after the period covered here. Pictures of 'sugar-loaf' hills were used to show relief in almost all the maps included here, or various methods of shading (like the 'hairy caterpillars' on map 1B) at the very end of the two centuries.

Maps have ancestors just like people, and tracing the origins and 'family tree' of a particular map (as in Appendix 2) can be a fascinating exercise. There is romantic interest to be found in the eventful personal stories of the early map-makers, in their rivalries and occasional co-operation. The subject is endless. The problem is what to leave out. Almost every paragraph could be extended into a book (and sometimes has been). Those wanting detailed justification and a more complete story must consult the references given in notes for each chapter and the books in the final bibliography.

Originally Lancashire was mapped only as part of a larger area, and our story must begin with early maps of the British Isles. The earliest printed depictions are based on data collected by Ptolemy, an astronomer working at Alexandria from about 120AD to 160AD. Almost nothing else about Ptolemy is known with certainty, but medieval manuscript copies of his works on astronomy and astrology survived. In particular his *Geographia* established our current method of locating places by angles reckoned at the centre of the Earth, latitude measured north/south

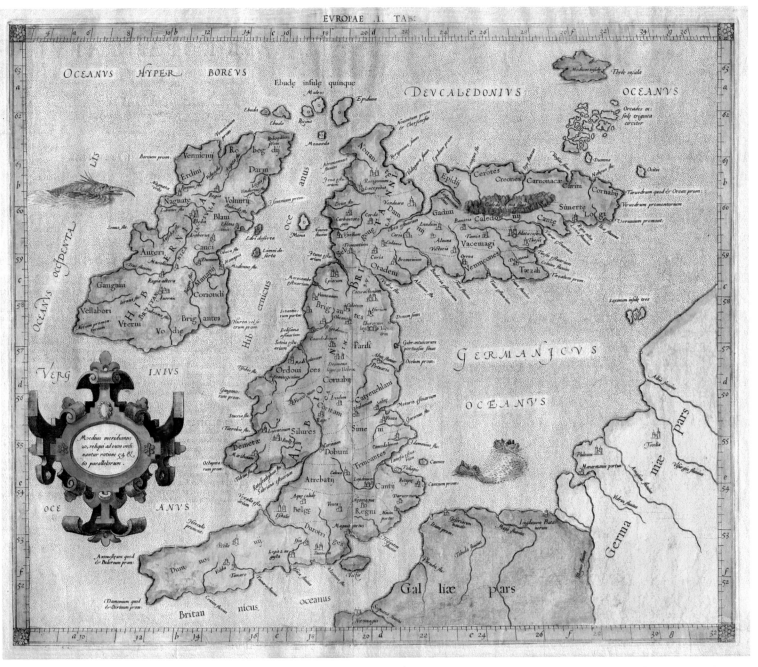

Fig. 1 Map 1A 'Europae I Tabula' by Gerardus Mercator, from *Tabulae Geographicae Cl. Ptolomaei...* (G. Kempen, Cologne, 1578). [383mm x 315mm, 15.2" x 12.4"]

from the equator and longitude measured east/west from a prime meridian running between the poles. *Geographia* catalogues latitude and longitude values for about 8000 places across the Old World, a list from which Ptolemy's maps were reconstructed and printed from the fifteenth century onwards. Map 1A (Fig. 1) appeared in the most careful edition, published in 1578 by Gerardus Mercator (discussed as a cartographer in the next chapter). Ptolemy's information on Britain, an obscure island on the edge of the world, is understandably inaccurate and very few of the places named can be identified with any certainty. For example, historians John Horsley in 1732 and John Whitaker in 1771 identified Ptolemy's 'Moricambe estuarium' with the bay containing the Lancaster and Kent Sands and hence the current name Morecambe Bay was introduced on maps and charts, but this is based on no specific evidence from Roman times.[1]

By the time of the Domesday Book (1086) many of the boundaries and settlements of what would become the County Palatine of Lancaster were established. Alas, no original maps from these times have survived. Indeed it is not totally certain that any existed, though it seems likely. Map 1B (Fig. 2) showing 'Lancashire ... According to the Doomsday Survey' was produced in 1831 by John and Charles Walker from what meagre evidence was available. As for other large maps illustrated in this book at reduced size, a strip extending south from Lancaster is included at close to actual size to indicate the detail on the original map, very scanty here in the area south of the Ribble which was devastated during the Norman invasion. But it would be wrong to think this map shows the boundaries of Lancashire in 1086, or even to think that the county then existed as a unit. North of Amounderness the lands of Earl Tostig formed part of Yorkshire, from which Lonsdale and Kendal were extracted when division into Hundreds was evolving for county administration. The origin of the name 'Hundred' is obscure, but may refer to an area supporting a hundred households, or one required to supply a hundred warriors to the army if summoned in emergencies. Some counties have other terms for such divisions of the shire, like Ward or Wapentake.

Lancashire was a late addition to the partitioning of England into Shires, emerging from the Royal Honour of Lancaster by 1168. Some Lancashire Hundreds were merged in the twelfth century, leaving only six, namely Lonsdale, Amounderness, Blackburn, Leyland, West Derby and Salford (as indicated on Map 1B). To the

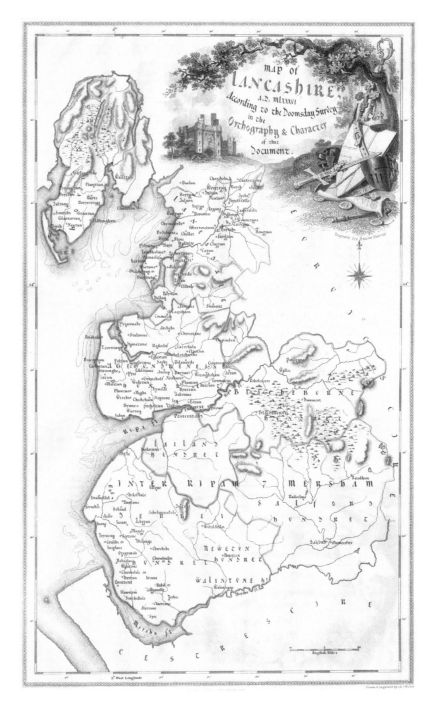

Fig. 2 Map 1B 'Lancashire A.D.1086. According to the Doomsday Survey...' by J. and C. Walker (1831), from *History of the County... of Lancaster* by Edward Baines (Fisher, Son & Co., London, 1836). [207mm x 349mm, 8.1" x 13.7"]

confusion of many map-makers, Lonsdale Hundred was in two separate parts, north and south of the Sands, communicating via the short (but perilous) route across Morecambe Bay. Sometimes the isolated northern part was referred to wrongly as Furness (Fells) Hundred, probably via confusion on an unpublished map (2K in Fig. 12) used by John Speed when designing his Lancashire map (3C in Fig. 16, printed in 1612), where the Hundred boundaries first appeared in print. By that time Hundreds had little real function, although until 1886 they were responsible for any damage done by rioters and never have been formally abolished as county divisions. They were shown on maps until the Victorian era.

The original design for a map might be drawn entirely from a new survey, but nearly always incorporates details from previous maps and often is totally copied from previous work. For wide circulation that manuscript draft must be copied. Before printing was invented the only possibility was a laboriously hand-copied duplicate, making complex maps rare, unreliable and very expensive. However, it is probable that manuscript maps of many types were in general use for local and national administration, though very few survive today. A notable one for Lancashire is Lord Burghley's map showing the houses of gentlemen with notes on their probable loyalty.[2]

Fascinating as many manuscript maps are, here we can include only the most detailed surviving early map of Britain, usually known as the 'Gough Map' (after the owner who first made it known). This manuscript was drawn in 1360-70 on two joined sheets of vellum (calf-skin) to show England, Wales and Scotland, with east at the top. We know nothing about the author. The original map is now in the Bodleian Library and is almost illegible, but careful studies using infra-red and ultraviolet light have clarified most of the details and replica copies have been published.[3]

The area from the Mersey to Hadrian's Wall as shown on the Gough map is sketched in Fig. 3, with place-names in modern form. The coastline is almost straight with rivers running parallel inland, in particular omitting Morecambe Bay, a form copied on maps until 1550. The lines joining places are probably main travel routes, though elsewhere on the map this is less certain, with distances noted in old miles of about 2500 yards (originally in Roman numbers). Two routes from the south into Lancashire are indicated, one through Warrington to Carlisle via Preston and Lancaster (now the A6) used from Roman times, and one from Chester to Liverpool via the Mersey ferry run by Birkenhead Priory.

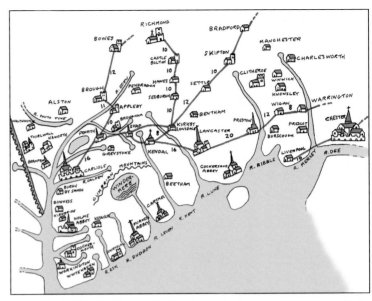

Fig. 3 North-West England on the Gough manuscript map, 1360-70, now in the Bodleian Library, as a sketch by the author with modern place-names, based on the frontispiece in Whitaker's *Descriptive List...* (1938).

There are also two familiar ways from Yorkshire, both entering Lancashire via Kirkby Lonsdale, and one from Westmorland via Kendal. It is likely that manuscripts similar to the Gough map existed for official use in various parts of the country and copies circulated among scholars, of which a late example, once owned by King Henry VIII, is the *Anglia Figura* of *c.*1540.[4]

Fifteenth- and sixteenth-century maps in Northern Europe were often printed from woodcuts, where most of a flat wooden surface was cut away to define details via thin raised lines, which were coated with ink and pressed on the page to print the image. Carving small delicate text letters on woodcuts is virtually impossible and the lettering for place-names was cast on thin metal strips and glued to the wood, or metal type was inserted into slots cut in the block. The main advantage of a woodcut is that in a single press such illustrations (including maps) can be printed along with text set in metal type. The woodcut method was used to produce editions of Ptolemy's *Geographia* from 1482, particularly in Germany. The Italian editions in general were copper plate engravings.

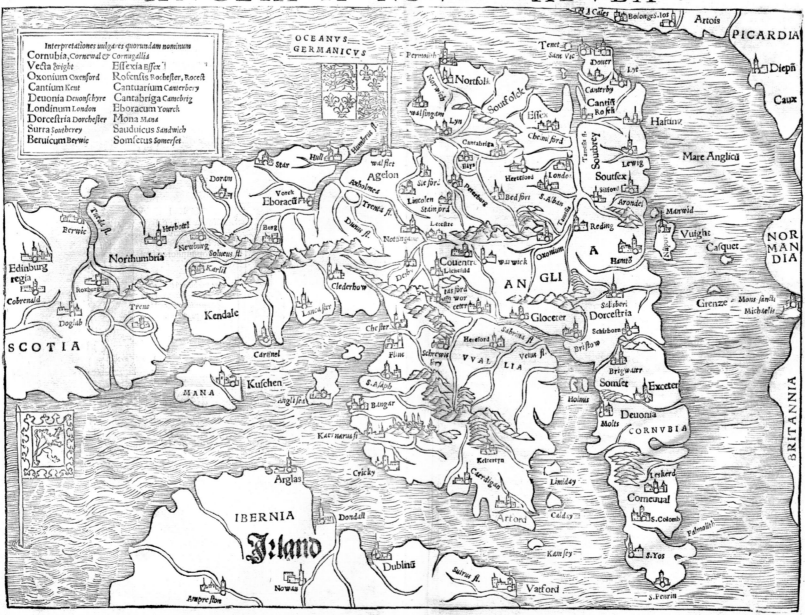

Fig. 4 Map 1C 'Anglia II Nova Tabula' woodcut from *Ptolemy's Geographia* by Sebastian Münster (H. Petri, Basle, 1540). [337mm x 247mm, 13.3" x 9.7"]

A little modern knowledge was introduced by some editors of Ptolemy, but the Basle edition produced from 1540 by Sebastian Münster (1489-1552) was unusual in containing genuinely modern maps, in particular the first printed maps of the continents, and a map 1C of England and Wales (Fig. 4) oriented with east at the top (see Box 1 on orientation) and with a coastal outline based on a source similar to the 'Gough' map. This was the best printed map of England available in 1540, with Cartmel, Lancaster and Clitheroe shown for the first time. The sea contains wave-like lines (hard to carve in wood) copying early manuscript style. It is included here for historic interest and to emphasise the rapid progress achieved by map-makers and printers soon after 1540, when everywhere copper plate engraving took over from crude woodcuts.

Many people can be involved in producing a set of maps, and the overlapping roles have been combined or shared in every possible way. The team could include a sponsoring financier, the surveyor and assistants, the compiler and map designer, the engraver, an author of explanatory text, publishers, printers, binders and retailers. For almost all maps the names of most people involved are unknown and the 'authorship' name used to identify a map or atlas can vary over any of the roles listed above in a very confusing fashion. Most suitably it is the map designer, but credit may be given to the engraver or the publisher, as often their names are put on the plate. The nominal authorship can be arbitrary and some rare maps are labelled with the name of a recorded owner, like 'Gough' for map 1B, which is also referred to as 'the Bodleian map' as if that great library in Oxford owned only one.

Decorative colour, familiar on manuscripts, was added to many early maps by hand-painting, using established conventions like the red for habitations derived from Roman tiled roofs. There were a few very early experiments with woodcut printing in colour, but these produced such crude effects compared to the familiar hand colouring that maps were not printed in colour again until after 1820. Many examples selected for the illustrations in this book are in 'original' hand colouring, done at the time of publication, which is not common. Most old maps were coloured later in old style, as is still being done today to suit map collectors.

Apart from a few clearly defined exceptions, like the woodcut 1C, all the maps illustrated in this book were printed using copper plates in a slow and complex operation, restricting production to

BOX 1   THE ORIENTATION OF MAPS

It can be hard to recognise the region shown if north is not at the top of a map, as in the 1540 woodcut of Fig. 4. However, north upwards is just a handy convention, imprinted by all the examples seen from our childhood, and exceptions to that format are found even today. At the beginning of map printing readers had no pre-existing expectation. Many early manuscript maps such as the *Mappa Mundi* at Hereford have east at the top, a convention thought to derive from the importance of the Garden of Eden being east of Jerusalem. Christian churches have the altar at the east end and from the Latin for east, 'Oriens', we get *orient* and *orientation* for this relative placement, though these words were used only after 1700.

The top is north on pre-Christian maps in Ptolemy's *Geographia* printed around 1500, starting a modern convention further emphasised by geographers using globes invariably with the north pole at the top. By the mid-seventeenth century a north orientation on the page had become standard on county maps, following the examples of Saxton and Speed who almost always used a north orientation. The exact relation of these maps to true north is discussed in Box 7 on Magnetic North.

In some cases the major factor determining orientation is the shape of the land depicted. Since Lancashire (like Britain) is somewhat long and narrow, the county can be shown at a significantly larger scale by turning it with north at one side across a double page spread, almost doubling the effective area for showing detail. Thus when William Smith drew Lancashire with west at the top for map 2K (Fig. 12), he could use a scale of just over four statute miles per inch rather than Saxton's five miles per inch. A very late example of the same unusual orientation is included as map 4L (Fig. 41). South at the top is rare, but not unknown.

Of course lettering and titles on a map can be viewed in a direction different from that used to read the main text. If the reader is willing to revolve the book through a right angle to view an illustration, maps can be placed across a double page with north at whatever side becomes the top after rotation, usually the left. This concept, now obvious, was applied to county maps for the first time by Richard Blome in 1673 (Fig. 27), and to full folio-sized maps by Robert Morden in eight cases for the Gibson edition of *Britannia* in 1695.

Many later mapmakers used a similar page layout for tall counties, to optimise scale on a given page size. Turning the book through 90° is not hard with a small volume such as the Blome county atlas. However, there is much more awkwardness and difficulty in performing such rotation with an open folio atlas like Gibson's *Britannia*, measuring about 600mm x 450mm (24" x 18") and weighing over 4kg [9lbs]. So for most large atlases north orientation in normal viewing is the standard format.

at most a few hundred copies in each edition (see Box 2). Thus all early maps are effectively 'limited edition prints' and maps were not common items. Also it is estimated that at least three quarters of all the maps ever printed have been destroyed by wear and tear of use, fire, paper rot and many other hazards. Some printed maps are known from a single survivor and others only from references to their existence, all originals having perished. Another problem is that many early atlases were 'broken' into individual original maps for sale to collectors. Today this is done only if an atlas is disintegrating and incomplete, as whole early atlases are so rare they are now worth more than the sum of their parts, but an unfortunate effect of previous practice is that for many loose maps the exact provenance is uncertain (prompting interesting detective work).

Most maps were reissued several times from the same engraved plate, perhaps revised slightly or even altered so much as to seem totally different. Occasionally a different but almost identical new plate was copied from the original. Authorship and exact date of printing can be unknown, unclear or quoted incorrectly. Complexity and confusion are normal. All these factors lead to a regrettable but inevitable vagueness in the discussion of some maps. The Bibliography indicates some of many specialised reference works written to aid identification of old maps, while Appendices 1 and 2 give further guidance.

NOTES

1   See William D. Shannon, 'From Morikambe to Morecambe: Antiquarians, Periploi and Eischuseis', *Transactions of the Cumberland & Westmorland Antiquarian & Archaeological Society*, Third Series, 12 (2012), 37-54, and the original Horsley and Whitaker references in the Bibliography.

2   William Shannon & Michael Winstanley, 'Lord Burghley's Map of Lancashire Revisited, *c.*1576-1590', *Imago Mundi*, 59:1 (2007), 24-42.

3   View online at www.goughmap.org and printed copies via the Bodleian Library; part as frontispiece in H. Whitaker, *Maps of Lancashire 1577-1900* (Manchester University Press and the Chetham Society, Manchester, 1938).

4   British Library, Cotton MS Augustus I.i.9; shown in C. Delano-Smith and R.J.P. Kain, *English Maps: a History* (British Library, London, 1999) p.62.

BOX 2   THE USE OF COPPER PLATES FOR PRINTING

This method was used for almost all map production until 1820. In the 1470s Italian goldsmiths had applied established skills to engrave copper plates for map printing, allowing more size and subtlety than competing methods, but printing required a rolling press completely different from the style used to print with woodcuts or raised metal type. Using two separate presses increased the complexity and expense of illustrating books, but improved quality and raised sales. Many weeks of meticulous work went into making the finest plates. Lines of varying depth and width were cut into a finely polished copper surface using a sharp steel blade, allowing very fine detail and delicate decoration to be included. Apprentices attended to some of the routine details, such as drawing borders and shading, but the finest map work was done by artists as skilful as any other craftsmen.

In some cases lines were etched by acid through scratches in a wax coating, but this was uncommon for maps, as was indenting letters or standard symbols into the copper using a punch, though even in the fifteenth century both methods were sometimes used. The title, distance scale and various notes were placed within elaborate decorative frames called 'cartouches', offering free scope for artistic design in the fashion of the day. Engraving skill was sorely tested to show geographical features clearly and to label those features unambiguously in tiny uniform script. All engraving was done with left and right reversed in 'mirror writing', difficult in particular for small lettering in the many place-names, but proficient engravers made few errors. An intricate large plate required so much work it was hugely expensive, the equivalent of several thousand pounds in today's terms.

The copper plate was heated and covered with thick sticky ink, then rubbed clean, leaving ink only inside the incised lines. In the rolling press damp paper was squeezed very hard against the plate to pick up the image. There is a 'plate mark' around the map at the edge of the paper compressed by the copper, which should be looked for as a sign of authenticity. Early plates were kept as small as possible to reduce cost, with very narrow blank margins between the engraved area and the plate mark (as on Fig. 1).

Correction and improvement involved gentle hammering on the back of a plate to raise an erroneous area slightly, then polishing off unwanted features to restore flatness before inserting new details. Thus plates were used in successive 'states', sometimes unrecognisably related to the first issue. Fine engraved details disappeared after only a few hundred uses of the plate, worn away during inking, but re-emphasising lines by deepening the grooves could 'retouch' or 'refresh' a worn plate. Sometimes plates cracked and were repaired by riveting. All such signs of age help in dating the printing. Eventually worn-out or obsolete plates were sold as scrap copper for recycling.

2   The Era of Invention (1550–1600)

THE PUBLICATION OF THE FIRST ATLAS

New measuring instruments were developed to advance surveying methods and expand cartographic activity in the sixteenth century. Scale plans became more common, based on plane table plotting of measured directions from a baseline of known length, while the next century saw greater precision through more careful triangulation.[1] Printing made the use of maps more familiar to the educated and by 1550 demand was increasing. From then until about 1680 the centre of world map production was firmly established in the Netherlands, the rich hub of world trade. At Antwerp in 1570 Abraham Ortelius (1527-1598) published the first example of what we now call an 'Atlas', defined as a volume containing maps all by a single publisher at a uniform size, printed and bound as a coherent description of an area ranging from the world to a single country. Ortelius called his book *Theatrum Orbis Terrarum* (Theatre of the World) and for the next century 'Theatre' competed with 'Atlas' as the defining title for a book of maps (see Box 3).

Ortelius compiled data from many sources and commissioned well-decorated map plates in his recognisable individual character, many engraved by Frans Hogenberg (1535-1590). The Ortelius plates were used for about 45 editions of the *Theatrum* from 1570 until 1612, with the printed text on the back of maps and on extra pages newly typeset for each edition, in various languages including English in 1606. Like nearly all early maps the plates themselves had wording in Latin, the language of scholars in all nations. About 7300 individual Ortelius atlases were created in many separate editions, typically of 50 to 500 copies.[2]

The first edition contained only 70 maps, including one of the British Isles, but by 1600 the atlas had nearly tripled in size. A map of England and Wales (2A, Fig. 5) was introduced in 1573. It is based on information from Humphrey Lhuyd (1527-1568) and hugely improved relative to Fig. 4, but inaccuracies are obvious,

BOX 3   THE FIRST ATLASES AND THEIR MAKERS

Abraham Ortelius (1527-1598) started as a map colourist, working with his sister to hand-paint maps to clarify and decorate them, a respected profession still practised today. He branched out into book dealing, with making and selling maps becoming his main interest, and in 1570 he produced *Theatrum Orbis Terrarum*, the most expensive book published by then, costing six florins for the uncoloured set of map sheets, or as a bound hand-coloured atlas sixteen florins, two month's wages for a skilled craftsman and equivalent to over a thousand pounds today. Ortelius sold atlases mainly as status symbols for kings, dukes and similarly rich customers throughout Europe. He never married and had no sons to inherit the business on his death. The map plates passed to Jan Baptiste Vrients (1552-1612), who replaced some for his late editions of the atlas, including a fine new map of England.

Gerardus Mercator (1512-1594) was a close friend and colleague of Ortelius and unique in combining so many roles in map publishing. He was a perfectionist, taking many years to collect all available information, carefully collating and evaluating details, designing and engraving his own superb maps with exquisite delicacy. He even invented new forms of script ('copper-plate writing') to improve legibility and clarity, described in his treatise on handwriting printed in 1540.*

From 1569 Mercator concentrated on designing and making plates for his major work, *Atlas, sive Cosmographicae Meditationes de Fabrica Mundi ...* (i.e. 'Atlas, or Thoughts of a Cosmographer on the Creation of the World ...'), named in honour of a mythical creator of the first globe map, 'the Titan, Atlas, King of Mauritania, a learned philosopher, mathematician and astronomer'. This multi-volume world history and geography had his 1578 edition of Ptolemy's *Geographia* and an account of the Creation as the opening, with volumes of modern maps as continuation, but it was far from complete when Mercator died in 1594. In 1595 his son Rumold (1545-99) issued the remaining finished maps (including Britain) and collected his father's maps into the Mercator 'Atlas', but though a lot more accurate than the Ortelius *Theatrum*, it covered only the main parts of Europe, contained fewer much less decorative maps, and was almost as expensive. So it had limited appeal for the general public.

In 1604 Mercator's grandchildren sold the plates to Jodocus Hondius (1563-1612), who expanded and decorated what became the 'Mercator-Hondius Atlas'. By 1606 this contained 144 maps and was so successful that the Ortelius/Vrients *Theatrum* stopped publication in 1612, the year in which Jodocus Hondius died, leaving development of his atlas to his sons and son-in-law Jan Jansson (1588-1664). The 'Mercator-Hondius-Jansson Atlas' dominated the luxury trade until about 1640.

* Reproduced in *Mercator*, by A.S. Osley, Faber and Faber (London, 1969).

Fig. 5 Map 2A 'Angliae Regni Florentissimi Nova Descriptio...' by Humphrey Lhuyd (1573), from *Theatrum Orbis Terrarum* by Abraham Ortelius (C. Plantin, Antwerp, 1592). [448mm x 364mm, 17.5" x 14.4"]

such as the almost straight Lancashire coastline from the Kent to the Mersey, Clapham in the centre of Bowland Forest and reversed quartering in the royal coat-of-arms. Considerable mapping errors are not surprising when information on Lancashire from a Welshman was edited by a Belgian and engraved by a German.

After Ortelius died in 1598 the atlas was issued by his heirs for three years, then Jan Baptist Vrients (1552-1612) bought the plates and rights of publication. Although Vrients expanded the atlas with a few new maps, including one of England, its design was too old-fashioned to attract sales, via the very features which make the maps so attractive to us today. At the start of the seventeenth century quaint antiquity had no appeal and the Ortelius atlas prospered only while it had no rivals.

THE COMPLETE CARTOGRAPHER

Gerardus Mercator (1512-1594) was the most important cartographer since Ptolemy and arguably of all time. He contributed greatly towards establishing map-making as a science, particularly via 'Mercator's projection', still used to construct a high proportion of our maps. Mercator founded the first great family map-making firm, with sons and grandsons joining him in engraving maps for his lifelong task, an atlas which began with the Ptolemy edition of 1578 (map 1A) and continued with sections on modern geography issued from 1585. It was not until 1595, just after the great man's death, that his family published that first eponymous 'Atlas', so establishing the name now employed to describe all books of maps (see Box 3). The final section of Mercator's Atlas contained regional maps of England based on the Christopher Saxton wall-map of 1583, including map 2B (Fig. 6) showing our North-West region in bright colouring contemporary with its 1595 printing.

The superb work of the famous cartographer is well displayed here, especially in the full size section of the map. Sea-shading laboriously engraved in subtle 'shot-silk' style gives a spectacular impression of waves, perhaps inspired by the wavy lines introduced by Münster for sea areas in imitation of manuscript maps, and the sea coast is emphasised with the short horizontal shading lines used for many years on most maps. An emphatic title cartouche is present on the left, but the only other decoration is the almost obligatory

sea-monster in the Irish Sea (itself copied from the Mercator map 1A in Fig. 1). Geographical accuracy is emphasised by edge calibrations showing latitude (about 1° too far north) and longitude using a prime meridian in the Canary Islands at the western edge of the old world, as introduced by Ptolemy. Though the spelling often differs from modern practice, place-names are nearly all correct, evidence of Mercator's perfectionism, which included adding small 'tails' onto many circular location symbols, pointing towards the correct adjacent name, greatly reducing ambiguities. Unfortunately this practice was not copied subsequently.

The maps created by Mercator were issued for many years by his successors (see Box 3). To compete with the Blaeu Atlas launched in 1635 (as described in the next chapter), Henry Hondius or Jan Jansson altered the Mercator map 2B to a final state used from 1636 until 1642 (including an English edition in 1636), in which it lost sea shading, a ship replaced the monster, the Isle of Man had a more correct shape (copied from John Speed), and the title cartouche was 'modernised' to seventeenth-century style. However, there was no change to the geographical detail in Lancashire. The fine details are still so clear in these late editions that only a few hundred copies of this splendid map could ever have been printed.

ATLAS MINOR

Large expensive atlases sold only in small numbers to the wealthy, prompting publication of cheaper more popular books for the educated middle class. In 1607 the Hondius family reduced their folio maps to under a sixth of the original area for their *Atlas Minor*, which included 2C (see Fig. 7) with our county titled 'Castria' (instead of 'Lancastria') via the word splitting in Mercator's title cartouche in 2B (Fig. 6) which was copied for 2C. It is shown in an early edition (1609) and in the final condition (1637) when the last issues were printed in London, where the plates had ended up for use in *Purchas His Pilgrimes* (1625) and other works, after the Hondius family had finished with them. By then sea shading and all subtle details have disappeared due to the plate wear obvious in Fig. 7, proving these maps had been printed in unusual numbers, perhaps over two thousand copies. Small atlases proved so profitable that other reduced copies of Mercator maps were made in Amsterdam, including the three further versions of 2B shown in Fig. 8 all reduced to half their original linear scale.

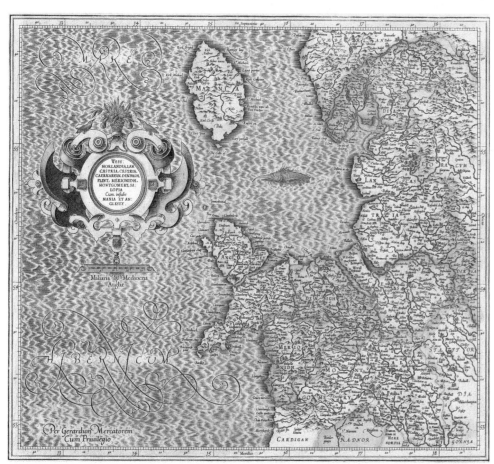

Fig. 6 Map 2B 'Westmorlandia, Lancastria, Cestria...' by Gerardus Mercator, from *Atlas sive Cosmographicae Meditationes...*, Part III (A. Busius, Dusseldorf, 1595) [390mm x 336mm, 15.4" x 13.2"]; also the Lancashire section at actual size [118mm x 165mm].

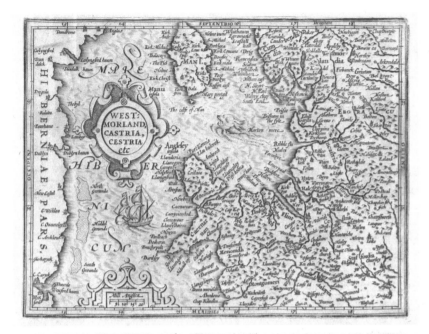

Fig. 8
Regional Maps based on 2B

Top: 2D (1616)
Petrus Bertius edition
(J. Hondius II, Amsterdam, 1618).
[123mm x 83mm, 4.8" x 3.3"]

Centre: 2E (1628)
Jan Jansson edition
(J. Jansson II, Amsterdam, 1630).
[187mm x 132mm, 7.4" x 5.2"]

Foot: 2F (1630)
Johan Cloppenburg edition
(J. Cloppenburg, Amsterdam,
1630).
[238mm x 170mm, 9.4" x 6.7"]

Fig. 7 Map 2C 'Westmorland, [Lan] Castria, Cestria...' (1607) by Jodocus Hondius I, from *Atlas Minor Gerardi Mercatoris*; **top** (Jan Jansson I, Arnhem, 1609) [169mm x 124mm, 6.7" x 4.9"]; **foot** (Michaell Sparke, London, 1637 after much plate wear [171mm x 124mm, 6.7" x 4.9"].

The first set (see 2D) was at post-card size for the final editions in 1616 (Latin) and 1618 (Latin and French) of a miniature world atlas by Petrus Bertius (1565-1629), a brother-in-law of Jodocus Hondius the elder. These small plates were also issued in 1639 by Willem Blaeu's heirs in an 'epitome' (or summary) of Camden's *Britannia*. For the *Atlas Minor* Jan Jansson replaced the worn-out original plates (e.g. 2C) by a new slightly larger and more detailed set used from 1628 until 1651, including 2E. Even larger plates (at a third of original area) were finely engraved for an epitome of the Mercator atlas by Johan Cloppenburg issued from 1630 until 1673. Map 2F in this set reverted to the original Saxton Isle of Man form, despite the previous use on 2D and 2E of a corrected form introduced by John Speed in 1611. The popularity of the Mercator regional maps is shown by entries in *A Descriptive List of the Printed Maps of Lancashire, 1577-1900* by Harold Whitaker.[3] He noted 29 issues of the folio Mercator map 2B and 22 printings of the various reduced copies (in much larger printing runs) among the 80 editions of Lancashire maps he identified up to 1642, which omitted the three printings of 2D by Bertius.

THE START OF ENGLISH COUNTY MAPPING

The first national atlas for our country, or indeed of almost any national region, was produced by Yorkshireman Christopher Saxton (see Box 4), who began the use of individual counties as the basis for mapping England and Wales, a localised style of mapping unique to our nation. His example was followed for the next 300 years as county atlas after county atlas was issued, with maps showing each county but almost no details of its neighbours across the border. We know that Saxton completed his survey of England and Wales for the Elizabethan government in about seven years, though details of his appointment and methods of mapping are scanty and speculation abounds.[4] Single map sheets for the counties were available once the engraving was completed (in 1577 for Lancashire) and in 1579 the entire atlas was published with a map of the whole kingdom, 24 maps for individual counties, six maps showing two counties and four maps for groups of up to five counties. Queen Elizabeth granted Saxton a patent in 1579 giving him the sole right for the next ten years to print and sell maps of her realm, to encourage and reward him 'in this his so profitable and beneficiall an enterprise to all manner of persons'.[5]

BOX 4   THE PIONEER OF COUNTY MAPPING

Christopher Saxton (*c.* 1543-1610) was probably educated by the Vicar of Dewsbury, John Rudd, previously chaplain to Henry VIII and a lifelong map-maker. We know Saxton was working with Rudd in 1570, but little else about his early career. He was appointed to perform the first official national survey by Thomas Seckford, Master of Requests to Queen Elizabeth, almost certainly by order of William Cecil, Lord Burghley (1520-1598), who recorded extra local details on the only known proof copies of the county maps. Work started between 1571 and mid-1573. Seckford paid the survey costs, getting a well-paid official post in 1579 as a reward. All the maps include the Seckford coat-of-arms with his appropriate motto 'Diligence adorns the World'.

Unfortunately there is no record of the surveying methods used by Saxton, but these are indicated in a Privy Council letter of July 1576 ordering Welsh Justices of the Peace and others 'to see him conducted unto any towre Castle highe place or hill to view that country, and that he may be accompanied with ii or iii honest men such as do best know the cuntrey ...'.* At such viewpoints he may have used an early version of the theodolite to record angles of sight relative to a magnetic compass, for scale drawing on a plane table.† It is likely he surveyed Lancashire in the summer of 1576, completing his work within three weeks before passing on to other Northern Counties. The whole kingdom was surveyed in from five to eight years. The first individual maps were produced in 1574, Lancashire in 1577, and the complete set was collected in 1579 in an untitled volume containing 34 maps of English and Welsh counties and a general map of England and Wales. This was the main basis of mapping for England and Wales until nearly 1800.

By 1583 Saxton had compiled his data into a huge wall-map on twenty sheets showing England and Wales at eight miles per inch, proudly including his tiny home village of Dunningley in Yorkshire. Then he retired into relative obscurity for the rest of his life, living at Dunningley and working from 1586 as an estate surveyor, seldom outside the West Riding. He was employed by the Duchy of Lancaster in March 1610, but was dead about a year later, the details sadly as imprecise as those for his birth.

* TNA, Privy Council Register:11. Reprinted with other documents and discussion of known details for Saxton's life and work in a facsimile of the 1583 map by R.A. Skelton, *Saxton's Survey of England and Wales*, Nico Israel (Amsterdam, 1974).

† See analysis by Gordon Manley, 'Saxton's Survey of Northern England', *The Geographical Journal*, 83 (April 1934), pp 308-16. That orientation on magnetic north does not prove that Saxton primarily used compass bearings was noted by J.H. Andrews, *Maps in those Days*, Four Courts Press (Dublin, 2009), p 103.

As already mentioned, Saxton established the mapping of our kingdom on a county basis, with only a few details shown for neighbouring areas beyond the boundary. The lack of consistency of such inclusions with entries on the corresponding county map reveals that each county was surveyed, designed and engraved without cross referencing to the others around it. Such signs of haste are perhaps inevitable when all the work was performed in at most eight years, an absurdly short time for a first national survey at such detail. However, in view of the longevity of resulting errors it is unfortunate that more care was not taken in final editing. Despite such carping, the Saxton maps were a splendid achievement, the size of the advance being evident upon the comparison of any area with the Ortelius map 2A by Lhuyd.

In particular the high quality of Saxton's cartographic work is well displayed in the Saxton map 2G of Lancashire (Fig. 9), engraved in England by Flemish refugee Remigius Hogenberg (1536-1588?), brother of Frans Hogenberg, the main engraver for Ortelius. His engraving style is typical of map design and decoration in the sixteenth century, not fully of the quality later achieved in Amsterdam but still a fine artistic feat as well as a good presentation of geographical data. The map is oriented on magnetic north around 1576. The distance bar at lower left indicates about four miles per inch, but those are 'long miles'. If we assume a long mile of 2400 yards, which is consistent with the distances shown on these maps, the 1760 yard statute mile is close to three quarters of that and the Saxton map scale corresponds to just over five statute miles per inch, the best scale for Lancashire on any printed maps commonly available before 1750.

No roads were shown by Saxton, although bridges were indicated. There was an extensive road network used for local travel and movement of goods by cart, but clearly Saxton did not consider them important enough to be included.[6] Before the eighteenth century people made long journeys as slow affairs on foot or horseback across mainly open countryside, with local guides escorting the travellers on routes like modern bridleways as part of the horse-hiring deal, a service still being advertised for Lake District visitors in the nineteenth century.

Hills were shown clearly in the conventional 'sugar-loaf' form, illuminated by a summer sunset in the west, but with scant regard for accuracy of position or of form. Some attempt was made to indicate relative heights. Ingleborough is depicted as several miles high, befitting the hill then believed to be the highest in England, and Pendle Hill is shown little smaller. By comparison the hills in the Lake District section of Lancashire seem modest in height and are shown with little attempt to indicate true locality. Rivers feature prominently, clearly indicating valleys and the water drainage system. However, the two lakes of Windermere and Coniston Water have an incorrectly sinuous form, which differs completely from their representation on Saxton's Westmorland and Cumberland map, where 'fosse flu[men]' (modern Force Beck) was omitted and Esthwaite Water was included, in converse to the Lancashire map.

It seems that Saxton paid scant attention to rural wildernesses and concentrated his efforts on the well-populated regions, where a range of symbols indicates settlements from groups of buildings for market towns like Lancaster and Preston to small circles for hamlets. However, no city symbols appear in Lancashire and the others were not used with consistency, as a comparison of Manchester and Garstang reveals. The extensive mosses were stippled (less obviously at first than in the retouched version shown in Fig. 11) to warn travellers of these dangerous areas of marshy wasteland. Manor houses of wealthy land owners and the aristocracy were shown clearly, these being Saxton's most likely customers, and parklands were indicated, usually by a ring of palings. Although he showed many parish churches and chapels, several are missing including some quite important ones. It is likely this was not only a consequence of haste in the survey, but also due to lack of space for more names on the relatively small scale map, and possibly it was Hogenberg during the engraving who was responsible for a lot of the omissions.

Original copies of Saxton maps in all editions are rare, even though the maps were reissued in small print runs for about 200 years. The date of printing can be judged by the amount of modification performed from the original state, in a sequence reconstructed by Harold Whitaker from what evidence was available.[3] The alterations are indicated by colour coding of the details in Fig. 10, which as background has an edition of the map in 1770 when all the changes were complete.

For his Civil War edition, William Web altered the title to 'The County Pallatine (*sic*) of Lancaster, 1642' and the Royal coat-of-arms to the Stuart version with a unicorn supporter instead of the Tudor dragon. Probably around 1665 an unknown owner made major changes to the plate, adding the Lancaster town plan, coats

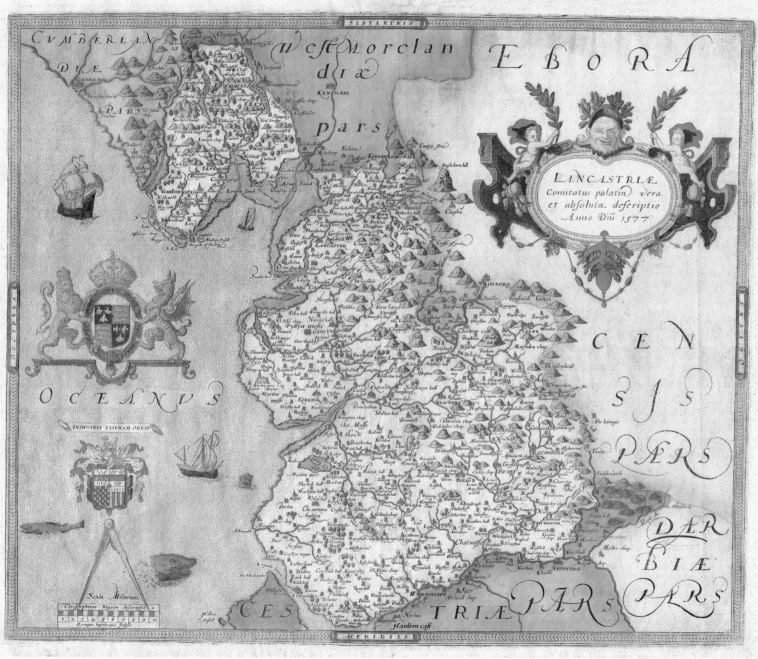

Fig. 9 Map 2G 'Lancastriae Comitatus Palatin...' by Christopher Saxton (Saxton, London, 1577). [456mm x 371mm, 18.0" x 14.6"]

of arms and the names and boundaries of the Hundreds (all copied from Speed's map 3C), as well as reference letters, the initials CR and extra towns. The date 1665 was entered in the title, but no edition seems to have been published near that year, perhaps due to the plate owner dying in the Great Plague of 1665 or the whole batch of printed copies being destroyed by the Great Fire of London in 1666. The state is inferred from amendments appearing in a few Saxton atlases issued before 1690 by the next owner, Philip Lea, whose further gradual changes included by 1689 the first overtly political information on county maps via crowns to label parliamentary boroughs and crosses to indicate markets. By 1690 he had inserted more towns and several main roads (in general from the work of John Ogilby described in Chapter 3) and by 1693 a new title in its final form. The several editions by Lea are referred to as 'Saxton-Lea' maps which are relatively common in the state illustrated as 2H in Fig. 11 (given a separate reference in view of the many changes from the original state 2G in Fig. 9). Some of these additions can be noted in Fig. 18, which includes small sections from the 1577 and 1693 versions.

Around 1720 George Willdey added his own imprint 'Sold by Geo: Willdey at the Great Toy, Spectacle, China-ware and Print Shop...' within a small box below the title. Thomas Jefferys removed this imprint in 1749 (but left the box) for the last state, which he sold until about 1765. Around 1700 the Saxton plates were bought by Cluer Dicey and Co. and reissued until about 1775. The relatively light plate wear on that Dicey edition (used as background for Fig. 10) indicates that well under a thousand copies of the Saxton map were printed in all the issues from 1577 to 1775.

After publishing his atlas Saxton assembled all his county data to create a map of England and Wales on twenty sheets at eight miles per inch to fill an area 1.73m x 1.40m (68" x 55") when assembled. Typically such a large map is referred to as a 'wall-map', as that is where it would be displayed. (A much later example of a wall-map is shown as Fig. 58). The large Saxton map was published in 1583 and reprinted a few times with revisions; it was used by Mercator as a source for his regional maps as noted above, and by Thomas Jenner in 1644 for his *Quartermaster's Map* as mentioned later. We can also note here that the general map of all England and Wales in Saxton's atlas was the source for county maps on playing cards of 1590, represented by map 2J in Fig. 21 in the next chapter, where it is more relevant.

THE ATLAS THAT NEVER WAS

County atlases sold by John Overton from *c.* 1670 to 1700 contained some unusual county maps in antique style with no indication of the designer or engraver. A few very early prints of these maps were found, and in 1926 Edward Heawood recognised that a set of 12 county maps had been engraved just after 1600, including one of Lancashire.[7] A later printing of this is shown as map 2K in Fig. 12. These maps became known as the 'Anonymous' series and their origin was a cartographical mystery which seemed impossible to solve.

Eventually the engraver was identified via a note of 1622 by antiquarian William Burton that what must be the 'Anonymous' Leicestershire map was 'graven at Amsterdam by Iodocus Hondius 1602'.[8] The similarity of style indicates that all twelve plates were made by Hondius, who was the leading engraver of his day. We know that well before 1608 he was hard at work for George Humble and John Sudbury on the large set of plates for the John Speed county atlas. It seems this replaced an earlier county atlas project commissioned from Hondius, but abandoned after plates for only 12 counties had been engraved. John Overton acquired the plates by 1666 from the stock of another London map-seller, Peter Stent, who himself had issued some loose copies of the maps before dying in the Great Plague of 1665. Stent probably purchased the plates on the death of George Humble in 1640. So we can guess that by about 1604 Humble had bought the plates to withhold them from use and prevent competition with his Speed Atlas, plate ownership being the only effective form of copyright control at that time.

The main clue to the designer and commissioner of the 'anonymous' series was that the Cheshire and Lancashire maps are closely similar to manuscripts by antiquarian William Smith (1550-1618).[9] Smith went to Nuremberg in 1575 as keeper of the Goose Inn, and during a decade there learned German mapping methods including the use of a table of symbols (as in 2K). He returned to London and was appointed Rouge Dragon at the College of Heralds in 1597. Authorship by Smith was proved in 1958 when R.V. Tooley found that four further manuscript maps in Smith's handwriting implausibly had survived in Holland since 1602, clearly some of the fair copies prepared for use by the engraver.[10] Fascinating glimpses into the engraver's methods are given by these papers, where the ink drawing has been traced in pencil on the other side of the paper to reverse the image on the copper, and a punch has been used to mark the position of towns and villages

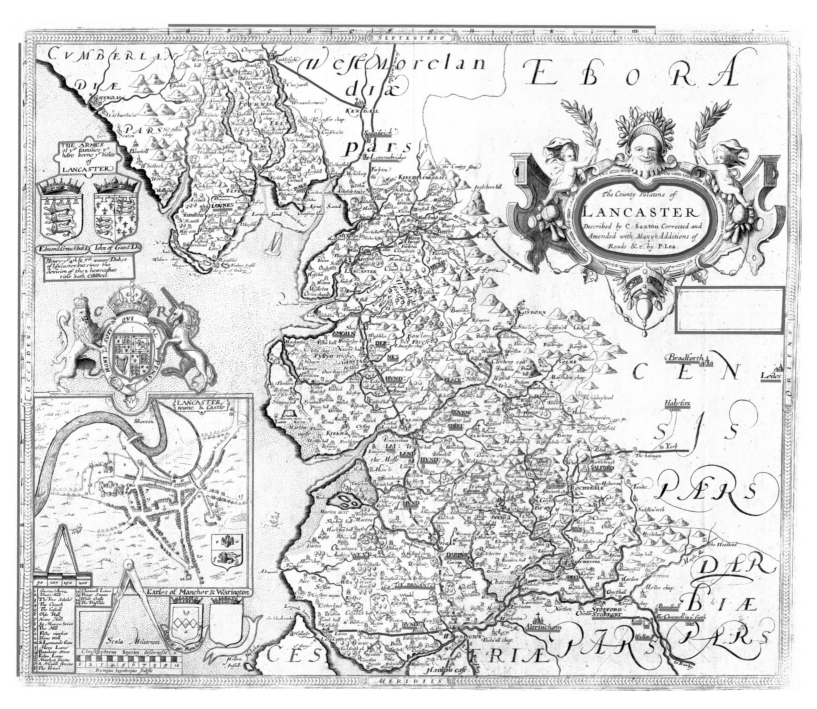

Fig. 10 Map 2H The final state of the Saxton map plate (*c.*1770) with colour coding to indicate successive changes for various states.

GREEN: in 1642 by William Web (title, Royal Arms).

RED: in 1665 by an unknown owner (town plan, Arms, names, Hundreds...).

BLUE: from *c.*1683 to 1693 by Philip Lea (roads, borough signs, title).

MAGENTA: in 1720 by Willdey (imprint in box) in 1749 by Jefferys (imprint removed).

Fig. 11 Map 2H 'The County Palatine of Lancaster…' by Christopher Saxton (1577), as amended by Philip Lea (P. Lea, London, 1693). [466mm x 378mm, 18.3" x 14.9"]

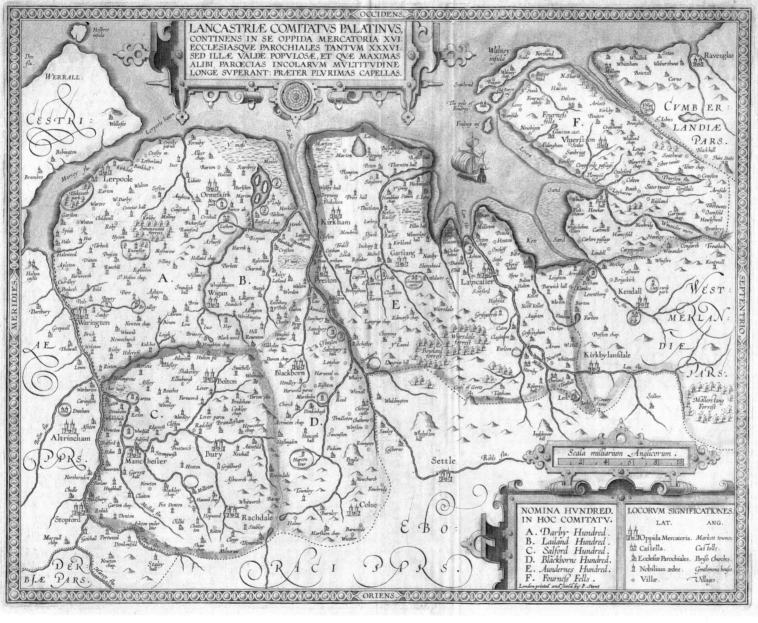
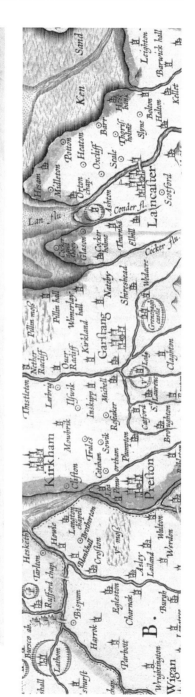

Fig. 12 Map 2K 'Lancastriae Comitatus Palatinus…' (1602) by William Smith (formerly 'anonymous'), loose sheet issue (Peter Stent, London, *c*.1660). [462mm x 355mm, 18.2" x 14.0"]

through the paper. Presumably Smith decided against competition with his friend John Speed in producing a new county atlas and to recoup his investment sold to Humble the twelve plates already engraved for him by Hondius.

Only a very few prints of the 'Anonymous' maps in first state from 1602 are known (for Lancashire only one), and later issues by Stent and Overton are also very rare. A Lancashire map 2K as printed by Stent in about 1660 is shown as Fig. 12. The only change from the first state is a tiny imprint inserted below the list of Hundreds, saying 'London printed and sould by P. Stent'. For third state Overton issues from *c.* 1670 this imprint was changed to 'London printed and sould by I:Overton overag: – ainst Sepulchers church'.

This Lancashire map by Smith is of great interest, as the only large-scale version of Lancashire published between Saxton in 1577 and Bowen in 1752 not essentially a tracing of the Saxton map with additions. By having west at the top on the standard double folio page (as on the manuscript maps of Lancashire by Smith and for Lord Burghley), the scale is larger than that of Saxton and his imitators, about four statute miles to the inch, the largest scale until 1752 (see Box 1 and Appendix 3). In general the details are in agreement with Saxton, though different spellings and altered details show that Smith did not merely copy Saxton. The engraver Hondius made a curious error by wrongly interpreting a hill symbol on the source manuscript (presumably similar to the British Library version), so that on the printed map Farleton Knot is replaced by a small lake as source for the River Keer (just south of Kendal). However, a marshy waste in that area may be what was indicated. In some small details Smith corrects Saxton; for example, the hamlet of Abram in much more correctly situated near Wigan, rather than halfway towards Warrington as placed by Saxton and 'Septentrio' is true north, not magnetic north.

The division into hundreds is indicated for the first time, using code letters on the map and a table as key. But Smith does this incorrectly, in particular by omitting Lonsdale Hundred, included with 'E. Aundernes Hundred' and with the detached portion named as 'F. Fourness Fells' in the table, implying that to be a Hundred. Probably (via use of Smith's map by Speed) this is the origin of such confusion over Lonsdale Hundred for nearly 200 years. The Lonsdale Hundred is correctly labelled in other contemporary sources, including Smith's own manuscript map of Lancashire in the British Library.

The Liverpool antiquarian Matthew Gregson (1749-1824) commissioned a printed map 'Lancashire, 1598 WSR' as his own copy of the British Library manuscript map by Smith. This map 2L (Fig. 13) was included in the second edition of his *Portfolio of Fragments ...* of 1824, the year Gregson died after falling from a ladder in his library. However, the inclusion of anachronistic names not present on the original (e.g. 'Morcalm Bay' and 'Soutport') and many other inaccuracies make this 'copy' so misleading as to be worse than useless as a record of the original manuscript. However, it is noteworthy as the first map of Lancashire designed for lithographic printing.[11] It was drawn on the stone by James Wyld (1790-1836), who in *c.*1812 introduced lithography for English map printing while working for the Quarter-Master General's Office.

A later *Portfolio* edition in 1869 contains an apparently identical map, still signed 'Ja^s·Wyld del^t', but close inspection reveals it to be a completely new drawing with the same errors as the 1821 edition.[12] Unfortunately Bagley and Hodgkiss copied many erroneous details from the copy by Gregson (in the 1869 version rather than the 1821 issue as cited) and used these as the basis for their discussion of the William Smith map and their table of names on it and other maps.[13]

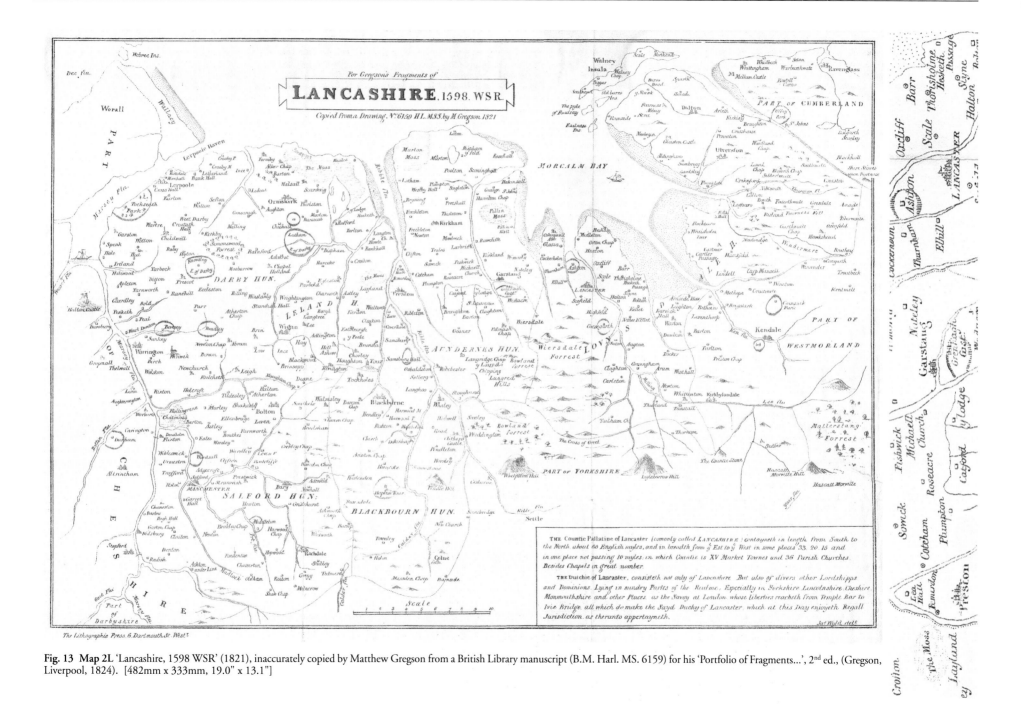

Fig. 13 Map 2L 'Lancashire, 1598 WSR' (1821), inaccurately copied by Matthew Gregson from a British Library manuscript (B.M. Harl. MS. 6159) for his 'Portfolio of Fragments...', 2nd ed., (Gregson, Liverpool, 1824). [482mm x 333mm, 19.0" x 13.1"]

NOTES

1   The methods of plane table surveying and triangulation are outlined by Rachel Hewitt, *Map of a Nation* (Granta, London 2010), pp.15-7, 67-70.

2   Detailed analysis is given in M.P.R. van den Broecke, *Ortelius Atlas Maps* (HES, Tuurdijk, 1996).

3   Harold Whitaker, *Maps of Lancashire 1577-1900* (Manchester University Press and the Chetham Society, Manchester, 1938) lists all printed county maps of Lancashire (as known then) in chronological order of individual editions, including early regional maps based on Mercator and a few others. In particular he describes the successive states of the plates (including an analysis of the various alterations to the map by Saxton) and other details from which the date of issue of individual maps may be determined.

4   Ifor M. Evans & Heather Lawrence, *Christopher Saxton: Elizabethan Map-maker* (Wakefield Historical Publications, London, 1979); William Ravenhill, *Christopher Saxton's 16th Century Maps* (Chatsworth Library, Shrewsbury, 1992); J.H. Andrews, 'A Saxton Miscellany', *Imago Mundi*, 65, 1 (January 2013), 87-96.

5   TNA, Patent Rolls, 19 Eliz., pt.9 (no. 1159), m.21. See Skelton ref. in Box 4.

6   Or so vital that William Cecil decided enemies of England should not get the knowledge. Even today maps omit details for reasons of national security. John Norden included roads on a few county maps published just after 1590.

7   Edward Heawood, 'Some Early County Maps', *The Geographical Journal*, 68, 4 (October 1926), 325-37.

8   William Burton, *Description of Leicestershire* (1622), in the preface; second edition reprint (Whittingham, Lynn, 1777) is at http://cdm15407.contentdm.oclc.org/cdm/ref/collection/p15407coll6/id/11597 (accessed 29 July 2013).

9   For Lancashire, British Library Harley MS 6159, dated 1598, which can be viewed via the British Library Online Gallery.

10 Described in a discussion of the Smith maps by R.A. Skelton, *County Atlases of the British Isles 1579-1703* (Carta Press, London, 1970) pp.19-22. This book lists the editions of county maps before 1700 and complements the Whitaker list described in note 3 above, with information more recent but less specific to Lancashire. The notes by Skelton were corrected and extended by Donald Hodson in three further volumes referred to later in this text.

11 This versatile printing method was invented just after the period reviewed and is not discussed here. It was not until nearly 1850 that lithography allowed printing at approaching the quality via direct use of engraved metal plates.

12 James Wyld the Elder died in 1836, of overwork according to R.V. Tooley, *Dictionary of Mapmakers* (Map Collector Publications, Tring, 1979) p.675. Probably Wyld's name was blindly copied for the second version, along with the rest of the 1824 map, but just possibly the 1869 drawing was by his son, James Wyld the Younger (1812-1887) at the very end of his engraving career.

13 J.J. Bagley & A.G. Hodgkiss, *Lancashire: a History of the County Palatine in Early Maps* (Neil Richardson, Manchester, 1985) pp.19-21.

3   The Era of Decoration (1600–1690)

Seventeenth-century maps are often masterpieces of engraving, in some cases the geographical content being only an excuse for the insertion of florid lettering and elaborate decoration to fill blank areas with coats of arms, portraits, drawings of people, titles, notes and distance scales in decorative frames. Seas are full of ships or monsters and the land covered with trees (for forests), stylised hills and building signs for cities. The Saxton set of maps provided the only source material throughout the period, with no systematic introduction of new material until Ogilby added surveys of strips along main roads towards the end of the century.

CAMDEN'S *BRITANNIA* – TUDOR MASTERPIECE

William Camden (1551-1623) was a Herald-at-Arms and a master at Westminster School. All his spare time, in particular between leaving University (without a degree) and beginning teaching, was spent travelling the country to record historical and geographical information, sketching inscriptions and examining monuments. In 1586 Camden published the first edition of his famous *Britannia*, a county by county account of the topography and history of Britain. In the preface Camden recorded that ten years earlier he was persuaded to develop his travel notes into this seminal work by his friend Abraham Ortelius, who visited England in 1576-7 as an asylum seeker from the 'Spanish Fury' which afflicted Antwerp.

The *Britannia* text was reprinted, translated, abridged, plagiarised, revised and extended for the next 200 years as the principal description of Britain, just as the Saxton Atlas was copied for the same period as a source of maps. The first four editions had no maps, and the fifth had only general historical maps of the whole country, but the sixth edition in 1607 (the last in Latin) included the earliest complete set of maps published for individual counties, all separated rather than grouped as they had been in many of the Saxton maps. Saxton is named as designer on most of the maps,

and possibly he personally authorised this use by Camden. Six maps are attributed to John Norden (1547?-1625). The maps are usually referred to as 'Saxton-Kip' (e.g. Westmorland) or 'Saxton-Hole' (e.g. Lancashire), as on the plates the engraver is named as William Kip (34 maps) or William Hole (21 maps).

The original books were not coloured when issued. Map 3A (Fig. 14) is from a 1610 printing with later (but old) hand-colouring. The details on Saxton's 2G have been copied on a smaller scale to fit the size of the quarto book, giving a scale of about six-and-a-half statute miles per inch. The surveyor and engraver are named beneath the distance scale. The title cartouche is closely modelled on the original Hogenberg design for Saxton, though cropped a little at the right edge, and in the title '*olim pars Brigantum*' (meaning 'formerly part of Brigantia') refers to the pre-Roman tribal regions into which Camden grouped the counties for his book. Hole introduces a large compass rose as decoration, directed to the 1576 magnetic north used for Saxton's orientation. Latin text appears on the back of the 1607 edition, but the verso is blank in the 1610 edition (the first in English) when the maps were reprinted unchanged. Plate numbers (52 for Lancashire) were added at bottom left for the final 1637 edition. *Britannia* was a best-seller, and its maps are relatively plentiful compared to other maps four centuries old, thus inexpensive in view of their age and interest. Further important sets of county maps appeared in revised editions of Camden's *Britannia*, in 1695 (discussed in chapter 4 for map 4A) and in 1789 with maps by John Cary. Also several texts based on Camden's *Britannia* included county maps.

A MAPPING ODDITY

Among the foremost county maps for eccentricity are those illustrating the attempt by Michael Drayton (1563-1631) to rewrite Camden's *Britannia* as a poem. There are many real maps of fictitious places (like 'Treasure Island'), but the Drayton maps are almost unique among printed maps as semi-fictitious depictions of real places, somewhat in the style of a mediaeval *Mappa Mundi*. Drayton had devoted his life since 1598 to the composition of his poem *Poly-Olbion*, a useful source of much unique historical information. The first part containing eighteen 'songs' on the charms of the southern English and Welsh regions was published in 1612-3, with allegorical maps perhaps to designs by Drayton himself.

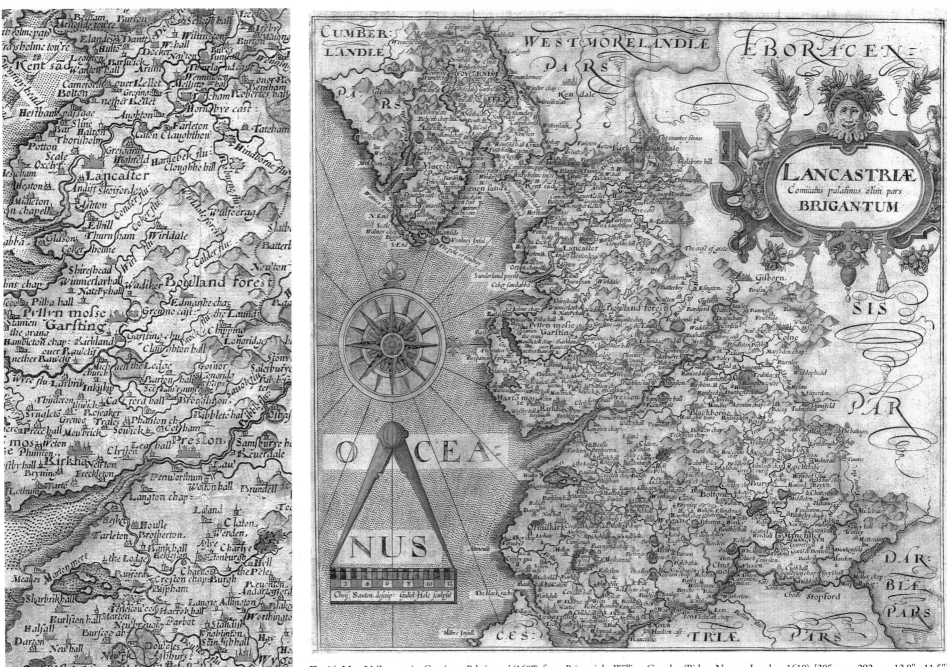

Fig. 14 Map 3A 'Lancastriae Comitatus Palatinus...' (1607), from *Britannia* by William Camden (Bishop Norton, London, 1610). [305mm x 292mm, 12.0" x 11.5"]

However, the author was bitterly disappointed by its negligible impact on the book market. Literary merit in small doses did not compensate for the tedious monotony of ten thousand lines of verse lacking any kind of narrative or dramatic theme. William Shakespeare was said to have died in 1616 of fever following a night out drinking with his friends Michael Drayton and Ben Jonson, possibly all drowning their sorrows as poorly acknowledged authors.[1]

Drayton continued work on *Poly-Olbion* in the same style and in 1622 published a second volume covering the counties 'betwixt the two famous rivers of Thames and Tweed' according to the title, with twelve more songs and maps including 3B for Lancashire (see Fig. 15). It has been suggested that this second part is so rare because only enough copies were printed to match the unsold remainder of the first part still in stock after ten years, with booksellers reasoning that now the work was complete these could be moved on via something like a 'Buy One Get One Free' offer.

Poly-Olbion was not reprinted until limited editions for scholars in the late nineteenth century, but the very decorative maps have always attracted interest. They were engraved by William Hole and are the nearest thing to soft pornography in county maps, featuring naked nymphs in rivers and various ladies in flimsy transparent dresses. The 'Bowland Lady' who represents that hunting forest on the Drayton map was taken for the logo of Bowland College in Lancaster University.

SPEED - THE MOST DECORATIVE MAP-MAKER

As a young man John Speed (1552-1629) moved to London, where he married and fathered eighteen children. He spent many years working there, presumably in the family business. His father was a member of the Merchant Taylors' Company, which admitted Speed himself in 1580, although this does not mean he was 'bred a tailor' as has been oft repeated since stated in 1769.[2] The company included many with no direct tailoring connections and we do not know in what business the Speed family worked. In his spare time Speed studied theology and history, developing a 'very rare and ingenious capacitie in drawing and setting forthe the mappes and genealogies'.[3] In 1598 sponsorship via Sir Fulke Greville assured his income and historical work became full-time. The results included a genealogical table and map of Canaan, included in all copies of the King James Bible which brought Speed wealth via

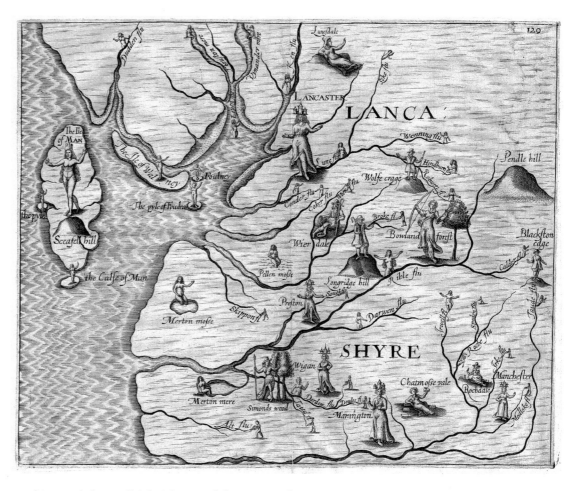

royalties, and above all *The Theatre of the Empire of Great Britaine* which brought lasting fame. This magnificent first atlas for the complete British Isles was published in late 1611 or early 1612 and reissued for over 60 years.

The maps themselves were reprinted from the original copper plates until perhaps 1780, nearly 200 years, and are still being reprinted today by modern methods of copying. Speed's ingenious additions to geography provided the decorations which make these maps among the most visually attractive ever produced, especially when finely coloured. The main sources of topographical information were the Saxton maps, though Speed used any others available and in particular collaborated with his friend William Smith on the

Fig. 15 Map 3B 'Lancashyre' by William Hole, from Part 2 of *Poly-Olbion, or a chorographicall description of... this renowned isle of Great Britaine* by M. Drayton, (Marriott, Grismand & Dewe, London, 1622).
[305mm x 240mm, 12.0" x 9.4"]

map of Cheshire where both men had been born. Speed mapped each county of England and Wales separately and so affirmed Saxton's county basis for mapping as the norm, thereafter unquestioned until about 1800. His text notes on the counties were abridged from the 1610 English translation of Camden's *Britannia* and other sources. Publisher George Humble (in partnership with his uncle John Sudbury) spared no expense by commissioning copper plates from the greatest living engraver, Jodocus Hondius (1563-1612) of Amsterdam, who had spent the ten years after 1583 in England as a refugee. His craftsmanship combined with Speed's genius for design to create maps of great interest (see map 3C, Fig. 16).

The inclusion of detailed plans of the county towns was the most significant new cartographic feature. About two-thirds were from street surveys performed by Speed himself (indicated by inclusion of a distance scale of 'pases'), including the plan of Lancaster drawn when Speed visited the town on 17 August 1607.[4] Each map is decorated with appropriate additions in blank spaces around the county. Portraits of York and Lancaster 'Wars of the Roses' monarchs are a unique and valuable embellishment on the Lancashire map, and the sea area is enlivened with ships, monsters and even a mermaid with mirror and comb, like an early bathing beauty. As usual the 'sugar-loaf' hills show little accuracy of position or form, though some attempt was made to indicate relative heights, so that Speed shows the peaks of Pendle and Ingleborough as a few miles high, though not so lofty as depicted by Saxton.

All the maps (except the Farne Islands) are oriented with north at the top, usually labelled explicitly (in some cases as *Septentrio*) or via a compass as on the Lancashire map. However, the Speed county maps and their descendants (like those by Jansson and Blaeu) lack the calibrations of latitude or longitude Speed included on his general maps, which would have shown what 'north' really means as a precise direction. Presumably the map owners were not concerned about this being an approximation, the magnetic north of many years previously (see Box 7).

The Lancashire map is closely based on Saxton and was drawn to a similar scale, indicating that the base map sent to the engraver was copied directly from a Saxton print. In the title of the published map (and in the signature by Hondius) the map is dated 1610, which was not altered during the first 100 years of printing. Some proof copies from a few years earlier have survived for various counties (including Lancashire, dated 1608), and from them it is interesting to see that

Hondius left the more routine details to be filled in later, presumably by assistants, including the 'shot-silk' sea-shading (a style copied from Mercator maps) and the decorative borders.

Speed shows the Lancashire Hundreds as county divisions for the first time and seems to have used the unpublished Smith map 2K for these details, though he corrected some of Smith's boundary errors. In the 1608 proof only the 'Lailand', 'Salford' and 'Fournisfels' Hundreds are named, indicating that Hondius (or Speed) was seeking clarification for the other names. By 1612 names of the other Hundreds had been squeezed in awkwardly, though the word 'Hundred' was not added for West Derby until after 1616 and was permanently omitted for Blackburn.

The 'Fournisfels Hundred' confusion from the list on Smith's table would never be erased, though in similar capital lettering 'Loynes' and 'Dale' were added lower down in Furness and 'Hundr' across the bay beside Lancaster and the Hundreds are listed correctly in the text printed on the verso of the map. The splitting of Lonsdale Hundred by Morecambe Bay and ambiguous labelling by Speed would confuse later plagiarists for nearly 200 years. Even as late as 1789 Harrison listed 'Fourness or Loynsdale' as the northern Hundred name (map 5Q).

It appears plate engraving was nearly complete by 1608, the year when the main publisher George Humble was granted a royal privilege to print and sell the atlas for the next 21 years. Privilege was an early rather ineffective form of copyright, backed by the king and granted only to cartographers who had demonstrated such originality in their productions that they deserved encouragement in their advancement of the science of mapping. Usually the privilege was granted in the year the work was published, and we must guess that the publication delay of two years arose from serious problems, possibly a funding crisis or illness of the engraver Hondius, who died in 1612.

Humble would have been charged about £10 (at 1600 prices) for engraving each complex large plate, and the atlas contained nearly seventy.[5] Total capital outlay (perhaps a million pounds today) was so large that at least a thousand copies of a folio atlas would have to be made and sold before the operation would become profitable overall. It has been estimated that a team of extremely efficient workmen handling large copper plates in a rolling press could print at most ten sheets per hour, yielding around fifty copies of the atlas

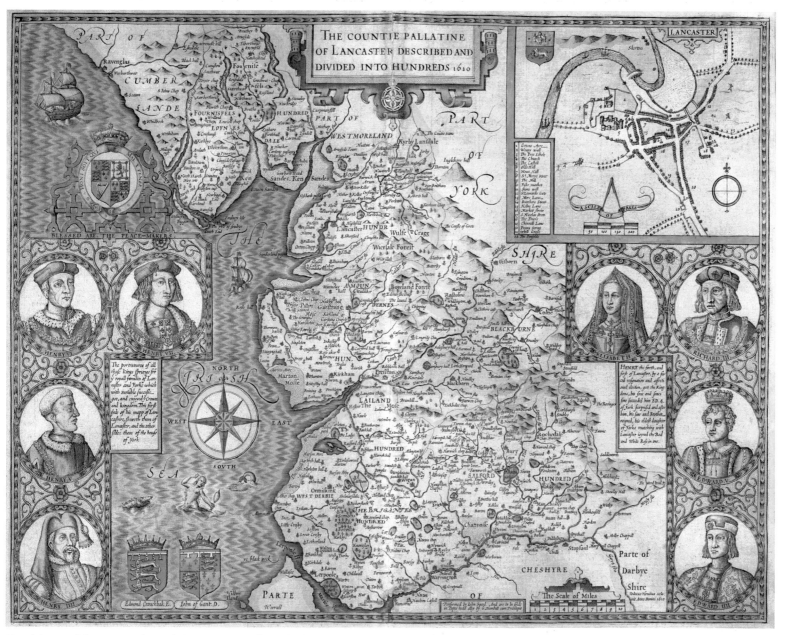

Fig. 16 Map 3C 'The Countie Palatine of Lancaster...' (1610), from *The Theatre of the Empire of Great Britaine* by John Speed, as issued with contemporary colouring (G. Humble, London, 1632). [495mm x 369mm, 19.5" x 14.5"]

per month.[6] Text was printed separately, usually in advance of the map printing. It would take several years of non-stop work to print a thousand copies. No wonder so many map-makers and publishers went bankrupt and so many projected atlases never appeared.

From 1608 onwards several early states of the Speed map of Lancashire were published, with plate changes even during the period of 1611/12 while it was in use for printing the first atlas edition. The most significant correction is of an error in the Saxton map 2G for the course of the River Irwell, west of 'Pilkinton Park' between its junctions with the rivers Roche and Croale. Several additional place-names were inserted on the Speed map in this region between Manchester and Bolton at the same time.[7] Relevant areas from the Saxton map and two Speed versions from 1611 and 1632 appear in Fig. 18.

The River Irwell error was never corrected on the Saxton plate and the route shown for the Irwell on later maps (such as on Morden's map 4A, as illustrated in Fig. 25) gives a clear indication of the copying being either directly from Saxton or indirectly via Speed. Another error by Speed is the location of 'The Colledg' (serving Manchester Collegiate Church, now Chetham's Library) which is shown near the junction of the Irwell with the Medlock, rather than with the Irk well to the north. This mistake was copied on various maps right up to 1768.

In 1627 an uncoloured copy of Speed's *Theatre* cost 30 shillings [£1.50] in sheets or £2 bound, a substantial sum at the time, equivalent to at least a thousand pounds today. Hand colouring would approximately double the price, depending on the quality of painting ordered. Though most Speed maps on sale now are coloured, few had colour applied when first issued and nearly all the colouring found today is recent. Original seventeenth-century colouring is usually more hurried and careless (see the haphazard place symbol painting in red on Fig. 16), which in view of the amount of work involved and the large number of maps in an atlas is not surprising. In later times outline colouring of maps involving much less work became standard. The maps were issued until 1619 by John Sudbury and his nephew George Humble, until 1632 by George Humble alone and until 1659 by his son Sir William Humble (knighted for supplying the exiled King Charles II with £20,000).

The plates were then sold to other publishers and printed without change (apart from names in the imprints) when issued by Roger

Rea around 1665 and by Basset and Chiswell around 1676. Henry Overton performed the overdue deletion of 1610 dates on the maps and added main roads (with other small alterations) for issues from *c.*1720 in the state illustrated in Fig. 17, where we can see a large crack in the plate across the river in the Lancaster town plan area. The appearance and growth of this crack would help to establish dates for the prints of the Speed map after 1700, but its existence has not been described in the reference books on county maps. Overton advertised his atlas and the single maps of northern counties in particular during 1715 and 1745 to exploit demand during the Jacobite invasions. The last printing of the Speed maps from the original plates was by Cluer Dicey in 1770-80 and thus the Speed Atlas was in print for over 160 years.

It was noted in the preface that during the wetting and drying cycle of printing the size of the paper can change, causing small variations between dimensions of individual maps. However, it seems that such disparities also may be due to the copper plates themselves being slightly stretched via the pressure repeatedly applied in the rolling press during many cycles of printing. Sizes measured on lines through the centre of Saxton maps owned by the author are 456mm x 371mm for 2G of 1577 (Fig. 9), 466mm x 378mm for 2H of 1693 (Fig. 11) and 467mm x 381mm for 2H of *c.*1770 (Fig. 10), suggesting very significant plate stretching in the 200 years of use. Similarly the Speed map 3C is 493mm x 368mm for 1612, 495mm x 369mm for 1632 (Fig. 16) and 501mm x 371mm for *c.*1720 (Fig. 17), where the plate crack in the Lancaster town map due to pressure is growing in classic metal failure fashion from a deep straight groove engraved for the frame around the street list. The small Hondius map 2C (Fig. 7) also shows slight lengthening during 30 years of heavy use. Further checking of other examples is needed to confirm this effect and information from readers would be welcome.

The Speed *Theatre* was always a very expensive book. Samuel Pepys greatly valued his copy, and recorded in his diary that he was 'mightily troubled, and even in my sleep, at my missing four or five of my biggest books, Speed's Chronicle and Maps, and the two parts of Waggoner [Waghenaer], and a book of cards [charts]', when they seemed lost during the confusion of moving his property endangered by the Great Fire of London.[8] Fortunately the books were in a hamper mistakenly taken by his neighbour. Pepys expressed his great joy by a very generous present of five shillings [25p] to the servant who returned them, nearly a month's wages for the man.

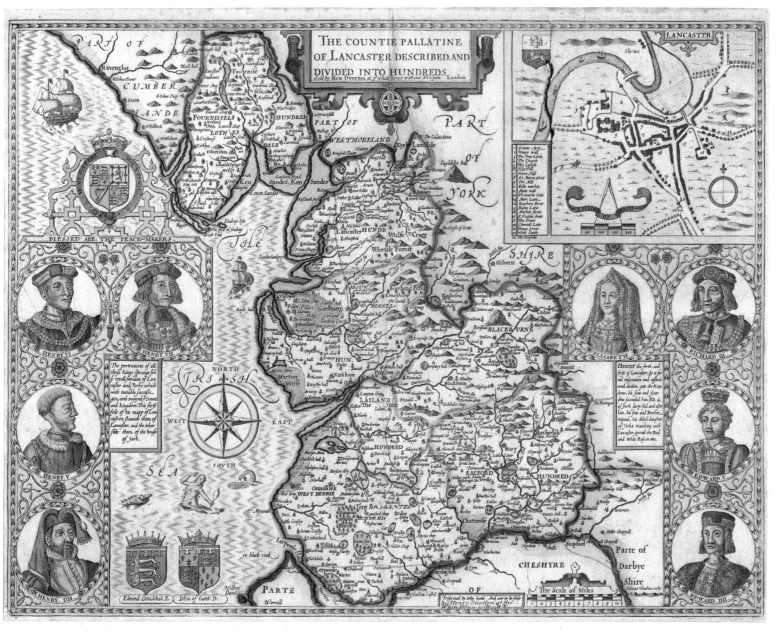

Fig. 17 Map 3C 'The Countie Palatine of Lancaster...' (1610) by John Speed, late state from *England Fully Described...* (Henry Overton, London, *c.*1720). [501mm x 371mm, 19.7" x 14.6"]

THE FIRST MINIATURE COUNTY MAPS

Great folio atlases were bought by aristocrats and wealthy men like Pepys. Many cheaper miniature atlases were published for the growing middle class market, some covering the world like the Hondius *Atlas Minor* (map 2C), but also some containing English county maps for British customers. The earliest contained maps which been unpublished for nearly 20 years after being engraved for an unknown purpose around 1600 as small copies of the Saxton maps (with similar county grouping) by Pieter van den Keere (1571-1646), who signed his maps Petrus Kaerius. His sister Colletta had married Jodocus Hondius while all of them were asylum seekers in London during conflict in the Netherlands, like Ortelius. These maps are only about 120mm x 85mm (5" x 3½").

The miniature 'Lancastria' map (3D) in Fig. 19 is a rare first state from a Latin summary by Regnerus Vitellius of Camden's *Britannia* issued in 1617 by Willem Blaeu in Amsterdam, the only known atlas edition of the Kaerius maps with the Latin title as originally engraved. Here van den Keere copied 'Maxchester' for 'Manchester', because the name was engraved on Saxton's map with the River Medlock across the letter N (see Fig. 18), but he avoided Speed's later error of turning 'Carnforth' into 'Cranforth', although just possibly this was a deliberate change by Speed as a very old form of the village name was 'Chreneforde', as used in the Domesday Book. For the 1639 edition of this work Blaeu's heirs had to use the small Bertius regional map set including 2D, as described above, because by then the Speed publisher George Humble had purchased the van den Keere plates, perhaps via Hondius.

Humble acquired the plates to illustrate the small atlas *England, Wales Scotland and Ireland described from a farr larger voulume by John Speed*, an abridgement of the Speed *Theatre* on pages about 150 mm x 100mm (6" x 4") printed in London by Humble from 1627 or possibly a few years earlier. Hence the van den Keere maps are mainly known from their use here and are usually referred to as 'Miniature Speeds', although independently derived from Saxton. On 40 of the plates by van den Keere the Latin titles were altered to English and these were supplemented by 23 new maps of similar design covering various omissions and replacing grouped counties, though not Cumberland and Westmorland which were still together on the original plate, as with Saxton. Only the main map titles had been translated for the new English customers, and there were still many Latin names to perplex unscholarly purchasers.

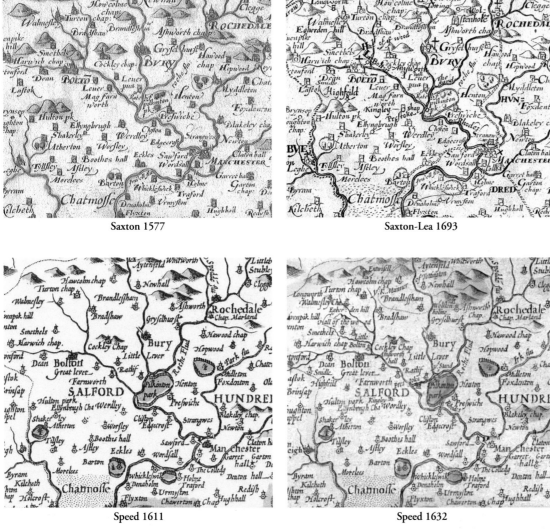

Saxton 1577   Saxton-Lea 1693

Speed 1611   Speed 1632

Fig. 18 Comparison of a South Lancashire area around Bolton and Manchester, as shown by Saxton 1577, Saxton-Lea 1693, Speed 1611 and Speed 1632. [Each section originally 90mm x 80mm]

Despite such faults in the maps, the 'Miniature Speed' atlas sold well until 1676.

Another miniature atlas, *The abridgement of Camden's Britannia...*, was published in London by John Bill (1576-1630) with text and maps in English. It came out in 1626, a year before the 'Miniature Speed', and contained small county maps very similar to those used by Humble, on an identical scale. Bill had been apprenticed in 1592 to publisher and book-seller John Norton (1557?-1612) and was employed by Sir Thomas Bodley to travel around Europe buying books for his library. From 1604 until his death Bill was established in London as the King's Printer.

When a plagiarising author is ignorant of the area depicted, one would expect an essentially arbitrary selection of places to be included on a smaller map, with insignificant hamlets included and relatively important places omitted, and van den Keere's selection of places does seem to depend erratically on where they would fit a blank space. However, comparison of the Lancashire maps by van den Keere (3D) and Bill (3E) in Fig. 19, and of similar pairs for other counties, shows almost complete agreement in the choice of places included, although the Bill spellings differ from those of van den Keere and display rather more errors. This similarity is unlikely to be by chance and it seems that the basic designs for Bill were based on suitable small maps in the 1617 Camden abridgement from Blaeu rather than directly from Saxton.

Fig. 19 shows how Bill introduced some extra fictitious coastline at the foot of 3E, omitting the Dee estuary so that Flintshire extends directly from the Wirral. That extra coast is needed because the Bill map 3E is rotated nearly 10° clockwise relative to the van den Keere map 3D, thus removing part of Cumberland and introducing Flintshire. Bill used a roughly true north orientation to suit the main originality in his maps, latitude and longitude calibrations placed along the edge on a county map set for the first time, and not used again for county maps until 1695. Latitude values are similar to those on the Saxton wall-map of England, but longitudes are about 1° larger. Either the prime meridian in the Azores used by Bill was further west than Santa Maria, the location used by Saxton, or he had better information on the relative position, as Greenwich is 25° east of Santa Maria, rather than the 24½° shown by Bill or the 23½° by Saxton. The Bill atlas was unsuccessful, presumably due to competition from the 'Miniature Speed', and only about 200 copies were printed. Thus Bill maps are very rare.

Fig. 19

Top: Map 3D 'Lancastria' by Pieter van den Keere (*c.*1600), from *Guilielmi Camdeni, viri clarissimi Britannia...* by R.Vitellius, (W. Blaeu, Amsterdam, 1617). [120mm x 83mm, 4.7" x 3.3"]

Foot: Map 3E 'Lancashire' by John Bill, from *The abridgement of Camden's Britannia With the maps of the severall Shires...* (J. Bill, London, 1626). [115mm x 82mm, 4.5" x 3.2"]

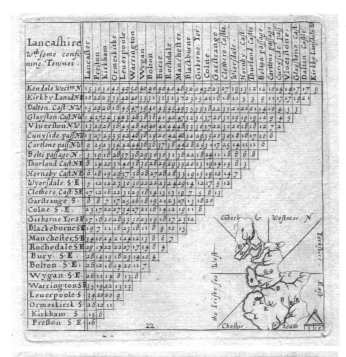

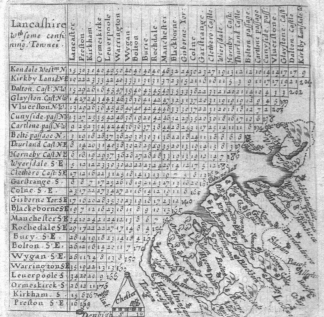

Fig. 20

Top: Map 3F 'Lancashire' (1635) by J.van Langeren, with distance table in *A Direction for the English Traviller*, first issue (Mathew Simons, London, 1635)

Foot: Map 3G 'Lancashire' (1643) by Thomas Jenner, from *A Book of the Names... in England and Wales* (Thomas Jenner, London, 1657). [engraved area is now 105mm x 104mm, 4.1" x 4.1"]

Fig. 21 Map 2J the 1590 playing card 'Lancashire' by William Bowes. [map is 38mm x 38mm, 1.5" x 1.5"]

DISTANCE TABLES

The triangular distance tables which are such familiar features in road books were devised and first published by map-maker John Norden (1548-1625) in his final work, *England, an intended Guyde for English travailers* of 1625. Mathew Simons (publisher to Milton) printed a small guide book in 1635, probably the first road book with maps, where engraver Jacob van Langeren borrowed the county distance tables from Norden (with corrections) and used the space below each table for a tiny county map. This was copied directly from extremely rare playing cards of 1590 designed by William Bowes, illustrated here for Lancashire as Fig. 21 and discussed at the end of this chapter with the other playing card maps.

Very few sets of English County maps show all the counties at the same mapping scale. The earliest was this 'thumbnail' map series, extremely miniaturised at 40 long miles per inch in both the Bowes version and in the van Langeren copy. This illustrates the distance tables only in a limited and obscure way via letters to indicate some of the towns (see 2J on Fig. 21 and 3F in Fig. 20). The values in the tables are not actual measurements along winding roads, but very approximate direct separations in the customary 'long miles' of about 2400 yards, using 'over-sands' routes across bays where available. Distances from London were added for a reprint in 1636, as an extra diagonal line of numbers below the table (to be seen on 3G).

Extra map demand during the English Civil War prompted Thomas Jenner in 1643 to replace the rather useless 'thumbnails' with more suitable larger maps (3G in Fig. 20) very uncomfortably squeezed into the triangular space with engraving right to the plate edge, and at strange undefined orientations, about north-west for Lancashire and many others. These county maps were copied from sections of the John Speed general map of England and Wales on a variable scale, such as 23 long miles per inch for Lancashire and 16 for 'Westmerland' (*sic*). The Speed general map itself was based on the Saxton 'Anglia' which had been the source for the earlier 'thumbnail' maps. In this final form the tables were reprinted several times up to 1676. As another Civil War enterprise, in 1644 Jenner published a set of large regional maps (reprinted until 1752), like the Mercator regional map 2B based on the Saxton wall-map of 1583. The two northern sheets were engraved anonymously and the other four were earlier etchings by Wenceslaus Holler. They were mounted on linen and folded (into 210mm x 110mm, 8.3" x 4.3") to be 'Portable for every Mans Pocket' according to the original title, probably the first example of that convenient map form. From the title of a later edition they became known as the *Quartermaster's Map*.

THE DUTCH MAPS OF LANCASHIRE

Antwerp, home of Abraham Ortelius and his printer Christopher Plantin, was reduced in importance during the Eighty Years War with Spain (1568-1648) which also forced Dutch mariners to voyage further away to seek wealth and so stimulated interest in maps and charts. In 1604 the world centre for cartography shifted to Amsterdam when the 'Mercator-Hondius' Atlas was published there by the excellent engraver Jodocus Hondius (1563-1612), beginning a new career as a publisher in the flourishing Dutch Republic. He died a few years later, but atlas printing was continued by his sons Jodocus the younger (1594-1629) and Henry (1597-1651), working with their brother-in-law Jan Jansson (1588-1664) who married into the Hondius family in 1612. Soon afterwards Willem Blaeu started his rival business, also in Amsterdam, and a golden age for decorative map printing began in that city (see Box 5).

In 1645 Blaeu copied a fine set of English county maps from Speed for the fourth volume of his atlas, which included geographical text from Camden's *Britannia*. Decoration here is more elegant, without the previous scarcely relevant detail filling all the plate, so reducing engraving time and cost. The Lancashire example (3H) on Fig. 22 shows the superb neatness of the work for Blaeu, in a very different style from the Speed map engraved in the same city by Hondius only 40 years earlier. Lettering is neater and less flamboyant, and sea monsters have become extinct. Many of these maps were coloured in the Blaeu printing house itself before binding, but the date and origin of colouring is always difficult to assign. In the example shown in Fig. 22 it seems clear that the colouring is original, as a modern colourist is unlikely to make such egregious errors in painting the Royal coat of arms.

In general coats of arms were copied from Speed, but on many maps Blaeu inserted additional blank shields (which were copied by Jansson). It is likely that Blaeu intended to insert the Lancashire arms on the space above the title. Similar blank shields appear for other counties and all remained mysteriously blank in later editions. It has been suggested that these spaces were intended for purchase by sponsors, or that atlas purchasers were expected to insert their

BOX 5   THE BLAEU AMSTERDAM ATLASES

The main founders of Dutch map publishing were Jodocus Hondius I and Willem Blaeu (1571-1638). Before starting a globe and instrument manufacturing company in Amsterdam in 1599 Blaeu had studied astronomy in Denmark with Tycho Brahe. He made such good sea charts that he became official hydrographer to the Dutch East India Company, a post inherited by his eldest son, and developed a greatly improved printing press for text. In a market dominated by the Mercator-Hondius-Jansson publishing house, at first Blaeu printed few land maps, but the balance crucially changed in 1629 when four members of the extended Hondius family died. This included Jodocus Hondius the younger, who had quarrelled with his family and launched his own business by making nearly 40 new map plates. Under the noses of the distracted Hondius clan, Blaeu snapped up these plates as a foundation for his own atlas. Henry Hondius and Jan Jansson began to update and expand their obsolete plate set in a competition which would last 40 years, but unfortunately the rivalry was fought out mainly via the quantity and style of the maps, rather than cartographic content.

In 1635 Willem Blaeu and his sons issued volume one of *Theatrum Orbis Terrarum, sive Atlas Novus*, so titled to pick up lingering respect for Ortelius. Other volumes followed as more plates were added, issued after Willem Blaeu's death in 1638 by his son and heir Johan Blaeu (1596-1673). In 1645 volume five contained a fine set of English county maps and volume six in 1654 added maps of Scotland and Ireland. By 1662 Johan Blaeu had expanded his *Atlas Novus* into the *Atlas Major*, eventually 12 thick folio volumes with 590 double page maps and 3000 pages of text in a choice of languages, one of the finest publications of all time. About 300 copies were printed and somehow it was commercially viable, even though its price of 450 florins would be about £20,000 in today's terms. The *Atlas Major* was a status symbol for show, with emphasis on decoration and size, rather than a work for actual use, for example most owners would get little benefit from the county atlas of Scotland and detailed maps of China.

The great Blaeu firm in Amsterdam had everything needed for printing, with at least nine letter-presses for text, six rolling presses for maps, a type foundry and an engraving shop. But in 1672 a fire destroyed their print works and almost all stock of engraved copper plates, causing 382,000 florins damage [£12 million at modern prices]. Johan Blaeu died soon afterwards and although the Blaeu firm continued in business until 1695 by selling already printed map stock, the fire put the greatest map-makers in the world out of production for ever. Yet overall the Blaeu disaster was beneficial, by stimulating atlas makers in other countries to develop more constructive approaches to cartography based on quality rather than quantity, on information transfer rather than embellishment. Instead of being a status symbol, an atlas became an accurate tool for scholars, as originally intended by Mercator.

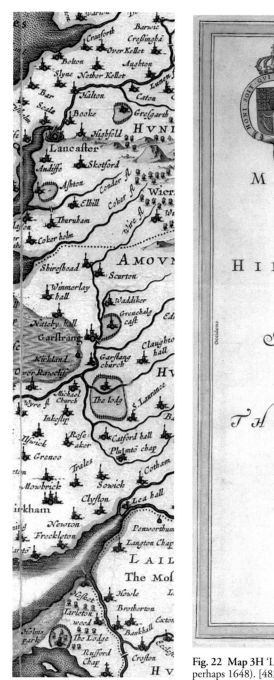

Fig. 22 Map 3H 'Lancastria Palatinatus, Anglis Lancaster et Lancas shire' (1645) by Johan Blaeu, from *Theatrum Orbis Terrarum, sive Atlas Novus* (Blaeu, Amsterdam, edition unknown, perhaps 1648). [483mm x 375mm, 19.0" x 14.8"]

own details, but no regular system is apparent. Most place-names are accurately copied and associated with symbols, but note the totally wrong west coast on the Wirral Peninsula at the lower margin. When tracing the design from Speed the Blaeu designer included more of Cheshire at the foot to achieve a less cramped effect, but apparently did not have the Cheshire map handy and just invented a shape for the extra bit of coastline. A similar more extensive fault is found on the John Bill Lancashire map 3E. The Blaeu map was reprinted until the plate was destroyed by fire in 1672.

When Jan Jansson took over sole ownership of the Mercator-Hondius atlas in 1636, he prepared six English county map plates, including a Lancashire map on Fig. 23 issued from 1636 to 1642 in state 1 (3J) with a figure of Poseidon for decoration and an elaborate title top right. Probably the blank cartouche at lower right was intended for a distance scale, never inserted. Flamboyant swash lettering covers Yorkshire. Engraving is more decorative and almost as proficient as the best for Blaeu, and lettering is much smaller and neater than in the Speed map copied, but Jansson (or his engraver) was more confused than Blaeu and unfortunately made 'double-Dutch' of more Lancashire place-names. There are some errors in association of name and symbol, mainly arising from the large script and ambiguous placing of town names on the Speed plate. For example, in the area between Chat Moss and Bolton (see Fig. 25, where the Speed and the Dutch maps are compared) Jansson wrongly associated names and town symbols as a chain of errors, moving Prestolee to Ratlif [Radcliffe], Ratlif to Farnworth, Farnworth to Highfield - leaving Highfeild (*sic*) without place symbol - and duplicating Ellynbrugh Cha[pel] where Hulton Park was correct. The name Chatmosse was misread as Channosse by both Jansson and Blaeu, which on inspecting Speed's map is not at all unreasonable.

Eleven more counties had been engraved for Jansson by 1644, and when Blaeu published his English maps in 1645, Jansson quickly completed his own set of county maps and revised previous plates to have decoration in a uniform style similar to Blaeu's. Thus in his first complete English atlas of 1646 (and all later editions) the Lancashire map (orginally 3J) was in a second state 3K (Fig. 24), so different that here a second reference is used for the same map (exceptionally, like 2G and 2H). In particular this state has a new title within a cartouche highly decorated in a baroque style. However, Jansson retained the long rhumb lines (or loxodromes) extending across the sea from a compass rose, still oriented on the

obsolete magnetic north. These decorations were carried over from marine charts where they were originally meant to help navigators in setting their course. Jansson failed to correct his 1636 copying errors from Speed. Fig. 26 illustrates the confusion with more problems in the Lune valley near Hornby, originally arising from the engraver Hogenberg's lack of clarity on the Saxton map. When Speed (or Hondius) copied this he omitted the small circle across the river near Hutton which indicated the location of Borwick Hall and associated the name Barwick with the symbol for Arum (modern Arkholme), leaving Arum as a name floating without an indicated location, though this could have been checked quite easily from Speed's Westmorland map where Arum and Barwick are placed correctly (see Fig. 37). The double symbol Saxton gave to Hornby (village and castle) was included, but Melling was incorrectly moved to the park boundary and the name for Tatham ('Tatehᵖm', on Saxton) was omitted; the Speed map seems to have two symbols for Wennington and a spare one at Hornby.

Jansson followed Speed's error over the position for Barwick but left out Arum. He apparently decided to check later on the unnamed Wennington, Thurland castle and Tatham (similarly unlabelled on Speed), but forgot to do so as no names ever appear for them. He incorrectly labelled Hornby village as the castle. Blaeu also copied Speed errors, miscopied Barwic, omitted Arum, labelled Thurland but attached its cast(le) to Wiñgton (Wennington) and ignored Hornby village. All the maps derived from Saxton and Speed copied the unlikely double course of the Lune near Melling around an island about a mile long and wide, which may be an exaggerated flood channel which existed only briefly while Saxton visited Lancaster in 1576. Saxton correctly named Carnforth, but that was altered and contracted to Cräforth on the Speed map, copied as Cranfarth by Jansson and Cranforth by Blaeu. Saxton had included the very prominent Warton Crag as a sugar loaf hill, but this was omitted by Speed and his followers.

About 1640 Jansson stopped linking publications to his cartographic ancestors Hondius and Mercator and began using the Latinised imprint of 'Joannes Janssonius' for his maps and atlases. He tried to keep up with Blaeu by reworking old plates and producing new ones, publishing maps of similarly high quality in his *Novus Atlas, sive Theatrum Orbis Terrarum*, a title as deliberately similar to that used by Blaeu (*Theatrum Orbis Terrarum, sive Atlas Novus*) as the maps themselves. Dutch maps are often unsigned and

Fig. 23 Map 3J 'Comitatus Lancastrensis, The Countie Palatine of Lancaster' first state (1636) by Jan Jansson II, from *Appendix Atlantis* to the Mercator-Hondius Atlas (Jansson, Amsterdam, 1636). [484mm x 361mm, 19.0" x 14.2"]

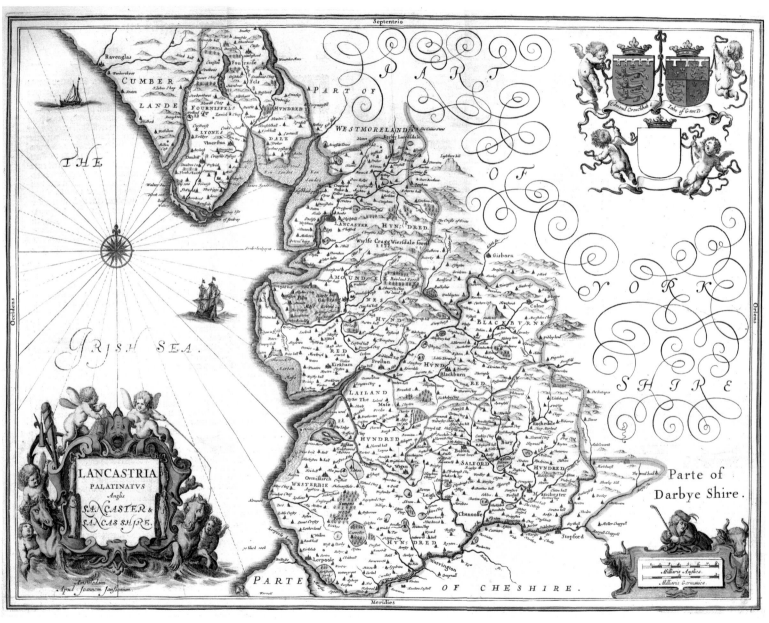

Fig. 24 Map 3K 'Lancastria Palatinatus, Anglis Lancaster & Lancas shire' second state (1646) by Jan Jansson II, from *Novus Atlas, sive Theatrum Orbis Terrarum* (Jansson, Amsterdam, 1652).
[486mm x 362mm, 19.1" x 14.3"]

it can be hard to distinguish from style, content and decoration if they are by Jansson or by Blaeu. One clue is Jansson's weakness for cherubs with ribbons, as at top right on 3K. It is surprising that no significant revisions were made on either of the Dutch county map sets during many years of use for printing (apart from Jansson's decoration changes in 1645-6), but of course those atlases were intended more for ornament than for use. The expansion of Blaeu's *Atlas Major* finally defeated Jansson, whose stock was sold to other Amsterdam publishers after he died in 1664. In particular, about 1694 the county map plates went to Pieter Schenk and Gerard Valck, who revised them and added their own imprint for later issues (probably as loose sheets). Eventually those Jansson plates, and 19 similar Blaeu plates which had survived the fire, found their way to London, to be used there occasionally until about 1730, to print map collections by David Mortier and Joseph Smith (who possibly just imported loose prints taken from the plates in Amsterdam).[9]

So the Amsterdam map plates had an active life of nearly a century and modern reprints preserve the admired Dutch artistry. There were many other atlas productions by European cartographers, but apart from Jansson and Blaeu none featured a Lancashire map to earn inclusion here. However, Pieter van Aa did publish some very rare county maps in 1714, also from Amsterdam, and his series may have included Lancashire. His maps are remarkable only for having elaborate engraved borders about three times larger in area than the maps they surround.[10]

BLOME, UNJUSTLY CONDEMNED?

In contrast to universal praise for Speed and the Dutch atlas maps, the atlas publications of Richard Blome (1635-1705) have attracted adverse comments for 300 years. Today it is difficult to see how Blome is much more at fault than other publishers in copying from the usual suspects, but for example in 1780 Richard Gough called his atlas 'a most notorious piece of plagiarism'.[11] Blome adroitly operated just within the limits of legality and if living today would probably have become a prominent media tycoon. The second volume of his *English Atlas* (1670) was the first world atlas produced entirely in England, though plagiarised from the great French cartographer Nicholas Sanson (1600-1667). In view of the financial difficulties involved it was a major success to get such books published at all.

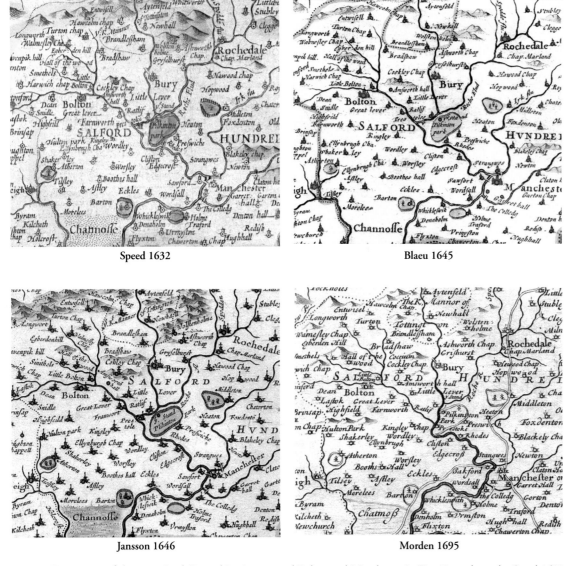

Speed 1632

Blaeu 1645

Jansson 1646

Morden 1695

Fig. 25 Comparison of the same South Lancashire Area around Bolton and Manchester in Fig. 18, as shown by Speed 1632, Blaeu 1645, Jansson 1646 and Morden 1695. [Each section originally 90mm x 80mm]

Blome produced two sets of county maps. The large ones illustrated his *Britannia*, which was published in 1673 as the third volume of the *English Atlas*, with a hack text summarising Camden's *Britannia* and with maps based on Speed at about half the area of that folio volume. In his preface Blome denigrated the Speed maps with the ingenious suggestion that they were so good 'that with usage they are (or soon will be) become useless' via plate wear, and he dismissed the Camden work (last reprinted in 1637) as 'a very dear Book, scarce, much out of print, and never like to be reprinted'. In fact the Speed maps were reprinted for another century, despite plate wear, and only twelve years later a new edition of Camden's *Britannia* much improved by Edmund Gibson would appear (as discussed in the next chapter).

All Blome's publications were financed in part by soliciting sponsorship in return for fulsome dedications on the maps. It cost up to £4 to get your name and coat-of-arms included on a map, but that did not guarantee its appearance in all copies as in some cases dedications were changed on the plate, while in others a new label was pasted to the page over the original. The accuracy of the dedication was also suspect, as we see on Map 3L (Fig. 27) where the griffin and stag supporters of the Derby coat-of-arms have exchanged sides and the motto '*Sans Changer*' is misprinted.

It is worth noting that this is the first new county set designed and published in England for nearly 70 years. Though not outstanding in craftsmanship, the anonymous engraving for Blome is clear and decorative. Wenceslaus Hollar signed the first county map in the atlas and may have engraved some others. For the first time some of the counties, including Lancashire, are oriented in upright 'portrait' format to optimise scale, with north at the left side of the book as on Fig. 27, rather than the wide 'landscape' format used for all the previous map illustrations in this book. Thus the book must be rotated to view the map, allowing Blome to use a map scale in 3L only slightly smaller than Speed's in 3C. Despite the greatly reduced page size, almost all the detail on the Speed map could be included. In view of this relative success it is strange that Blome's large maps are so relatively scarce. They were never reissued except as a very small edition in 1677, probably composed of remainders from the first printing in 1673.[12]

The exact history of the other set of county maps by Blome is not clear. They are smaller, about half the area of the first set. Although there is evidence from imprint dates and dedications that their

Saxton 1577

Speed 1632

Blaeu 1645

Jansson 1646

Fig. 26 Comparison of the North Lancashire Lune Valley Area, as shown by Saxton 1577, Speed 1632, Blaeu 1645 and Jansson 1646. [Each section originally 90mm x 80mm]

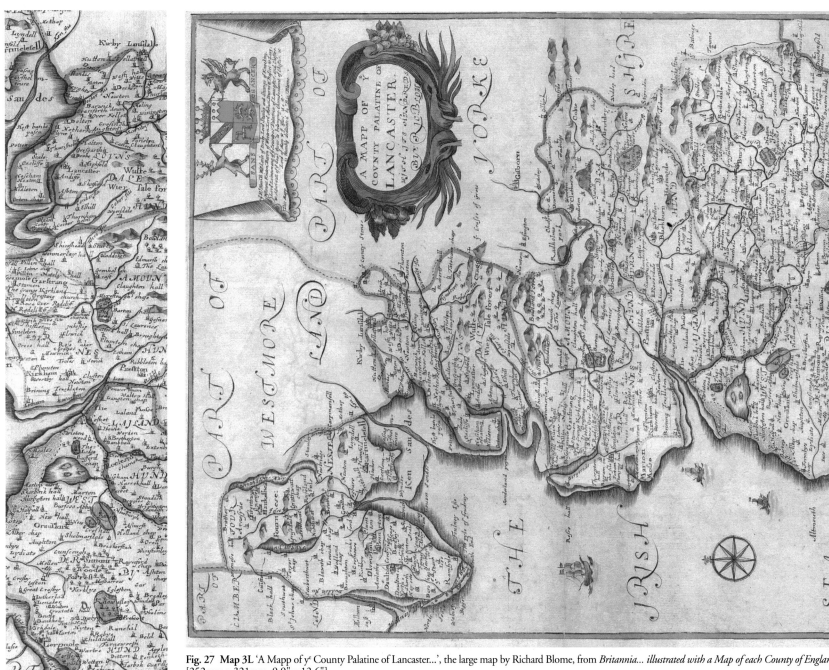

Fig. 27 Map 3L 'A Mapp of yᵉ County Palatine of Lancaster...', the large map by Richard Blome, from *Britannia... illustrated with a Map of each County of England* (R. Blome, London, 1673). [252mm x 321mm, 9.9" x 12.6"]

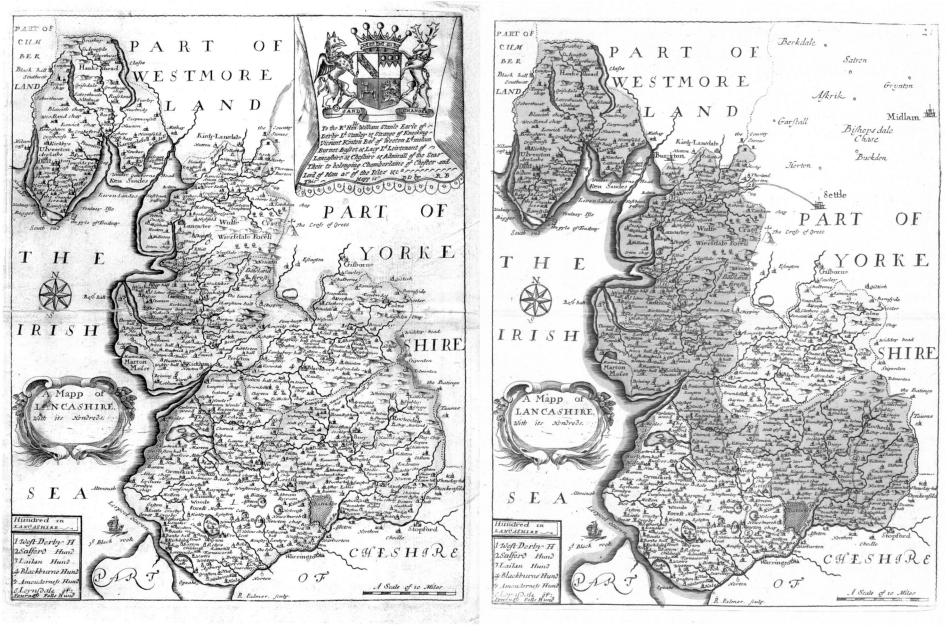

Fig. 28 Map 3M 'A Mapp of Lancashire, With its Hundreds', the small map by Richard Blome; **left** first state from *Speed's Maps Epitomised* (R. Blome, London, 1681); **right** final state from *England Exactly Described...* (Thomas Taylor, London, 1717). [193mm x 243mm, 7.6" x 9.6"]

Fig. 29 Playing Cards with County Maps (all reduced to about half of linear scale).

3P 'Lancaster Sh[ire]:' by Robert Morden, from his pack of playing cards (Morden, London, 1676)
(a) state 1, (b) state 2, both issued in 1676. [map 56mm x 57mm, 2.2" x 2.2"]

(c) state 3 trimmed at top and mounted on a thin page (R. Morden & Joseph Pask, London, 1680).

(d) state 3, no stencil and mounted on a thick page (Homan Turpin, London, 1764 or later).

(e) **3R** 'Lancaster Shire' copied from Robert Morden (in second state example b here) by John Lenthall, from his pack of playing cards (Lenthall, London, first state, 1717).

(f) **3Q** 'Lanca= Shire' by William Redmayne, playing card, first issue (Redmayne, London, 1676).

engraving started earlier than the large maps, perhaps in 1667, they were not used for printing until issued without text as _Speed's Maps Epitomised_ in 1681 and reprinted in 1685. Lancashire (Map 3M in Fig. 28) was signed by Richard Palmer, who engraved it including a dedication and coat-of-arms similar to the large map, but with a _different_ misprint in the motto to again displease the ninth Earl of Derby, despite the supporters now being correctly placed. The final line of the dedication is squashed in to end 'This Mapp is DD [=dedicated] by RB [Richard Blome]'.

The original state of these maps included '... by Ric[hard] Blome' in all the map titles, but this was imperfectly erased from nearly all maps before publication, although Blome was still identified in many of the dedications, as noted above. The title cartouche is identical in design to that on the large map, clearly indicating direct copying. For the last issue of the map by Blome himself, a rare 1693 edition, the very prominent dedication to the Earl of Derby was removed, leaving a large completely blank area at the top right. Thomas Taylor next reprinted the maps in his _England Exactly Described_, filling the blanks with extra place-names in 1715 and adding roads in 1717 to create the final state of map 3M (also in Fig. 28), which was reissued by Thomas Bakewell from 1731 until about 1750. So, rather inappropriately, Blome's small maps of lower quality greatly outlived the better large ones in print and are more commonly available.

PLAYING CARD MAPS

The coincidence of there being 52 playing cards in a pack and 52 counties in England and Wales several times prompted publication of packs with one county on each card (see Fig. 29). The first was by William Bowes in 1590 (see Fig. 21), with 'thumbnail' maps at 40 customary miles per inch, too small to be useful, known almost entirely from later copying by van Langeren (Fig. 20). In this pack the usual suits were replaced by county groups in the North, East, South and West (Wales), and in each group the cards are numbered from I to XIII for counties in increasing size, with Lancashire (2J) as X (Ten) of North. These cards for the first time list the county dimensions, quoting values estimated from the general map _Anglia_ at 22 customary miles per inch in the Saxton atlas, which gave models for the 'thumbnail' maps by Bowes at about half that size.

Another slightly later pack by Bowes (*c.*1605) included suit marks, from which we see the allocation is north = clubs, east = diamonds, south = spades and west = hearts. These cards were generously filled with bizarre miscellaneous information, including the same county descriptions as the 1590 series and the maps at an even more reduced scale. This pack is known only from a unique proof set in the British Library, which is illustrated and discussed in the review of all playing cards showing British maps by Sylvia Mann and David Kingsley.[13]

Cards printed in 1676 by London publisher Robert Morden do have cartographic utility, being neatly engraved on a relatively large area, and some historical significance because in most cases this was the first time the county map included roads, within a year of them being surveyed for the first time by John Ogilby (Box 6). Very few county maps before 1675 showed any roads, but nearly every new map would feature them from then onwards, during the period when horse-drawn coaches became common and road atlases developed towards the prominent role they have today. The routes shown in Ogilby's *Britannia* include five through Lancashire: Warrington to Garstang on Ogilby's plate 37 as part of the road from London to Carlisle, continued for Garstang towards Kendal on plate 38 (see Map 3N in Fig. 30); Clapham to Lancaster concluding the road from York on plate 88; Blackstone Edge to Warrington via Manchester as part of the York to Chester road on plate 89; Manchester to Stockton as the start of a road to Derby on plate 90.

On each section of his strip-maps Ogilby indicated magnetic north for 1675, 3° west of true north and the same 'north' direction would appear on clones of his maps until nearly 1800. Changes in orientation for each road section are indicated by a new compass rose, and gradients are shown by drawings of hills astride the road, upside down for descents, looking very odd at first sight and surely confusing casual users, especially the low hills seen on some strips in 3N (Fig. 30). Bridges were recorded, as were landmarks visible from the road to show the traveller's progress. Some of these were clearly impermanent, such as whether the road was hedged or walled on one or both sides, but the maps were unchanged for 100 years, if one includes the reduced Ogilby editions copied so widely after 1719. County maps were gradually influenced by Ogilby's innovations, not only via the introduction of roads, but also his scale of one statute mile per inch and more subtly via his representation of large towns 'ichnographically' (as a street plan

BOX 6 THE FIRST ENGLISH ROAD MAPPING

John Ogilby (1600-76), the most colourful character in the history of cartography, published the first set of English road maps in 1675. Born near Dundee, he moved to London as a child and had achievements enough for a dozen lifetimes, as dancer, soldier, theatre manager, poet, book seller, publisher and cartographer.[*] He was totally impoverished twice, in 1640 by the Civil War and in 1666 by the Fire of London. His final venture was a multi-volume series on world curiosities, intended to include three atlas-like volumes on Britain, for roads, counties and towns. Only the first was published, but it was original enough to gain Ogilby permanent fame.

Ogilby invented (or re-invented) the 'strip-map' (see Fig. 30), a form still used today to show a route in great detail. In his preface Ogilby mentions the *Peutinger Table* diagram of Roman roads, implying his strip-map idea is from that tradition, but it is possible that manuscripts by Matthew Paris (?-1259) were a source.[†] From 1669 to 1674 Ogilby's surveyors accurately measured main roads in England and Wales with distance measuring wheels with 31½ inch (80cm) diameter referred to by Ogilby as 'Way-Wizers' or 'Wheel Dimensurators'. They performed 80 revolutions per furlong, recorded on a dial rotating (via gearing) once every ten miles. The survey teams recorded distances between places along 7,519 miles (12,100 km) of roads, noting place-names from county maps or by enquiries to bystanders (yielding strange phonetic records of their uncouth dialects). In 1740 these measurements were used to set up new milestones, some of which are still in place today.

Strip-maps were engraved for the roads on folio-size copper plates at a standard scale of one inch per statute mile, the first time this large scale had been used for printed maps and the first consistent use of the mile of 1760 yards introduced by Act of Parliament in 1593 but ignored by the people, who continued to use their 'customary' miles varying locally from about 2000 to 2600 yards. Ogilby thus supervised the first national survey work in England since Saxton a hundred years earlier, a venture which cost him £1400, raised from subscriptions and lotteries with his own books as prizes. The King and Queen signed up to give £500 each, but in typical royal style never supplied actual money. Instead Ogilby was granted relief from paper import duty. In 1675 *Britannia, Volume 1* appeared, containing 200 pages of text and 100 plates of maps. Ogilby died in 1676 a few months after his greatest achievement. The original plates were re-used only once, in 1698 for a final *Britannia* edition published in London by Robert Morden and Abel Swale.

---

* See K. S. Van Eerde, *John Ogilby and the Taste of His Times*, (Folkstone, 1976).
† Discussed by C. Delano-Smith and R.J.P. Kain, *English Maps: a History* (British Library, London, 1999) pp.150-1.

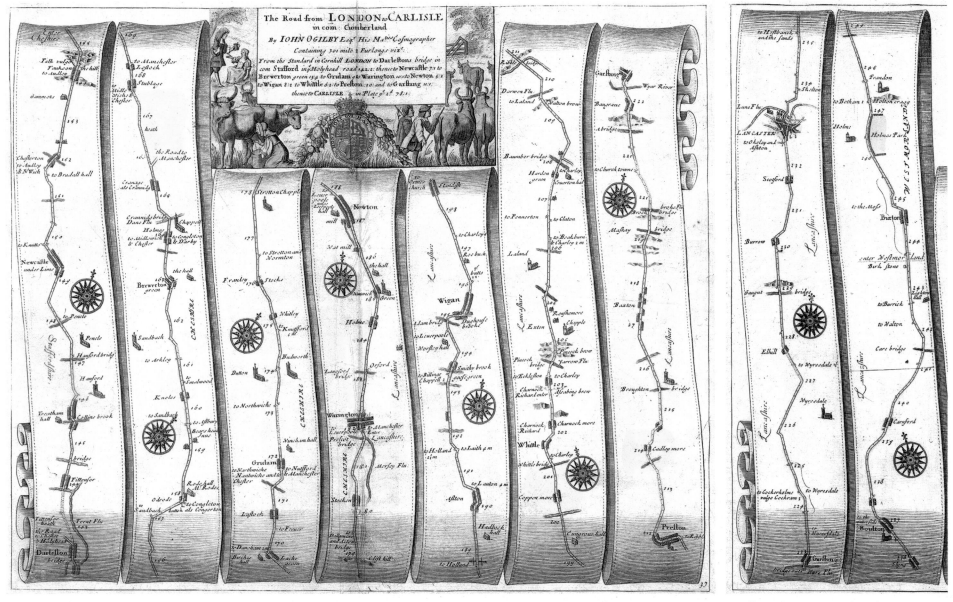

Fig. 30 Map 3N 'The Road from London to Carlisle' (1675), plate 37 in *Britannia, Volume the first* by John Ogilby (Morden & Swale, London, 1698 final reprint) showing Darleston (Staffs.) to Garstang [engraved area 413mm x 333mm, 16.3" x 13.1"] together with left hand section on plate 38 in the same volume, showing the road continuing through Lancaster to the border with Westmorland.

viewed from above, like Lancaster on Fig. 30) rather than 'scenographically' with a prospect view of buildings, as he depicted manor houses, churches and so forth.[14]

Morden indicated the magnetic north for 1676 on all his playing card maps and apparently used that as orientation for many of them, though the small scale makes exact direction uncertain. Clearly several counties were oriented off north to fit them on the card at a larger scale (including Lancashire very slightly rotated), with Cheshire at 40° west and Somerset at 45° east as extreme cases. For suits Morden grouped the counties geographically just as in the Bowes pack (although Warwick and Surrey exchange regions), but allocated suits differently to the regions, except for Clubs remaining in the north. Kings and Queens are illustrated by small portraits of Charles II and his consort, Catherine of Braganza. However, there is no apparent logic in the allocation of a particular county to an individual card in the suit other than some sequential continuity moving around each region. The Lancashire map 3P is on the Three of Clubs. Morden included two explanatory cards describing the pack and its use.

During 1676 Morden packs were issued with stencilled suit marks in the two states shown in Fig. 29(a) and (b). In addition to measurements in 'reputed' miles, Morden included distances to county towns from London in 'measured miles by Esqr. Ogilby with his leave'. Reissues were printed without suit marks as educational pocket-books, first as in Fig. 29(c) in 1680 by Morden and stationer Joseph Pask who described them as 'very useful for travellers and others, and to give Youth an idea of Geography'. So they can be considered to be the first maps sold for use by children, even though not designed as such. Here the cards were trimmed at the top before mounting on thin pages and are in a final third state with extra town names added and the lines for some roads doubled. Another edition *c.*1680 had two similarly trimmed maps per page mounted closely in a tall narrow format as *A Pocket Book ... Being a necessary and plain Direction for Travelling to any Place or Town in all England or Wales.* Revived a century later, Homan Turpin reprinted them in the third state seen in Fig. 29(d), probably between 1772 and 1787. For this final edition each card (without any suit mark) was cut to full size and mounted on a thick paper page.

Remarkably, a second set of playing cards with county maps was also issued in 1676 by William Redmayne. However, the 'thumbnail' maps on these are of no cartographic significance,

unless the replacement of Yorkshire by an ocean on the Lancashire map 3Q (shown in Fig. 29(f)) is found amusing. Presumably the engraver intended to indicate the Irish Sea, but got east and west confused. The allocation of cards to counties seems to be totally random in this pack. Lancashire is on the Ten of Diamonds. The Redmayne cards were reprinted around 1717 by the stationer John Lenthall, who around the same time also published a newly-engraved close copy of the Morden cards, including 3R, shown in Fig. 29(e). This was soon afterwards sold in a second state with decorative borders. The engraver retained the Morden numbering and included the suit marks on the plates, but the actual suit grouping is inconsistent with Lenthall's introductory explanation card describing the county allocation (which identically copied the details from Morden's similar card). Lenthall's engraver confused the intended distribution by exchanging Spades and Diamonds (except for the Kings and Fours) and arbitrarily reassigned two of the Tens (Surrey and Pembroke). These Lenthall packs were on sale until 1754 or later. All examples of playing card maps are very rare, due to the small initial sales and destruction of packs left incomplete after careless use for games.

NOTES

1   The sad aftermath to their revels was recorded in 1663 by the Vicar of Stratford-upon-Avon for 1662-81; *Diary of the Rev. John Ward* (Colburn, London, 1839), p.183 (and comments pp. 59-73).

2   Stated by James Granger, *A Bibliographical History of England...*, vol. I (T. Davies, London, 1779); for a modern biography of John Speed with the most recent scholarship see Sarah Bendall, 'Speed, John (1551/2–1629)', *Oxford Dictionary of National Biography*, Oxford University Press, 2004 [Online edition Jan 2008 at http://www.oxforddnb.com/view/article/26093]

3   Noted by the Merchant Taylor's Company in 1600, according to Arthur Hind, *Engraving in England in the Sixteenth & Seventeenth Centuries,* vol. II (Cambridge University Press, Cambridge, 1955), p.68.

4   Sarah Bendall, 'Draft Town Maps for John Speed's Theatre of the Empire of Great Britain', *Imago Mundi*, 54 (2002), pp.30-45.

5   In addition to the cost of the polished copper plate itself, in 1630 a fee of 100 carolus guilders (equivalent to about £14 then) was negotiated for the engraving of each plate in a set of 36. These were made to extend the Mercator-Hondius Atlas, as agreed by Henry Hondius and Jan Jansson in a contract reported by C. Koeman in *Atlantes Neerlandici*, II (Theatrum Orbis Terrarum, Amsterdam, 1969), p. 345.

6   See notes on printing methods by Peter van der Krogt in the introductory text with facsimile *Blaeu Atlas Maior* (Taschen, Cologne, 2005). The huge capital value of engraved plates is shown by the estimated costs of the fire which destroyed Blaeu's print house, 27,000 florins for the building and equipment, but 335,000 florins for the stock of around 1000 plates, as quoted by John Goss in *Blaeu's The Grand Atlas...* (Studio Editions, London, 1990) p.9. This implies that in 1672 a typical Blaeu copper plate was worth 300 florins, £10,000 today.

7   These changes were first noted and discussed in Diana Winterbotham, *John Speed's Map of Lancashire*, CNWRS Regional Bulletin, 9 (1995), pp.65-8. Her suggestion of 1614-16 for the amendments is a little too late, as they are all present on a print owned by the author from a Speed atlas firmly dated to 1612 publication.

8   See the Diary of Samuel Pepys, entries for 19-21 September 1666; available online at http://www.pepys.info/1666/1666sep.html (accessed February 2013).

9   The complex tale is told by Donald Hodson, *County Atlases of the British Isles, Volume 1 (1704-1742)* (Tewin Press, Welwyn, 1984) pp.31-40.

10 See illustration of 'Cumberland' by van der Aa in Y. Beresiner, *British County Maps* (Antique Collectors' Club, Woodbridge, 1983) p.41.

11 Richard Gough, *British Topography* Vol. 1 (London, 1780), p.37.

12 However, Hodson, *County Atlases of the British Isles, Volume 1*, p.145, reports a Willdey Atlas of *c.*1732 (B.L. Maps C.29.c.3) containing an inserted Blome map of Staffordshire with roads added and the title re-engraved. This indicates that there may have been an unrecorded attempt to update and reprint at least some of the large Blome maps after the 1677 issue.

13 Sylvia Mann and David Kingsley, *Playing Cards Depicting maps of the British Isles...*, Map Collectors Series 9, No 87, (The Map Collectors Circle, London, 1972).

14 A century later (from *The Large English Atlas* onwards) such representation 'ichnographically' would become standard for a large town on a county map, involving the use of an enlarged street plan (typically simplified from a large scale map) rather than the long-established conventional picture of schematic buildings viewed sideways. The terms 'ichnographically' and 'scenographically' are used by Ogilby in 'Decyphering these Roads upon Copper-Sculptures' in the Preface to *Britannia, Volume the First...*, by John Ogilby (Ogilby, London, 1675), note 5.

4   The Era of Imitation (1690–1750)

As mapmaking entered the eighteenth century, Saxton and Speed had firmly established an atlas of England to consist of county maps, based on Saxton's survey and with accompanying text from Camden's *Britannia* at various removes. The excellent maps produced in Amsterdam for Speed, and by the Hondius-Jansson and Blaeu families, are fine works of art and worthy contributions to cartography, so influential that county maps continued their decorative theme for the sixty years of this next era. However, these later maps became less distinguished and indeed were dismissed as 'with few exceptions, work of little artistic merit, and less originality' by the pioneer map historian Sir Herbert Fordham.[1] Nevertheless, they have the advantage of being the oldest original maps with easy availability, as growing demand from the middle-class travelling public caused non-specialist publishers to enter the map market by copying standard basic designs and printing multiple copies of them. They show the development of the road network in the earliest days of turnpike improvement and are decorative at affordable prices.

MORDEN AND THE GIBSON *BRITANNIA*

After 1637 Camden's *Britannia* was not reprinted for nearly 60 years, apart from plagiarised abridgements. About 1690 the young Edmund Gibson (1669-1748) began to lead a team of scholars (including Pepys, Evelyn and Aubrey) in newly translating Camden's Latin text and revising it to include the latest knowledge. His fine new edition, published in 1695, was illustrated with double-page folio county maps designed by Robert Morden, a cartographer, publisher and bookseller in London from 1668 until his death in 1703 and the designer/publisher of the playing cards reviewed in the previous chapter.

In his preface Gibson explained that the most up-to-date county map available (in many cases the Lea version of a Saxton map) had

been 'sent to some of the most knowing Gentlemen in each County with a request to supply the defects, rectifie the positions, and correct the false spellings'. In the immodest style of the age, Gibson claimed the resulting Morden maps to be 'by much the fairest and most correct of any that have yet appear'd'. This is a distinct exaggeration and perhaps it is as well for his soul that Gibson later spent over 30 years as an Anglican Bishop. However, the text translation and additions were excellent and the Gibson edition of *Britannia* was very popular, reprinted several times. So Morden maps are common and by far the least expensive of any folio maps first published in the seventeenth century. It is surprising that these maps were not sold loose or reprinted as a county atlas without text, but perhaps the publishers thought separate map sales would seriously reduce the market for the whole work.

Rather than the wide 'landscape' format generally used for folio maps before 1700, for eight maps in this *Britannia* (Scotland, Ireland, Buckinghamshire, Cambridgeshire, Lancashire, Northumberland, Oxfordshire and Staffordshire). Morden used an upright 'portrait' format (see Fig. 31), as Blome had introduced for Lancashire (Fig. 27) in 1673. However, Blome's volume was much smaller, about the size of this one. Morden for the first time required the reader to rotate a full-sized folio book though 90° for viewing maps with text running vertically up the normal page direction, which is not a trivial exercise with an open book half a metre wide weighing over 4kg. Presumably once north orientation had become the norm, Smith's method a century earlier of using an unusual orientation (Fig. 12) was no longer acceptable.

However, Morden did not exploit his new format by enlarging the Lancashire map itself, which has exactly the same scale and county outline as in all the earlier folio editions, and it is clear that the draft for 4A was traced directly from a Saxton-Lea map 2H of 1693 (Fig. 11), itself printed from the original Saxton plate as modified by Lea, in particular to include roads from John Ogilby's survey (and a few others). The Saxton-Lea source was a best choice for Morden because as yet roads had not been inserted on the Speed maps, but thus Morden missed some improvements Speed had introduced, such as the correction of the River Irwell course which on the Morden map appears in Saxton's incorrect form (see Figs.18 and 25).

Although Morden closely copied Saxton-Lea, on 4A he added coastal sandbanks in a realistic form from the 1689 Irish Sea chart by Captain Greenvile Collins. He also tidied up and in general much

Fig. 31 Map 4A 'The County Palatine of Lancaster' (1695), final state of the large map by Robert Morden, from Edmund Gibson's version of Camden's *Britannia* (R. Ware *et al.*, London, third edition, 1753), with modern colouring in original style. [345mm x 407mm, 13.6" x 16.0"]

improved the place-names, though some new errors were introduced. For a second state of the Lancashire map about 30 minor corrections were made, mainly south of the Ribble. The states can be distinguished easily from state 1 having 'Ken Sand(s)' named twice in Morecambe Bay, while for the second state 'Lancaster Sands' appears at the top near Cartmel (see Fig. 31) although it was the other name which should have been corrected. The plate had been amended by the time Gibson issued a new version of his translation in 1722 (as an extended revised text with most of the maps corrected), but about that time Moll copied a first state Morden Lancashire for his map 4F (published in 1724), which indicates that no changes were made until just before 1722. The plates had been used so heavily by 1753 that substantial retouching had to be performed to correct plate wear for an edition in that year. Fig. 31 shows the Morden map in this third state, in particular with hill and tree symbols strongly emphasised. The map was unchanged when reprinted for the last time in 1772.

Morden makes a big step forward by introducing latitude and longitude calibrations on the sides, previously used for Lancashire only by Bill on his small map of 1626. The latitude values are reasonably correct for the date, but the Lancashire map is oriented with true north about 10° anticlockwise from the vertical map direction, which remains aligned near to Saxton's magnetic north (11° east of true north in about 1575) even though by 1695 the compass deviation was 7° west (see Box 7). These are the first maps to make it clear that the top is not true north, by having the latitude calibrations offset 12½ minutes of arc between the right and left hand sides. It is also one of the first to show longitude measured from London, rather than from a point far off in the Atlantic Ocean. The 3° west longitude line is very nearly correct relative to an origin at St Paul's Cathedral (as implied on the Middlesex map), only about three minutes of arc east of the true position, which is much more accurate than on most maps published throughout the following century.

The almost unique calibration along the top edge of Morden's Map 4A is the time difference from London (correctly offset relative to longitudes at the foot), a reminder that before the middle of the nineteenth century each town in the kingdom had its own local time, loosely based on astronomical observations, getting earlier towards the west. So in Liverpool the clocks were about 12 minutes ahead of London and in Manchester 9 minutes ahead. Far in the

BOX 7   THE PROBLEMS OF MAGNETIC NORTH

A magnetic compass points towards *magnetic north*, and in general there is a significant difference between true north and that direction, known as the 'magnetic variation' or 'declination'. So even if a map orientation is 'north', there is the question of *which* north, true north, magnetic north, or something else. The Saxton county maps are oriented about 10° east from true north, near magnetic north in 1576, indicating this to be the reference direction he used for his survey work. Variation is nearly the same all over a small area like England, but changes significantly further across the world and before 1500 navigators began working out the pattern. Then in 1635 it was realised that the Earth's magnetic field varies with time as well as with place.[*] Magnetic north was moving to the west in England so that in 1660 a compass pointed directly at true north, reaching 14° west by 1720 and nearly 30° west by 1830. Then it returned eastwards to give the relatively small magnetic variation we have today. Around 2050 the variation will be zero again.

For 150 years county maps were copied from Saxton using his orientation and were indeed oriented on 'something else', the obsolete 1576 compass direction. This must have badly confused anybody trying to use a magnetic compass with maps in the 1600s and 1700s. John Bill was first to orient county maps on true north in 1626, but his maps (3E) were small and rare and this change was not clear. Robert Morden implied true north via the edge calibrations on his main map sets (4A and 4B), and Herman Moll inserted an explicit true north indicator when he revised Morden's small map (see Fig. 32). In 1695 John Seller clearly used our modern orientation on true north for his complete set of small maps (see Fig. 34), followed by Moll in 1724 (Fig. 36), and eventually by the mid-eighteenth century orientation on true north became standard.

True north was used by Ortelius and Mercator for their atlas maps. However, the Ortelius map 2A (Fig. 5) is oriented about 12° *west* from true north, giving it a very odd appearance to modern eyes, especially the unusual tilt of the English Channel with Sussex apparently well south of Cornwall. At the time the map was drawn magnetic north was 12° *east* from true north. The probable explanation is that when Ortelius received the draft map of England from Humphrey Lhuyd he incorrectly assumed it was oriented on magnetic north and so when copying it for printing he adjusted the orientation to true north by making a 12° clockwise rotation, not realising that this already had been done by Lhuyd (who was dead and unavailable for comment by 1573). So the correction from magnetic north to true north was done twice, giving the uniquely misleading orientation of map 2A.

[*] A. Jackson, A.R.T. Jonkers and M.R. Walker, 'Four centuries of Geomagnetic Secular Variation from Historical Records', *Phil. Trans. R. Soc. Lond. A*, 358, 1768 (2000), pp.957-90.

future the advent in 1830 of rapid rail travel between these two cities would make such differences highly inconvenient, eventually leading to the introduction of 'Railway Time' across the land around 1850 and the adoption of a national Greenwich Mean Time in 1880.

Almost all these maps by Morden show three distance scales, for long and short customary miles and something like statute miles (the shortest). As we have seen, the length of a mile was poorly defined in that period. The rod or perch in Lancashire was variously 8, 7½ or 7 yards, as well as 5½ yards to give 1760 yards for the statute mile (as defined for London in 1593, but not accepted elsewhere until well into the eighteenth century). On this basis Lancashire miles could be 2560, 2400, 2240 or 1760 yards. By taking one degree of latitude to define 69½ statute miles, the scales on all Morden county maps can be compared, but this reveals huge variations, with ranges of 3510-1950 yards, 3020-1720 yards and 2070-1440 yards for the three mile sizes.[2] For Lancashire we find 2289, 2044 and 1800 yards. It is not clear what conclusions can be drawn. Were miles really gigantic in Worcestershire and tiny in Surrey? The most likely implication is that the various scales are notional and Morden was very careless over these details.

THE SMALL MORDEN MAPS

Morden designed another set of county maps, published in 1701 not long before his death, very similar to those he made for the 1695 *Britannia* but a lot smaller and less detailed. Their history is not completely unravelled, but it is almost certain they were drawn and even engraved before 1693 as a first attempt at the new maps for *Britannia*, and probably they were the very first to show longitude based on London (rather than Morden's large set discussed above). 'New Proposals' appeared in 1693 to justify a rise in subscription price for Gibson's edition of *Britannia*, stating that the maps already produced to the original specification 'were not thought Large and Comprehensive enough, by some Judicious and Ingenious Gentlemen that assist in the work, Who think it Proper and Necessary to have the Maps of Every County full as Large as this sheet will admit, and ... the Undertakers ... Resolved to have the Maps so done ... Though the Expence (sic) will be at least 500 l. Extraordinary.'[3] That additional cost of £500 (or more) for the fifty folio maps implies that engraving each large Morden plate cost about £10 (in 1693 currency, perhaps £5000 today). The small Morden maps have been identified as the rejected set because of their

similarity of style to the large series actually used for the 1695 *Britannia*. Morden eventually printed the small maps in 1701 (see Fig. 32) with an anonymous text entitled *A New Description and State of England...*, followed by two further issues in 1704 of the same work.

The plates were revised by Herman Moll (according to the title page) and published as *Fifty Six New and Acurate* (sic) *Maps of Great Britain* ... in 1708. Similarity in style suggests that for many counties Moll may have done the original engraving of the plates for Morden, although he did not sign any. Fig. 32 also shows a later printing of this second state of 4B for Lancashire, with the addition of five extra place-names, the destinations of roads leaving the county, a distance scale where the 'English Miles' correspond to 2020 yards, and a true north compass indicator which explicitly shows the map axis still oriented on magnetic north for 1570. Another useful addition by Moll was an asterisk attached to some town symbols, for the first time clearly and correctly indicating the parliamentary boroughs which elected Members in Parliament. Philip Lea first attempted this when around 1689 he attached rather unclear 'crown' signs to the towns Lancaster, Clitheroe, Preston, Wigan, Liverpool and Manchester on a reissue of the Saxton map. Presumably Lea thought that Manchester *must* be a borough, but despite its large and growing population it had no parliamentary representation at this time, or for long after. He incompletely removed that erroneous crown for the 1693 Saxton-Lea edition (Fig. 11), but the borough sign was not awarded to tiny Newton until Moll inserted it correctly on 4B in 1708.

The small Morden maps next appeared in a publication with a complex history, *Magna Britannia et Hibernia...* which was the first example of an atlas designed as a magazine issued in monthly sections (costing one shilling). Very soon after the launch in January 1714 the rate of printing became irregular, as happened for almost all the many later examples of county atlases in instalments. Part 4 appeared in July 1715 after a long delay and eventually the series for England was completed after 17 years of erratic publication. Counties had been described in alphabetical order, reaching Lancashire in June and July 1719 (as parts 26 and 27) and eventually finishing with Yorkshire with part 92 in April 1731. The *Magna Britannia* journal then stopped, including nothing outside England and abandoning the original plan to cover the rest of Great Britain.

In 1720 the publishers collected sections printed by then into the first volumes (two of an eventual six) for atlas publication. The

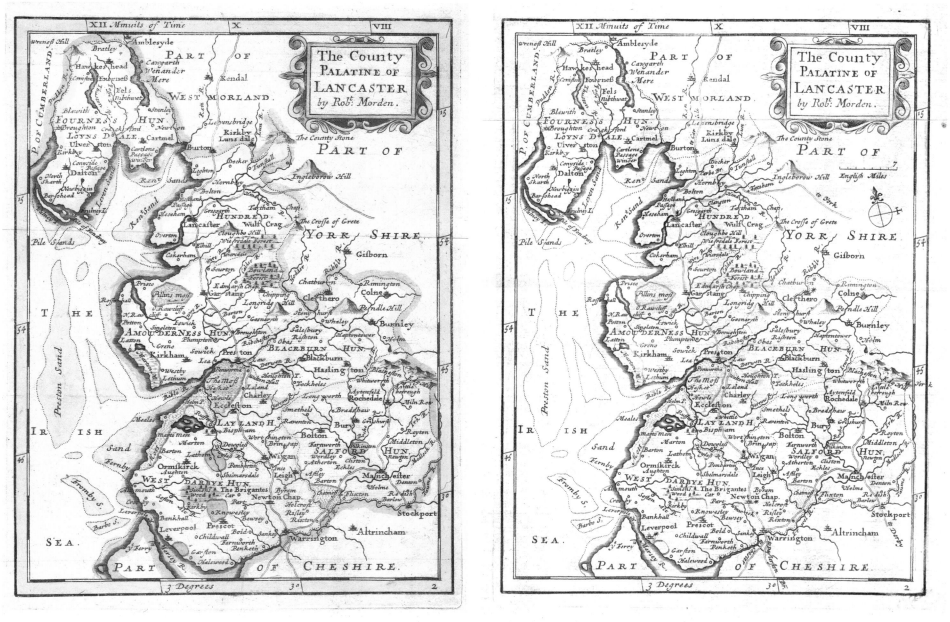

Fig. 32 Map 4B 'The County Palatine of Lancaster' (1701), the small map by Robert Morden; **left** from *The New Description and State of England*... (R. Morden, T. Cockerill & R. Smith, London, 1701) [150mm x 194mm, 5.9" x 7.6"]; **right** from *Magna Britannia et Hibernia*... Volume II, as revised by Moll (E. Nutt, M. Nutt & J. Morphew, London, 1720) [147mm x 194mm, 5.8" x 7.6"]

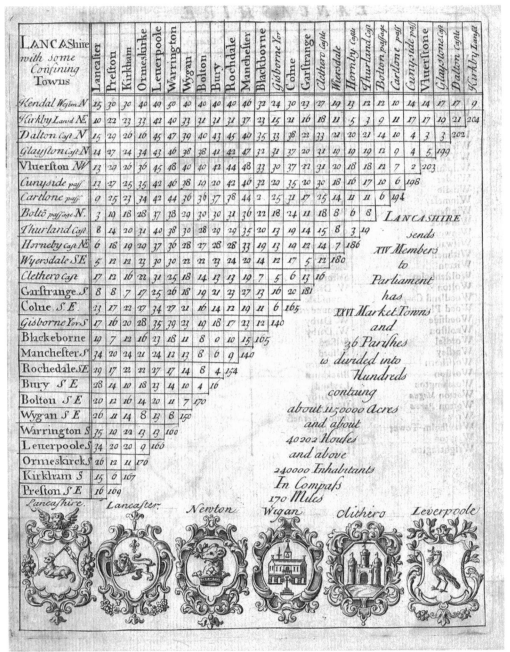

Fig. 33 Lancashire Distance Table (1719) from *Magna Britannia et Hibernia...* Volume II, (E. Nutt, M. Nutt & J. Morphew, London, 1720) [between outer lines 148mm x 186mm, 5.8" x 7.3"]

other volumes came out at about three year intervals as they were completed in the magazine. Each county was illustrated by the revised Morden map and a triangular distance table (see 4C Fig. 33) copied from the Jenner tables (such as 3G) containing the Norden distances of 1625, despite their use of long miles and clear inaccuracy. Indeed there are new errors, in particular for the inserted distances from London where Jenner's map overlapped entries on the distance table, for example on 4C a nonsensical 16 miles from London to Clitheroe, rather than 168, and similar errors for Bury and Thurland. The engraver clearly did not understand these numbers and presumably thought the coat-of-arms for Preston was sufficiently identified by proximity to that name in the table. 'Lancashire' was incorrectly inserted by a different hand as an amendment, and probably 25 years later this wrongly labelled coat of arms was copied on map 4K (Fig. 40).

The map plates, all complete books and the remaining stock of magazine parts (varying from zero to over 1000 copies) were sold off in 1738 for £200 to Caesar Ward and Richard Chandler, partners as booksellers with shops in London, York and Scarborough. By reprinting part 1 they made up about 140 complete sets and reissued them as six volumes in 1739. The surplus remaining parts were offered as text on individual counties, with the map. But success did not follow and many serious debts caused Chandler to commit suicide in 1744. Ward was forced to declare bankruptcy and the entire remains of *Magna Britannia...* were sold at auction early in 1746 for £38.50, including the map plates as scrap copper. The already printed sections were sold on again and the obscure London bookseller Joseph Marshall advertised parts for all but seven counties in 1751. Right up to around 1800 some individual county texts were still available.

JOHN SELLER MAPS AND SEA CHARTS

So many sea charts and atlases were imported into England from Holland in the eighteenth century that a 30 per cent import tax was imposed as a protectionist measure. Chart printing in Britain was first undertaken by non-conformist John Seller (1630-1697) who had survived a conviction and death sentence for high treason with five others in 1662, being pardoned after nearly a year in prison, though four of the others were executed. He had obtained about 60 badly worn engraved Dutch plates for sea charts as scrap copper, which in 1671 he 'refreshed' with English titles and began to sell as his *English Pilot*, thus inaugurating the London chart industry. However, most of the plates acquired by Seller had been copied by Jansson in 1620 from a Blaeu sea atlas of 1608 and already were at least sixty years out of date. Although Seller built up quite a large business on this insecure basis and was made Royal Hydrographer for life, even with the minimum of expensive updating and re-touching it was never a very profitable venture. He sold out in 1679 and by 1715 all his copper plates had passed to the chart-publishing dynasty of Mount and Page, who ignored their mainly 1608 origin and without revision used them (and Greenvile Collins plates) for printing charts until about 1800. One wonders how many shipwrecks resulted from their inaccuracy, and how many lives were lost.

Seller turned to county mapping and aimed to produce a very large-scale county atlas, in 1680 inviting advance subscriptions of one pound, with a further thirty shillings [£1.50] to be paid on publication. Six counties (not including Lancashire) were mapped at scales from one to four miles to the inch, but lack of finance ended that project in 1693. Seller settled for publishing a set of very small county maps in his much less ambitious *Anglia Contracta*, which was issued probably from about 1694; its publishing history is not at all clear. Seller also used the maps in his *History of England* of 1696 and 1703, and in an abridged edition of Camden's *Britannia* (translated from the Latin summary printed by Blaeu in 1617) published in 1701, reprinted in 1711 and possibly again about 1737.[4] Lancashire (4D, Fig. 34) is at 20 statute miles per inch scale, with the rivers emphasised. The land is shown in the Saxton format, imperfectly copied, with a small clockwise rotation (similar to that by Bill on 3E) to match the grid orientation by placing true north at the top.

The small Seller maps lack other details, but have originality via the introduction of grid lines and orientation on true north for the second time on county maps. For Lancashire the grid squares have sides of ten customary miles, apparently laid out from Lancaster. For the Home Counties the grid origin is St Paul's Cathedral in London which was chosen by Seller as the site for the British prime meridian in 1676 when for the first time on any English map he used a convenient local origin of longitude, rather than the distant zero at one of the various islands in the Atlantic Ocean traditional since Ptolemy. (Other map-makers used the London Stone in Cannon

Street and eventually Greenwich would become the national choice, later adopted by the world.) About 1787 these maps were reissued in a new state (shown later in Fig. 57), but despite that long interval it was modified only by the replacement of the title cartouche and the addition of a few place-names.

EMANUEL BOWEN'S FIRST COUNTY MAPS

In a few places we have referred already to the copying of roads from John Ogilby's *Britannia* of 1675 to update county maps. This book is not the place to tell the story of road mapping and here we

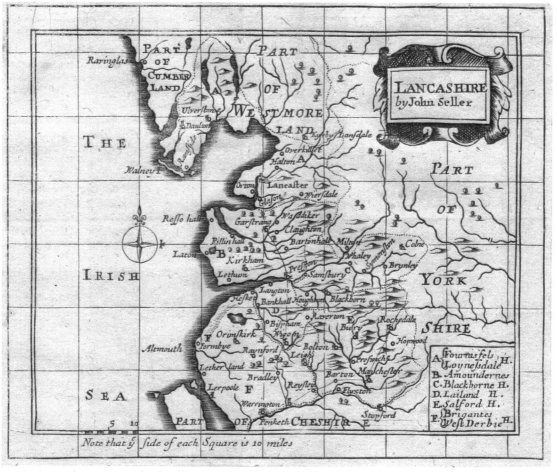

Fig. 34 Map 4D 'Lancashire' (*c*.1694) by John Seller, from *Camden's Britannia Abridg'd;...*(J. Wild, London, 1701). [131mm x 104mm, 5.2" x 4.1"]

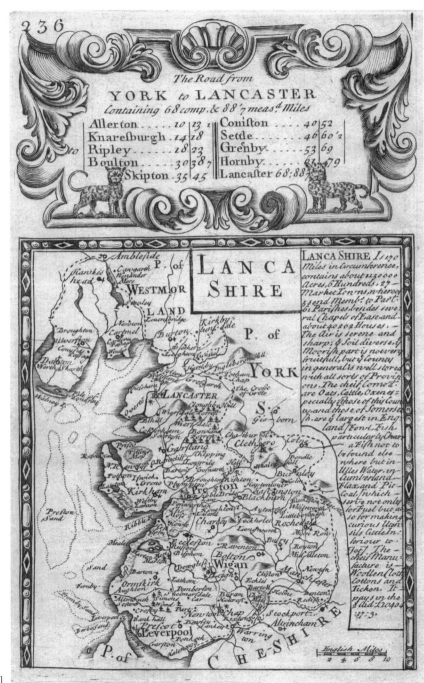

note only that the folio-size road 'strip-maps' published by Ogilby in 1675 were not copied as more portable reduced versions until 1719, a rather astonishing delay. Then three reduced clones from Ogilby all appeared within a few months. *Britannia Depicta, or Ogilby Improv'd* was the last, but turned out to be by far the best-seller among them, reprinted many times.

Emanuel Bowen (whose career is discussed in the next chapter) engraved the entire work on 278 small copper plates, including all the text and titles. The publisher was Thomas Bowles, who ran his father's London bookshop from 1714 until 1764 and (with his brother John) established family publishing businesses of great importance for over a century. Carington Bowles (son of John) continued their publishing of road maps and other works until his own death in 1793, succeeded by his son Henry. The road map engraving is of fair quality considering that all the plates were made in a year; work started late in 1718 when the proposals were issued and the book was published in February 1720. Unlike any other road books of this type, sections were headed by plates containing small county maps such as 4E (Fig. 35), all designed and engraved by Bowen.

The road strips were at two miles per inch, half the Ogilby scale, but contained the same details 'improved' by a fair attempt to correct eccentricities of spelling, and featured coats-of-arms and notes inserted rather untidily in all the spaces normally left blank around the strips. Such copious notes on maps would become a Bowen characteristic thirty years later. The young antiquary John Owen devised the notes, mainly extracted from text in Ogilby's *Britannia*, itself partly derived from Camden's *Britannia*. Thus many of the notes were fanciful or obsolete even when engraved, let alone seventy years later when still in print. 'Owen and Bowen' are usually citied as authors of the road maps to distinguish them from Bowen's many other works.

The *Lanca Shire* map 4E is based on the small Morden map 4B as revised in 1708. Distances are tabulated above it in the statute miles measured by Ogilby as well as the more familiar 'computed' miles of about 2300 yards. As in the revised 4B Bowen indicated all the six boroughs which elected two Members of Parliament (using a pair of asterisks) and this indication became common practice on later county maps. However, the text on the right of the map states there are five boroughs, perhaps via Owen counting them on the Saxton-Lea map, where Newton was not labelled. Although the

Bowen maps were reprinted unchanged until about 1780, much improved surveying was in progress, and by 1750 these county maps must have looked very old fashioned indeed.

HERMAN MOLL ADJUSTS THE BOUNDARIES

Herman Moll (1654-1732) came to London from Germany in 1678, not 1688 as stated by many authorities (from Chubb to Beresiner, till corrected by Tooley), settling there for his career as a celebrated map engraver and publisher of some notable cartography, such as the atlas *The World Described*. He was the first to propose an improved version of the Ogilby road atlas, and though his project was abandoned it may have stimulated the three versions actually published. It is probable that he engraved the fantasy maps included in early editions of Jonathan Swift's *Gulliver's Travels* (1726), where 'my worthy friend Mr. Herman Moll' is actually mentioned by the narrator Gulliver in Part IV, Chapter XI.

Moll influenced later county map sets via maps in *A New Description of England and Wales...* published in 1724 and reprinted without text early in 1725 with 'old style' 1724 dating. These reduced versions of Morden's large maps in the Gibson *Britannia* were the first significant county maps to use an orientation on true north, following the lead given by the small maps from Bill in 1626 and Seller in 1694. Their other notable novelty is that (as the atlas title explains) 'to render this Work more acceptable to the Curious, the Margins of each Map are adorn'd with great Variety of very remarkable Antiquities', a late example of superfluous decoration. Speed had included such details on some of his maps, but not consistently, and by 1720 archaeology was becoming fashionable. Lancashire on 4F (Fig. 36) is adorned with local Roman relics, mainly from Ribchester, successfully attracting the curious for nearly 300 years, though the drawings are not original.[5] The plate number (46 in the top left border) was introduced during the first printing runs in 1724-5. Moll has included single asterisks for parliamentary boroughs, but only for Lancaster, Preston and Liverpool. Perhaps he was unsure of the others and never got around to checking. Roads are shown, mainly from Morden, but routes from Poulton-le-Fylde to Garstang and Preston are shown for the first time. Distances along the roads are in the customary long miles. Some place-names have been copied incompletely or incorrectly, and Moll transcribed errors in the first state of the Morden map.

Moll recognised that previous map sets did not show county boundaries fitting together accurately without gaps, and in the preface he boasts his boundaries are 'regularly and methodically disposed'. However, this consistency was not achieved by research into the correct position, but by fudging. One local example is the Arnside area, which according to Saxton and Speed is in neither Lancashire nor Westmorland (see the extracts from two Speed maps in Fig. 37). Moll wrongly included Arnside in Lancashire, which was copied for later maps, and distorted the western boundary with Yorkshire. He correctly followed Morden's Westmorland map in excluding the waters of 'Winander Mere' from Lancashire, but it was well over 100 years before the boundary here was consistently established on maps. In the meantime on various maps Windermere was shown randomly in or out, or half and half as on Saxton, or with no clear boundary at all. Confusion over the Hundreds, with Lonsdale split into two parts, was still to be clarified, though not by Moll with a gap in his list of the Hundred names and his omission of the Leyland Hundred. But Moll does have latitude and longitude values correct enough for their date, though relative to Morden and reality he has moved the 3° west longitude about a tenth of a degree too far east.

The draining of Martin Mere is indicated for the first time. Between the future site of Southport and the River Douglas Saxton had noted a large area slightly below sea level which was under shallow water apart from three islands, labelling it 'Marton Mere' rather than the modern 'Martin Mere'. Some people declared it to be the largest lake in England. In 1692 Thomas Fleetwood obtained an Act of Parliament for its drainage and put 2000 men to work digging an embanked sluice 24 feet wide across the middle of the mere to the coast, where flood gates stopped the sea from entering at high tide. The newly drained land was used for farming, but the flood gates silted up and the area was still very liable to flood. Moll showed the sluice as two lines across a dry mere, though still containing three islands, but did not indicate the connection to the sea and perhaps relied on a text reference to explain what was signified. This would have confused readers of most editions as in general the maps were reprinted without text and without change, except for a plate number alteration to 23 when an alphabetical county sequence was introduced in 1747.

All these early issues are rare and lack of plate wear suggests very little use in all that time. Some of the faint guide lines used to line up text during engraving in 1724 (for example for 'IRISH SEA') are still

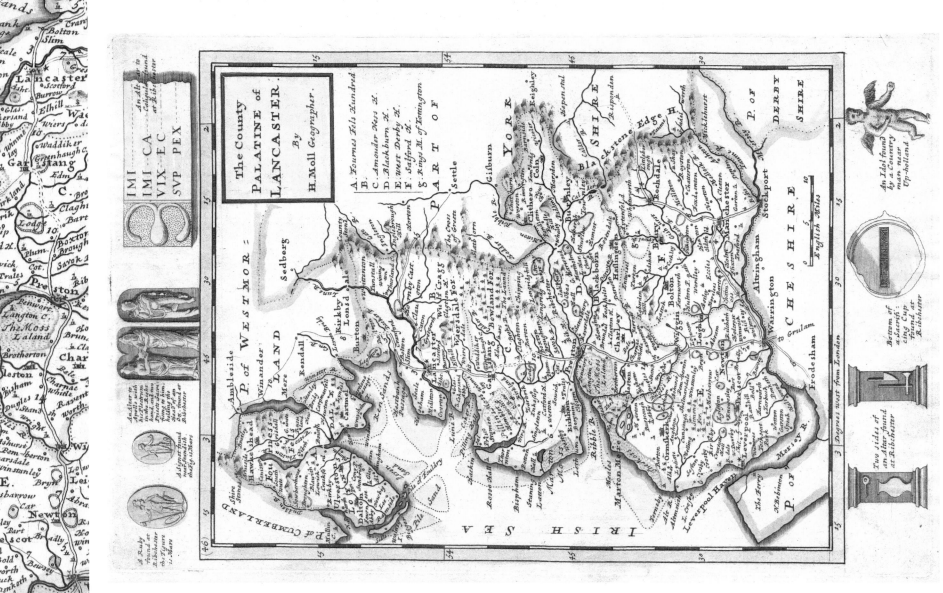

Fig. 36 Map 4F 'The County Palatine of Lancaster...' (1724) by Herman Moll, in *A New Description of England and Wales...* (H. Moll, C. Rivington and T. & J. Bowles, London, 1724).
[180mm x 243mm, 7.0" x 9.6"]

Fig. 37 Comparison of boundary regions in Speed's maps of Westmorland (**left**) and Lancashire (**right**), both excluding Arnside Tower from the county area being mapped and showing other inconsistencies. [Section 60mm x 40mm]

visible on a 1747 print, published by Thomas and John Bowles well after the death of Moll. For the final state used from 1753 the Bowles brothers cut down the plate to remove the antiquities and small details were added or changed (by Emanuel Bowen according to the title page) such as road distances put into statue miles. The Moll maps in this state were on sale until 1768, and perhaps later.

MAPS BY ROYAL COMMAND

A set of small maps was drawn by surveyor and engineer Thomas Badeslade (?-1745), mainly based on Moll (in particular for orientation and outline), and engraved by William Henry Toms (c.1701-1761) for the *Chorographia Britanniae* atlas of 1742, owned by Toms. In its day this was a best-seller, the first atlas at a convenient small pocket-size of 11 cm x 17 cm (4½" x 7") and a corresponding small price, namely 6 shillings [30p] for the bound set. The atlas was being advertised for sale until 1759.

The title page states that the maps were 'first Drawn and compiled ... by Order and for the Use of his late Majesty King George I'. If this is true, Badeslade must have created the draft maps between 1724 (when Moll's maps became available) and the king's death in 1727, making them fifteen years old when engraved by Toms. Explicit information is given on parliamentary representation in the column of useful information for the county, in addition to the usual asterisks for boroughs on the map, explaining that two members were elected to represent the whole county in addition to the two members for each of the six boroughs, giving the total of fourteen MPs. The note also stresses that Lancashire has only 36 parish churches, an unusually small number. All the information was engraved on the map plates themselves, instead of in separate typeset text normally included with an atlas.

These are the first county maps to use 'form lines' parallel to the coast (see 4G, Fig. 38) to emphasise the sea boundary, either via a borrowing which introduced this idea to English county maps, or as an original invention by Badeslade or by Toms. The form lines could have been used in this atlas because the customary short horizontal shading for coastal emphasis (to be seen on nearly all maps before 4G) had been adopted already to emphasis the land boundaries of the counties and a new way to emphasise the coast was needed. Many people find such heavy shading all around the counties makes them look too much like islands. Despite the date on the original map imprint 'Sepr. 29th. 1741' the first issue was in June 1742. Badeslade must have dropped out almost immediately, as Toms was sole owner of the atlas for that first issue, as indicated in the title and in advertising describing it as 'the cheapest and most useful Book ever yet published'.[6]

Engraving of the maps had not been fully completed for the first issue and Toms made changes to the plates at least twice during 1742 for further editions, doubling the number of towns show and adding two new roads for the second state, still with the original imprint dated 1741. The third state has a re-engraved imprint dated 'Sept. 29. 1742' no longer including Badeslade as a Proprietor, and another six towns were added, five of them around Manchester such as 'Traford'. The map was reprinted in that final state (with the 1742 imprint) during 1743, 1745, 1747 and 1749, and perhaps later, and is illustrated in Fig. 38 from an issue c.1746 with original colouring.

THE COWLEY MAPS

At the start of 1741 poet, dramatist and bookseller Robert Dodsley (1703-64) began *The public register or weekly magazine*, but there were only 24 issues, partly because Stamp Duty was levied on him by the authorities, who considered it contained 'news' whereas Dodsley argued (unsuccessfully) that his weekly summary of events was so delayed it was really 'history'. Less current contents were needed and six of the final issues contained county descriptions with maps, not including Lancashire. The magazine was then abandoned, but in November 1743 Dodsley published the complete set of county texts in a separate publication *The Geography of England* with county maps by John Cowley, Geographer to his Majesty. At this time works published close to the end of the year were usually post-dated and the title page states the year as 1744, the year when Cowley seems to have died.

Fig. 39 shows Lancashire by Cowley (map 4H), clearly based again on the small Morden map. Its most notable feature is the introduction of several roads not previously seen (for example, Manchester via Bury to Gisborn). The text at the foot 'D.W. Long from London' is not the name of a printer or engraver, but means 'D[egrees] W[est of] Long[itude] from London [St Paul's Cathedral]'. The maps were reissued unchanged by Dodsley in 1745 in *A New Sett of Pocket Mapps...*, but few copies were printed and the maps are rare. The title chosen shows that now portability for an atlas has become a selling point. Not much is known about Cowley, who seems to have been estate surveyor to the Duke of Argyll in the 1730s. He produced only a few other printed maps (of Scotland and elsewhere) in the period 1730-1745. Some authors identify him with John Lodge Cowley FRS (1719-1787), a mathematics professor at Royal Military College, Woolwich, but that John Cowley was surely too young to be Geographer Royal in 1741, and if precociously appointed to that role would not have been superseded by Emanuel Bowen within a few years.

THE 'ROCQUE' MAPS

The atlas with Cowley maps was first issued In November 1743 and in that month another county atlas was launched by printer Thomas Read, *The English Traveller* in weekly instalments, another title revealing the new sales angle. The text was edited from county descriptions originally published in the magazine *Magna Britannia* from 1708 to 1731 with the small Morden maps. Unlike most other cases of periodical publishing, Read did print to his intended timetable and for the first 40 weeks delivered to his subscribers the promised instalment. Almost all parts contained both text and a map copied from Moll, but nothing is known about the designer or engraver of these maps. The sequence of counties was alphabetical for both maps and text, but the text was too long for a single part and filled many weekly episodes for some counties (for example, eight for Essex). Thus in part 40 the text extended only as far as Gloucestershire, while the maps had got to Wiltshire. The further history of the work is unclear, but some parts were issued in 1744 and three collected volumes of *The English Traveller* containing the maps and text up to Shropshire were published in 1746. It is possible that Read completed his account of England in two further volumes, but no examples of them have been found.

The county map plates were next used in 1753 for *The Small British Atlas...* by John Rocque (1704-1762), whose name thus became

Fig. 38 Map 4G 'Lancashire North from London' (1741) by Thomas Badeslade and William Henry Toms, from *Chorographia Britanniae...* (Johnston & Toms, London, 1746), third state. [map 101mm x 140mm, 4.0" x 5.45"]

attached to these maps although his only certain connection was via republishing them, inserting road distances omitted when the Moll map was copied, changing the scale bars to show statute miles and revising some other details. Rocque was a Huguenot who had settled in England and introduced many good practices from French cartography, in particular the use of hachuring to indicate hills on his estate maps. His first known work in England was in 1734 as a royal garden designer, but by 1753 he was fully engaged in printing and cartography, creating some significant new maps. Unfortunately he had lost his shop and stock of plates by fire in 1750. His purchase of *The English Traveller* could have been an attempt to rebuild his business, but like many map-makers he was always on the edge of insolvency and died in poverty.

The Small British Atlas was republished several times by Rocque (and after 1761 by his widow Mary Ann). Finally the maps appeared in *England Displayed... By a Society of Gentlemen...* printed by Adlard and Browne for issue in weekly parts beginning from April 1769. This complete work and its separate parts were probably on sale well into the 1770s. The Lancashire example (map 4J in Fig. 40 left) shows a 'Rocque' county map in the final revised state. It has correct labelling of all the boroughs but otherwise is a very close copy of the Moll map 4F, even to the positioning of the names on the page and uncritical copying of Moll's mistakes. The sluice is shown across Martin Mere as introduced by Moll. This very late issue shows little plate wear, indicating few total prints made in 25 years use.

THE 'SIMPSON' COPY

With the publication in parts of *The Agreeable Historian... by Samuel Simpson, Gent.*, printed by Robert Walker from early December 1743, we find a remarkable entire duplication of *The English Traveller* by Thomas Read, discussed above as the source for the so-called 'Rocque' maps. Despite a few extra details, the text of *The Agreeable Historian* is so similar to *The English Traveller* that the use of a common source by agreement is almost the only possibility.[7] Yet why should two printers agree to compete so directly, when it would be hard for even one of them to make a profit? Even more mysterious is the creation, at huge unnecessary expense, of two separate sets of almost identical county map plates, traditionally labelled 'Simpson' and 'Rocque' for lack of any more relevant information.

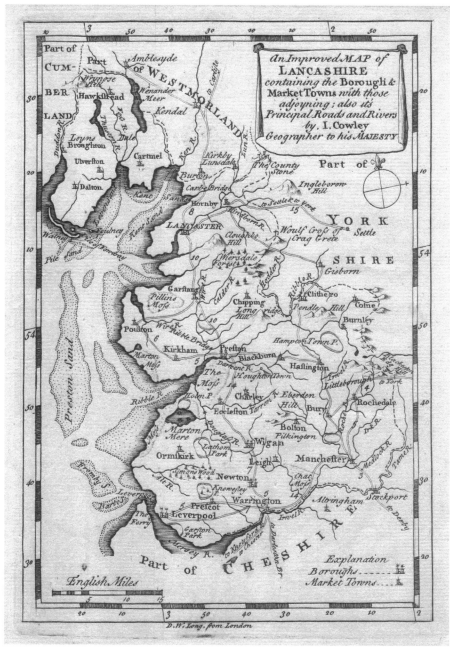

Fig. 39 Map 4H 'An Improved Map of Lancashire...' (1743) by John Cowley, Geographer to his Majesty, from *The Geography of England...* (R. Dodsley, London, 1744). [116mm x 169mm, 4.6" x 6.7"]

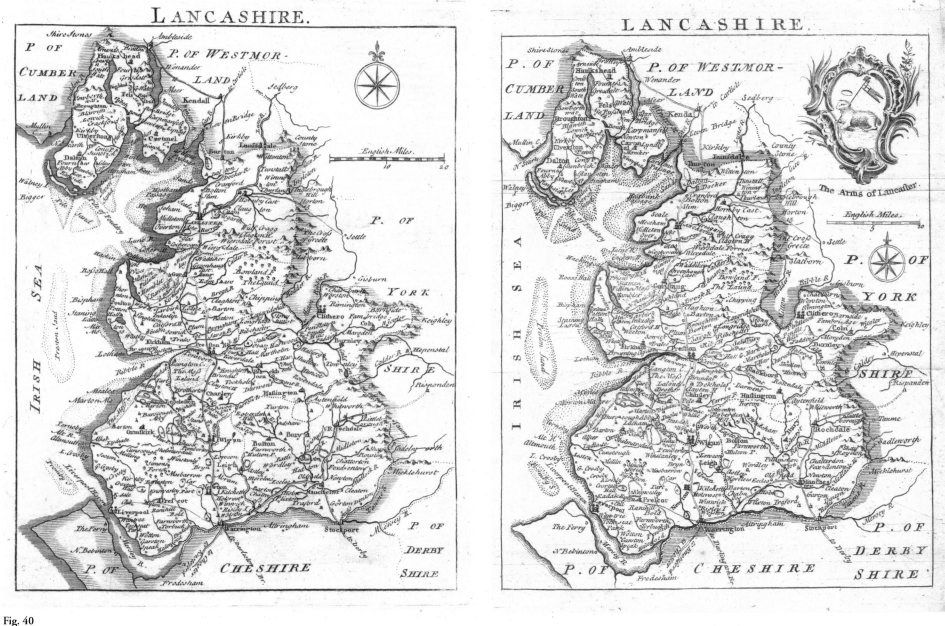

Fig. 40

Left Map 4J 'Lancashire.' (1744) first for *The English Traveller* by Thomas Read, modified for *The Small British Atlas* (1753) by John Rocque, as reprinted in *England Displayed* (Adlard and Browne, London, 1769). [154mm x 194mm, 6.1" x 7.6"]

Right Map 4K 'Lancashire.' (1746) from *The Agreeable Historian* by Samuel Simpson (Robert Walker, London, 1746). [152mm x 189mm, 6.0" x 7.4"]

The similarity can be confirmed by comparing the Simpson map 4K with the slightly larger Rocque map 4J (both in Fig. 40). They agree even on their correction of specific Moll errors (like the borough labels), their inclusion of other errors by Moll and the omission on 4K of the road distances on Moll restored in 1753 on 4J by Rocque. The Wirral is distorted on both in the same unique way. Small details indicate that 4K was copied from the first state of 4J, for example the omission of the road from Lancaster to Hornby, the misreading of Abram as Alram near Newton and of 'Chatm oss' as 'Chalm Oss'. The Simpson map additionally includes 'The Arms of Lancaster', actually those for Preston. Probably the 'Arms of Lancashire' were intended and the error arose via copying from the table in Fig. 33, which has that error. The strong inland boundary shading (as on the Badeslade and Toms map 4G) and the similar style of the lettering on both maps suggests William Toms as the engraver of both 4J and 4K, as do the form lines round the coast on 4K. However, form lines were fast becoming the standard coastal emphasis style at about this time. The scale bar on 4K (ten customary miles) shows what was on 4J in its first state, before Rocque changed it to the form seen in Fig. 40 (twenty statue miles). All these scale bars were ambiguously labelled as 'English Miles'.

The Agreeable Historian was collected into three volumes published in 1746. No other issues are known and the maps are scarce. Other than his name in the atlas title, nothing is known about 'Samuel Simpson', perhaps editor of the common text used by Read and Walker. Possibly he was the grocer Samuel Simpson (1711-88), Mayor of Leicester in 1751, noted for his erudition, or the name could be a pseudonym.

THE *GEOGRAPHIA MAGNAE BRITANNIAE* MAPS

An interesting small map of Lancashire (4L, Fig. 41) was published in the atlas *Geographia Magnae Britanniae* of 1748, with the Saxton outline and orientation, but with west at the top in similar fashion to the William Smith map 2K (Fig. 12), presumably again to optimise the scale. It must have been derived directly from a folio map, as idiosyncratically it includes places omitted in all the maps derived from the small Morden or from Moll. The sandbanks clearly indicate copying from Morden, while 'Cranford' and other details show this source was in the first state.

A more extensive road network is shown than previously, but the accuracy is suspect. In particular a false road is shown in a direct line from Blackburn to Lancaster. Again form lines are used around the coast. Latitude/time and longitude calibrations were copied from the Morden map and accurately numbered along three edges, but the numbers along the upper (western) edge are incorrect, with almost no offset from those on the lower (east) side. Clearly the engraver of 4L did not understand the orientation of the source map on 1576 magnetic north.

Unfortunately the map is unsigned and the atlas includes no information on map designers. However, it is somewhat similar in style to the other maps, two of which were signed by Thomas Hutchinson as engraver, and so the map is often called a 'Hutchinson', though that cannot be proved. It is also referred to by map dealers as an 'Osborne' after Thomas Osborne, the first publisher listed on the title page, or even more erroneously as by Samuel Wale, who engraved only the title page of the atlas.

THE KITCHIN AND JEFFERYS SMALL ATLAS

Yet another atlas in parts began publication in November 1748, but this was supplied more rapidly as at the price of sixpence [2½ p] each weekly issue contained small maps for four counties, each with a brief county description engraved with the map. As a unique experiment the whole set of four maps for a week was contained on a single copper plate and the paper sheet printed from it was cut into quarters before binding. Thus the plate mark on Lancashire map 4M (Fig. 42) extends round the bottom and right sides, but no plate mark is seen on the other two sides where the neighbouring maps (Monmouthshire and Worcestershire) were placed. The county sequence was arbitrary, presumably in the order the publishers finalised their information on each county.

At least half of the parts were issued on schedule, including Lancashire on 10 December 1748, and publication should have been completed in three months. No copy of this first edition is known to have survived, however, and precise dates for parts issued during 1749 are unknown. Delays are likely, because before the atlas was complete Kitchin and Jefferys had ownership instead of the original publishers.

Presumably sales were too low to cover expenses and it is tempting to guess that map-makers Kitchin and Jefferys were already involved as the engravers of the anonymous plates, which they were given in payment for their work when the publishers could not

Fig. 41 Map 4L 'A Correct Map of Lancashire' probably by Thomas Hutchinson, from *Geographia Magnae Britanniae* (S. Birt, T. Osborne, *et al.*, London, 1748). [161mm x 136mm, 6.4" x 5.4"]

meet their obligations. The county sequence was revised to be alphabetical when all the parts were collected in a book, *The Small English Atlas... by Messrs Kitchin and Jefferys*, published in 1749. Very few copies of this edition are known. Unfortunately the *Small English Atlas* did not generate much profit for Kitchin and Jefferys as it competed with the earlier and very successful Badeslade and Toms maps of similar size, and also with John Rocque's *Small British Atlas*. However, it was reprinted in 1751 and remained on sale for many years. The plates were sold on, probably when Jefferys died in 1771, and a very altered form of the maps (now on separate plates) was reissued in 1776 by Sayer and Bennett, both as *An English Atlas* with texts on counties, and as *The Small English Atlas* without text. These atlases were also on sale from the Bowles family and from various trading successors such as Laurie & Whittle and Robert Wilkinson until about 1825 when the plates were sold as scrap copper.

Thomas Kitchin (1718-1784) was apprenticed in 1732 to Emanuel Bowen (1693-1767), and married his daughter Sarah in 1739. He collaborated with his father-in-law for thirty years. Thomas Jefferys (1719-1771) was also a Bowen apprentice from 1735. So when they took on the atlas, Kitchin and Jefferys had been friends for a decade. Jefferys began independent work in 1744 and was responsible for some very important maps, in particular surveying, engraving and eventually publishing several large-scale county maps including Westmorland (1770) and Yorkshire (1772). However, well before then Jefferys had become overstretched financially, leading to his bankruptcy in 1766. With help from friends he recovered some of his business, which after his death in 1771 passed to his son Thomas Jefferys the younger (active until 1776) and his partner William Faden (1749-1836), who assumed full control in 1783 and went on to achieve great success, including engraving and publishing the first Ordnance Survey maps.

The Lancashire map 4M is based on the third state of the Badeslade and Toms map 4G, giving a similar suggestion of an island with ocean on the right instead of Yorkshire. This copying is confirmed by the inclusion of some relatively unusual place-names on both, such as 'Inkeslip' (a misprint for Inskip dating back to Speed), but there are differences which show that other sources were consulted. For example, the name 'Chadley' appears on 4M a few miles north of Preston where Badeslade shows 'Broughton' on 4G. This tiny place on the original road out of Preston seems to have been included to supply the missing name, or just to fill the gap, and was copied from the Owen-Bowen Road map (plate 92 in *Britannia Depicta*) where it appears as 'Chadley at Cadley Moor'. The name also appears on the almost contemporary map 5A signed by Kitchin, where the compass rose has an exactly similar form to that on 4M, suggesting that Kitchin was indeed the engraver for 4M. This would also indicate that by 1749 he was working on 5A, a more detailed map of Lancashire discussed in the next chapter.

It is hard to distinguish between the very similar (and inconsistent) writing styles of the various engravers, but here again there is a great deal of similarity between 4M and other work by Kitchin. Form lines appear around the coast in 4M and 5A, as on the Badeslade and Toms map, a concept Kitchin (and Bowen) would have picked up from there and later used for the 'Large English Atlas' discussed in the next chapter. Hence it became the style of coastal shading thereafter used most often for county maps. This is the first Lancashire map with a scale bar calibrated in statute miles rather than the longer customary miles, indicating a scale of just under 20 miles per inch. However, these are still labelled ambiguously as 'English Miles', like many previous maps, with no indication of the new idea. Better habits would be established in the next era.

NOTES

1 H.G. Fordham, *John Cary... a Bibliography*, (Cambridge University Press, Cambridge, 1925) p.xxxii.

2 The mean values are 2376, 2154 and 1909 yards, with standard deviations of about 10 per cent. Many of the values are incorrectly stated by R.A. Skelton, *County Atlases of the British Isles 1579-1703* (Carta Press, London, 1970) pp.196-8. For a discussion of measuring scales see A.W. Richeson, *English Land Measuring to 1800* (MIT Press, Massachusetts, 1966).

3 As reprinted in Skelton, *County Atlases of the British Isles 1579-1703*, p.193.

4 See Donald Hodson, *County Atlases of the British Isles, Volume III (1764-1789)* (British Library, London, 1997) pp.122-5. Note that even in 1701 the editor chose to translate the old Latin summary of Camden's *Britannia* rather than to abbreviate Gibson's newly published English version.

5 The drawings of antiquities for Lancashire were copied from Table 1 of C. Leigh, *The Natural History of Lancashire, Cheshire and the Peak in Derbyshire* (Leigh, Oxford, 1700), which also contains a regional map engraved by none other than Herman Moll.

6 See Donald Hodson, *County Atlases of the British Isles, Volume I (1704-1742)* (Tewin Press, Welwyn, 1984) p.155.

7 See discussion by Donald Hodson, *County Atlases of the British Isles, Volume II (1743-1763)* (Tewin Press, Welwyn, 1989) pp.42-3.

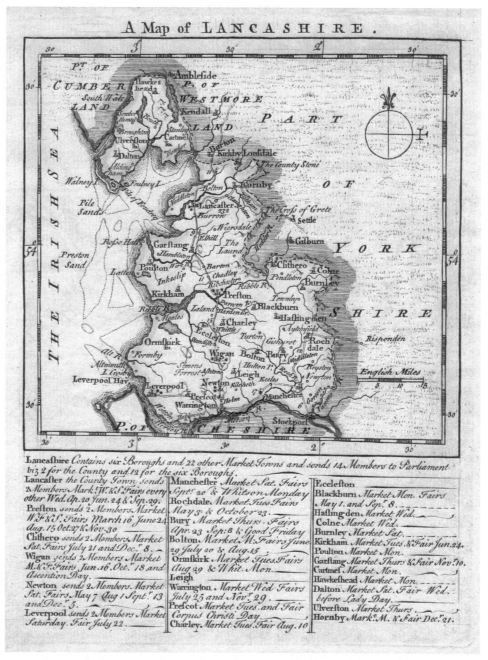

Fig. 42 Map 4M 'A Map of Lancashire' (1748), by T. Kitchin and T. Jefferys, from *The Small English Atlas* (Kitchin & Jefferys, London, 1751). [122mm x 111mm, 4.8" x 4.4"]

5   The Era of Innovation (1750–1788, and a bit)

County maps were still being plagiarised from Saxton in the first half of the eighteenth century, with good new surveys in only a few cases. However, serious attempts were made to improve the depiction of England and Wales from 1750 and the preferred county survey scale became one mile per inch, following its use by Ogilby for strip road maps and in part due to 'The Society for the Encouragement of Arts, Manufactures and Commerce' (from 1847 'The Royal Society of Arts'). In 1759 they offered gold medals and a gratuity of up to £100 for an 'accurate actual survey of any county upon a scale of one inch to a mile' based upon triangulation and showing correct coastlines, latitude and longitude. The honour of such an award was the incentive for the surveyors, not a gratuity much less than the cost of surveying (at least £1000). The 'one-inch' scale encouraged by the Society of Arts allowed detailed recording of topography and relatively precise plotting of towns and significant buildings without prohibitive cost on a map of handy size. For nearly 100 years the best commercial map-makers were involved in such surveying, although the Society of Arts judged several completed maps to be of insufficient quality and many mappings were not completed due to lack of sponsors.

While one by one the individual counties were being mapped at large scale, for the country as a whole Thomas Kitchin and his father-in-law Emanuel Bowen made the most of the information available by 1760 and dominated the period with maps in the *Large English Atlas*. At last innovation was being achieved and some progress was being made towards modern standards. Unfortunately Lancashire was one of the very last counties to be resurveyed, and throughout this period was depicted in a new distorted form. The specific termination year for the era in this chapter is determined by the appearance of the first one-mile-to-the-inch map of

Lancashire by William Yates, while the extra bit is concerned only with the later history of that map and its almost immediate copying by John Cary for his *New and Correct English Atlas*.

MAPS IN MONTHLY MAGAZINES

The surprising replication of almost identical county maps by 'Rocque' (4J) and 'Simpson' (4K) in weekly magazines during 1743-6 was repeated from 1747 when another map duplication occurred in monthly magazines. The *London Magazine* had been founded in 1732 and was under new guidance by Richard Baldwin junior when from November 1747 it began to publish a series of county maps by Thomas Kitchin (1719-1784). Up to ten maps appeared each year in apparently random sequence, comprising maps for all English counties by 1754 and nearly all for Wales by 1756. However, attention then shifted to covering the Seven Years War and the final five maps appeared only at long intervals to complete the series in 1763. Map 5A (Fig. 43) in November 1750 introduced a new depiction of Lancashire used throughout this era, incorrectly enlarged in width as a result of Kitchin's study of 'Astronomical Observations', as discussed in Box 8 and in the section on the *Large English Atlas* below.

These *London Magazine* maps were available loose, but never as an atlas, making maps in first state from 1750 rare. They were not reprinted until the unscrupulous London publisher Alexander Hogg acquired the *London Magazine* in 1785, with the long neglected Kitchin plates as part of the deal. Hogg deleted the original imprint and used the whole set in various works on antiquities between 1787 and 1798, amply supplying 5A maps in a second state, usually with severe plate wear.

An almost identical set of maps was published in John Hinton's *Universal Magazine*, starting a few months earlier than the *London Magazine* with a first issue in June 1747, but extending over a very much longer time period. In each year only about four county maps were published, in an alphabetical sequence reaching Lancashire in November 1751 (map 5B, Fig. 43). The publication rate became erratic in 1752 and decreased to only one or two per year until the series ended with a burst of six maps in 1765 and the final three in 1766, mainly of Wales.

The four maps in the first year were by Thomas Kitchin, followed by thirteen which were anonymous but in a style suggesting the

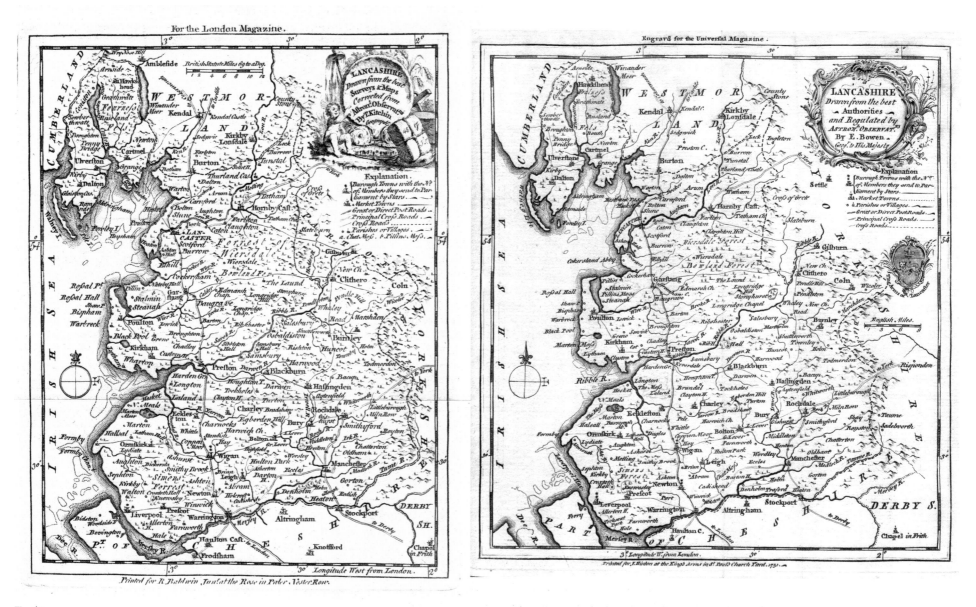

Fig. 43
Left: Map 5A 'Lancashire Drawn from the best Surveys and Maps Corrected from Astron[l]. Observat[ns] by T. Kitchin, as first printed in *The London Magazine* (R. Baldwin, London, November 1750). [150mm x 191mm, 5.9" x 7.5"]
Right: Map 5B 'Lancashire Drawn from the best Authorities and Regulated by Astron[l]. Observat[ns] by E. Bowen, from *The Universal Magazine* (J. Hinton, London, November 1751). [171mm x 182mm, 6.7" x 7.2"]

engraver Emanuel Bowen (1693-1767), who signed the next sixteen continuing the series, including Lancashire. Richard Seale (1703-1762) engraved ten plates appearing from mid-1759 onwards, and the final ten were again anonymous. Each subscriber could collate the map sections and arrange for their binding into an atlas, and a few such volumes are found in reference libraries, but it seems that no formal atlas edition was ever printed. The plates were not used again after the *Universal Magazine* publication, although back numbers of the magazine were available from Hinton until his death in 1781 and briefly from his successors.

Baldwin's more frequent *London Magazine* set was so far ahead of Hinton's alphabetically arranged *Universal Magazine* series that by January 1751 Baldwin had already issued all the maps Hinton published thereafter. However, the initial run of maps in each magazine is an almost entirely different selection of counties, with only one duplication in the first eighteen by Baldwin and three in the first fifteen by Hinton. This indicates that Baldwin's selection is not truly random, but was based on some sort of agreement between the publishers and engravers over sharing map design costs. Cooperation was simplified as all Baldwin's plates were made by Kitchin, while his father-in-law Bowen was engraving most of them for Hinton. Simultaneously Bowen and Kitchin were working together on Hinton's *Large English Atlas*, as discussed below.

The considerable costs of the actual engraving could not be shared, however, as each publisher wanted his own set of plates. In fact the plate duplication issue is even more complex, as from January 1749 a *third* set of plates was being engraved in Ireland for an independent reprinting of the *London Magazine* by the Exshaw family in Dublin, issued simultaneously with the London edition. These Irish plates are almost identical to the originals by Kitchin apart from an imprint on the lines of 'Engraved for S & I Exshaw Dub[n].' Only 28 maps were completed before this set was discontinued in 1852, with Lancashire in November 1750. Printed copies of this are very rare indeed.

Though in Fig. 43 maps 5A by Kitchin (1750) and 5B by Bowen (1751) are not identical, the similarity in writing, content and style is so great that only the signature reveals the cartographer. Kitchin learned engraving as Bowen's apprentice and similarity can be expected, but here Bowen copied directly from Kitchin. Both maps feature the stretched county shape first shown in 1750 on 5A and show 'Black Pool' as a town for the first time. Both maps use form

lines around a new coastal shape including a spurious elongation of the Naze promontory on the north Ribble coast near Warton, unique to this pair and a 1768 map (5J) by Thomas Bowen (son of Emanuel), itself copied from 5A. Another common feature is the use of statute miles on the scale bars, still just 'English Miles' for Bowen but explicitly labelled by Kitchin in the form that would became common practice as all other mapmakers followed this lead in using statute miles for map scales from 1750. Bowen lapsed into carelessness when copying the longitude scale, moving the values at the foot about two minutes east and repeating the same calibration length at the top, where the more scientific Kitchin has correctly indicated the tapering effect due to the Earth's curvature.

ANOTHER MAPPING ODDITY

The closest rival to the Drayton *Poly-Olbion* maps (3B) as the most unusual production in county cartography is the set of distorted 'bird's-eye views' by George Bickham, father and son, dubiously qualifying as maps only because they were originally labelled as such by their authors, for example 'A Map of Lancashire, North from London...' (Fig. 44). These relatively realistic landscape views from improbably high fictitious hills are combined with location labelling on the plate, partly justifying their inclusion in cartography. Employing a vista in perspective from a great height was relatively common in mapping town plans, in particular by Braun and Hogenberg from 1573 onwards, but rarely had this been employed for larger areas before these 'maps' of counties by Bickham, which perhaps inaugurated a high landscape-view theme dominant in prints for the rest of the eighteenth century.

George Bickham Senior (1684-1758) specialised in calligraphy and (like Gerardus Mercator) published works on lettering, while apparently George Bickham Junior (1704?-1771) managed their publishing business, in particular as a pioneer of engraving and publishing music. Both were equally skilled as artists, sharing the engraving of *The British Monarchy*..., their major work. In part it was intended for the education of children.[1]

Almost uniquely the entire book was on copper plates, with a great variety of lettering and decorations in the text, so that the entire book is a work of art containing some conventional maps as well as the famous county 'maps'. The various dates contained within it or quoted for editions reveal only that it had a very complex

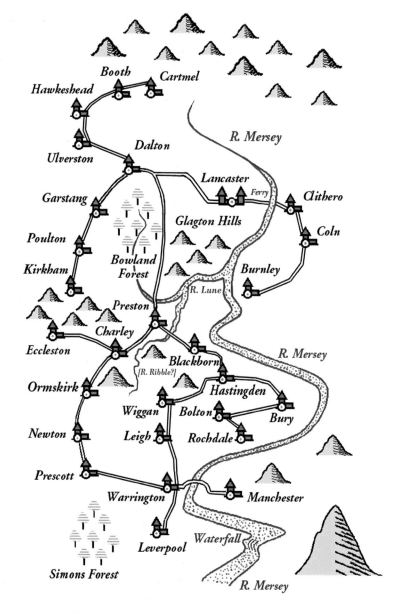

Fig. 44 Map 5C 'A Map of Lancashire' (1754) by G. Bickham Junior, from *The British Monarchy...* by G. Bickham (Bickham, London, *c*.1754) [142mm x 221mm, 5.6" x 8.7"] and the author's reconstruction of the scenographically implied geography in a more conventional ichnographic plan view.

history. It was published in 25 parts from 1743 to 1754, with the northern counties engraved last, and was on sale until about 1767 when the younger Bickham retired.[2]

The Lancashire 'map' (Fig. 44) by George Bickham Junior is dated 1754. From a fictitious mountain in North Cheshire the county is seen across the Mersey vanishing off into the Lake District. Place-names are scattered across the landscape, joined by what seem to be roads. An interpretation of the Bickham drawing as a more conventional map in plan view by the author of this book is offered alongside. The prints are mostly available in a second state reissued from 1796 as *A Curious Antique Collection of Bird's-Eye Views...* by Laurie & Whittle, who deleted all the descriptive headings naming them as maps and the geographical notes at the foot, leaving 5C labelled as just 'Lancashire'.

A MINIATURE MAPPING FOR CHILDREN

John Newbery pioneered publication of works for children and in 1759 issued maps of the counties at playing card size by map engraver John Gibson. This was a companion set to the 52 card miniature world *Atlas Minimus* by Gibson and Bowen published by Newbery in the previous year. That was reissued at least once with tiny standard playing card designs added to one corner, and possibly the same was done with the county maps, but unusually good eyesight would be needed to identify such a small detail on the card. The Lancashire map 5D (Fig. 45) was clearly based on one of the two maps in Fig. 43, but reduced to the scale of 32 miles per inch by Gibson, who was later involved in making the much larger Lancashire map 5F for the *Royal English Atlas*. The county map cards were advertised with other 'useful and pretty Books' for 'the little Gentlemen and Ladies of these Kingdoms' available 'at their old Friend, Mr Newbery's', indicating that these maps were the first specifically designed for children, but their effectiveness in that role is not obvious.[3] They were re-issued in an unchanged state until about 1790 by Newbery's descendants.

THE BOWEN AND KITCHIN *LARGE ENGLISH ATLAS*

The eventual copying of large-scale county surveys into a new county atlas was inevitable, but the timing of publication was difficult. Delay would allow more new county maps to be available, but waiting too long would let a rival get in first. About 1748

Fig. 45　Map 5D 'Lancashire' (1759) by John Gibson, from *New and Accurate Maps of the Counties* (T. Carnan, London, 1780). [56mm x 104mm, 2.2" x 4.1"]

the publisher John Hinton decided the time was ripe and commissioned work on *The Large English Atlas*. Consideration of this has been postponed to suit the 1760 date of the complete atlas, rather than the first appearance of the Lancashire map loose in 1752 near the start of work on this huge project. It is possible that the concept arose in discussions between Hinton and Emanuel Bowen and Thomas Kitchin, who (as described above) had been making county maps for Hinton's *Universal Magazine*, and who between them would produce nearly all the maps for his *Large Atlas*. Few original county surveys were published between 1736 and 1761 and with hindsight Hinton's starting date can be seen as a very good decision, with only Martyn's map of Cornwall of 1748 and a few one-inch maps new in the 1750s not included as sources.

By 1690 it was clear that a new national survey of Britain was needed. Philippe de La Hire (1640-1718) had performed a famous redrawing of the French national map in 1682, using astronomically determined values of latitude and longitude for parts of France, but even by 1750 nothing comparable had been achieved for England and after nearly 200 years Saxton still was the basis of map-making. From 1749 onwards the titles of nearly all the English county maps by Thomas Kitchin in the *London Magazine* claim them to be 'Regulated by Astronomical Observations', presumably as part of the process of revising the national map (as described in Box 8), while in the *Universal Magazine* series Bowen makes a similar claim only for the Lancashire map 5B, which he almost certainly copied from the earlier map 5A by Kitchin. From this it seems that it was Kitchin, rather than Bowen, who during 1748-50 performed this aspect of the planning for the *Large Atlas* by redrawing the map of England and Wales as had been done for France in 1682.

The bad data available to Kitchin resulted in considerable distortions of both latitude and longitude, in particular an overall enlargement for the breadth of Lancashire by about 25 per cent. The east side was located nearly correctly, but the west coast from Liverpool northwards is pushed about a quarter of a degree too far outwards, so that the meridian shown at longitude 3°15' is close to an actual 3° west of London, which is about 5' west of the Greenwich-based values used on modern maps. First used in 1750 on map 5A (Fig. 43), this distorted shape was correct north-south, but ten miles too wide east-west (particularly visible on the northern edge in Lonsdale, nearly doubled) and would be copied for the next forty years.

In cartographic literature the error for Lancashire is usually ascribed to Bowen, as author of the *Large English Atlas* map, and he almost certainly was involved, but only as friend and advisor to his son-in-law and former apprentice Kitchin. Easier and better methods of finding longitude were about to be discovered, however, in particular via the introduction of relatively inexpensive chronometers with sufficient accuracy, and by 1790 this error would be corrected. The outlines for the county in Fig. 46 show the successive attempts to describe the shape of Lancashire and clearly indicate the Kitchin/Bowen distortion as an anomaly in the series.

Despite such inaccuracies for other counties, the *Large English Atlas* contained the most original county maps since 1577, at the largest scale achieved to date. From Saxton (2G) onwards the largest one-sheet maps had been on the 'Royal' paper size allowing plates up to 50cm x 40cm (20" x 16") and a scale about five statute miles per inch for folio Lancashire maps, although an unusual orientation had allowed William Smith (2K) a somewhat larger scale. The *Large English Atlas* used the recently developed 'Imperial' or 'Atlas' size of paper, where an example owned by the author is trimmed to 74cm x 58cm (29½" x 23"), allowing the plate area to be increased to 71cm x 54cm (28" x 21½"). In addition, rotating the county to put the north-south axis on the larger dimension (like Smith 2K, Blome 3L and Morden 4A) allowed Lancashire to be 56cm (22") high without approaching the frame, limited in fact by the wrongly enlarged county width. Thus the useful map area was increased by a factor of more than three and a linear magnification by about 1.8 was achieved to allow a mapping scale of ten statute miles per three inches for the *Large Atlas*, nearly double the scale of the Saxton map. Smaller counties in the atlas were at an even greater scale, almost one mile to the inch for Huntingdon.

Though many features are recorded in an atlas for the first time, some of the large maps could not exploit this increased area by including a high density of new cartographic information, because as yet no land survey had provided that extra detail. Unfortunately this included Lancashire, as we see from 5E (Fig. 47, greatly reduced, and detail in Fig. 48). Roads and nearby details are added from Ogilby to inland areas based on Saxton, with a few other roads rather erratically inserted. Mid-eighteenth century emphasis is strongly away from decoration and towards cartographic information, with elegant and formal title cartouches. Decoration of the title depicts Lancashire's two principal industries, coal and textiles, also mentioned in a note on the county near the Ribble estuary. This emphasis on manufacture and trade at the dawn of the industrial revolution is very different from that in previous maps.

In the description of Liverpool at the top of map 5E it is noted that 'to obviate the Danger of the Navigation in and about this Harbour, and also along the whole Coast of this County... the Gentlemen and Merchants... raised a large subscription for defraying the expense of an Actual Survey... and employed the ingenious Messrs Eyes and Fearon in this important Service, which they executed accordingly with great Fidelity and Accuracy.' That coastal survey in 1736-7 by John Eyes (surveyor) and Samuel Fearon (hydrographer) was published in 1738 on two charts, which were the first printed charts to use Greenwich as the prime meridian. Emanuel Bowen himself had engraved the southern chart and on map 5E he copied their coastline (and sandbanks, rather approximately) for a much more correct western county shape than any previously shown, except on the small 5A and 5B maps which in effect are first drafts for 5E.

In particular Sunderland Point and the mouth of the Lune are much more as we would expect. It is possible that some of the differences in coastline are genuine changes due to the effects of erosion in the 160 year interval since Saxton's visit, rather than mere errors in the old survey or differences of method, such as Saxton taking the land outline at low tide in a salt-marsh which seems to be the case at the mouth of the Lune. Unfortunately the Smith map 2K of 1602 and Greenvile Collins' sea chart of 1689 are too inaccurate to help in deciding such details. Form lines around the coasts on maps in *The Large English Atlas* must have helped to establish the use of that new convention.

Individual loose maps for *The Large English Atlas* were published from 1749 to 1760, initially at a rate of one per month for the twelve maps in 1750, but the monthly schedule faltered and only nine maps came in 1751. Bowen designed and engraved thirty-two maps, eleven were by Kitchin and one by Richard Seale. Bowen's Lancashire map came in 1752, but only two other maps were issued in 1752-3 and Hinton sold his interest in the atlas to John Tinney. Map publication dried up for a while until Tinney resumed with eight maps in 1754-5, but he too found the task was too large to be undertaken alone and from 1756 shared the atlas costs with a consortium of other publishers, who took relative shares which can be deduced from priority in the sequence of names in various map

---

BOX 8 THE NEW NATIONAL MAPPING BY KITCHIN

Although both Seller and Ogilby completed a few improved county maps, as did others, no national projects achieved much beyond proposals. However, local progress was accumulating and maps at a scale of two miles to the inch or better had been printed by 1740 for half the counties of England and Wales, with ten counties at the one-inch scale, though the quality of such maps varied greatly.

An important aspect (first noted by Moll) of basing a national map on county surveys was the need for consistency across boundaries and in the latitude and longitude calibrations for adjacent counties, where there were many inaccuracies.* A revision was attempted by Thomas Kitchin just before 1750, the year when he engraved the general map of England and Wales for *The Large English Atlas*, stating in the title that it is 'Regulated by numerous Astronomical Observations Made by Members of the Royal Society'. The information Kitchin consulted for this regulation can be identified in notes on a larger four-sheet map of England and Wales he engraved for the Bowles family in 1752, namely detailed surveys for 18 English counties and much of Wales, ranging in date from 1596 to 1747 and varying in scale from three miles per inch to two-thirds of a mile per inch. Values for many latitudes came from 'Members of the Royal Society of London and others' and he got about sixty longitude values including five in Lancashire (Lancaster, Liverpool, Towneley, Warrington, Wigan). Similarly Johann Doppelmayr (1677-1750) of Nuremberg collected data in 1716-24 to create a new world map for Johann Baptist Homann, but found reliable positions for only 142 major places in the whole world, including 28 in France where astronomy was well supported. For Britain he listed only five, London, Greenwich, Oxford, Edinburgh and Dublin.

At that time accurate longitude measurement relied on careful observation of the moons of Jupiter with a top quality astronomical telescope, which had been done during 1676 in Lancashire by Richard Towneley FRS (1629-1707), a gentleman scientist who made many valuable observations. The position shown for Towneley Hall is correct, and it is probable that it was the first place in England to be astronomically located relative to the new Royal Observatory in Greenwich. However, Kitchin's other longitude values were too far west, by a quarter of a degree for Liverpool, Warrington and Wigan and a fifth of a degree for Lancaster. The Fearon and Eyes chart of the Lancashire coast had about double those errors in longitude and averaging from this may have affected Kitchin's interpretation of the results. Kitchin found similar inaccuracies in other places far from London, introducing significant distortions across most outlying parts of England and Wales.

* William Ravenhill, 'As to its position in respect to the Heavens', *Imago Mundi*, 28:2 (1976), pp.79-93.

imprints. However, the frequency with which these shares exchanged hands in the next half century is reflected in corresponding alterations to the imprint, leading to a very unusual multiplicity of states for *The Large English Atlas* plates, which uniquely defies any attempt to correlate the listing of issues in the various reference works with complete consistency. This is due in part to the several owners issuing the same maps with different title pages, often with incorrect dates.

Three anonymous maps (including the Lake Counties) completed the whole set of counties in 1760, when the entire *Large English Atlas* became available. Even though it was expensive at three guineas [£3.15], as the best atlas in print for England and Wales it achieved good sales in numerous editions until 1789 and publication continued up to about 1824. Thus the large maps are easily available. In 1768 Carington Bowles offered for 3 shillings [15p] each single county map dissected and mounted on linen, folded into a slip case for convenient storage and use whilst travelling. This is the first advertised appearance of what would be a popular format for large maps (as the *Quartermaster's Map* was not dissected). Unusually, the final fate of the plates for this atlas is known. Auction records presented by Hodson in *County Atlases...* show that the 47 plates were sold in 1825 as old copper at a shilling a pound for £28.45, which means a total mass of 258 kg [569 lb], or 5.5 kg [12 lb] of copper on average for each plate, which must have been awkward to handle during printing.

Rather than leave large inland areas blank, Bowen introduced spurious tree and hill symbols (see Fig. 48), and although the 'sugar loaves' are somewhat graded in size, the range used is much less than on the Saxton map 2H (which remained the source of the land relief suggested here). So the numerous little hills scattered at random give no real indication of the topography. Smaller versions derived later from the *Large Atlas* maps are even worse in this respect, and like all the maps in this atlas are characterised by copious engraved notes filling most empty space around the cartography, a style which Bowen copied from his work for the 1720 road map book *Britannia Depicta*.

Unfortunately these notes were sometimes well out of date. The description of Liverpool includes the Castle built by King John, long dismantled, and mentions the former Town Hall without saying this too had been demolished when 'very lately they have erected a magnificent Exchange', itself not completed when the

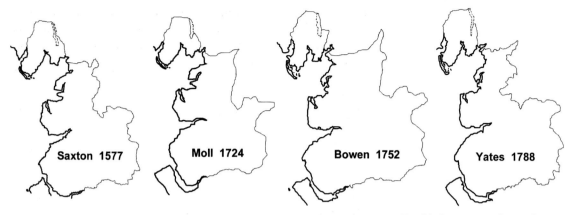

Fig. 46 Comparison of Lancashire outlines on maps published in 1577, 1724, 1752 and 1788 (all oriented on true north).

map was first published. Non-conformist Bowen also says of Liverpool, 'its trade is very extensive, particularly that pernicious and inhumane branch called the Slave Trade', a very outspoken criticism at the time of first publication. Some of these notes are amusingly inaccurate; for example the fantasy that the eight 'canoes' found when Marton Mere was drained were sunk by the Britons 'to keep them out of the hands of the Romans', when the boats almost certainly were of much less age.

THE REDUCED VERSIONS

Somewhat out of chronological sequence, two later Bowen and Kitchin atlases based on *The Large English Atlas* are considered next. As a volume about 60cm x 40cm [24" x 15"] weighing over 3kg [6½ lb], *The Large English Atlas* lived up to its name. The unexpectedly good sales after its completion in 1760 did not benefit engravers Bowen and Kitchin directly. Perhaps it was to share in the profits that in 1762 they began planning a handier volume of maps, done quickly and relatively cheaply as half-size copies of maps already designed. Kitchin perhaps suggested this and initially financed the project (from wealth acquired when he remarried), as he had a quarter share in the resulting publication, but the Bowles family and others were also involved.

Early in 1764 the map set was issued complete as *The Royal English Atlas*, like later atlases so named on account of the 'royal' paper size rather via any than sponsorship by a king. Three-quarters of the maps (33) were engraved by Emanuel Bowen, five were by Kitchin and three were by Emanuel's son Thomas Bowen. A further three, including Lancashire, are described in the title as 'by John Gibson,

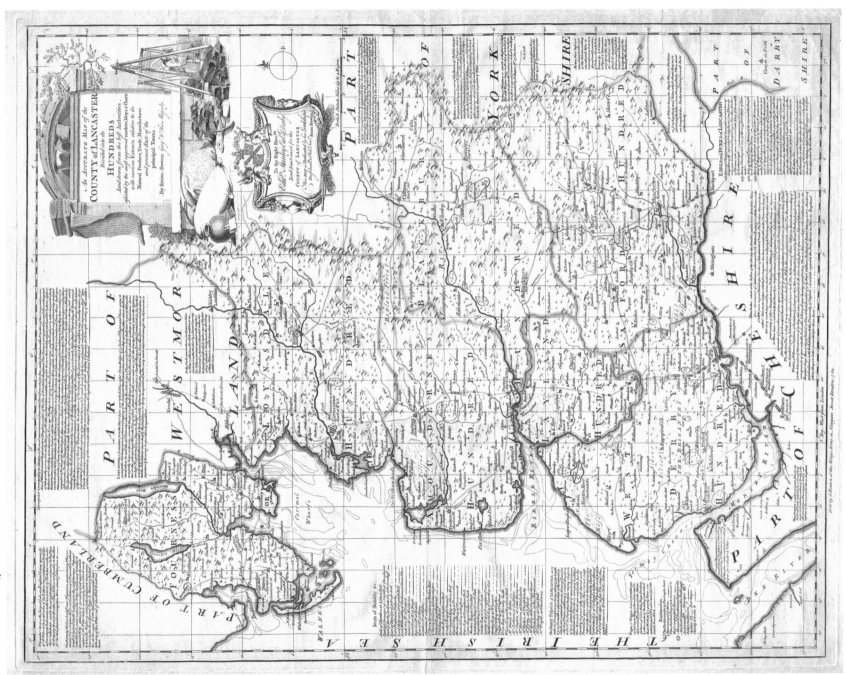

Fig. 47 Map 5E
'An Accurate Map of the
County Of Lancaster'
by Emanuel Bowen for
The Large English Atlas,
first edition before atlas
publication (J. Hinton,
London 1752).
[509mm x 668mm,
20.0" x 26.3"]

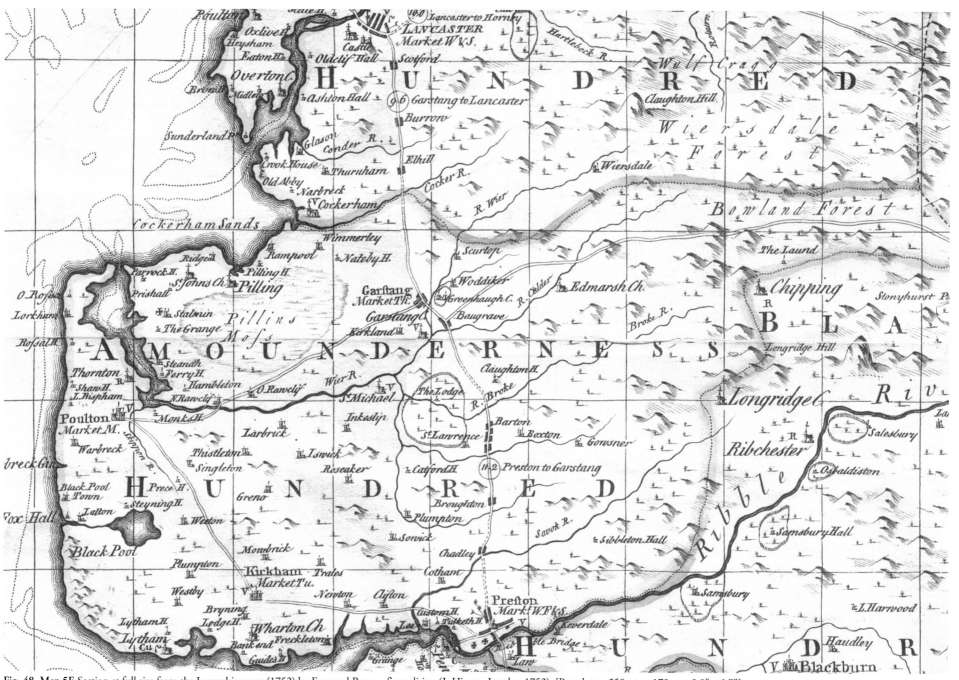

Fig. 48 Map 5E Section at full size from the Lancashire map (1752) by Emanuel Bowen, first edition (J. Hinton, London 1752). [Part shown 250mm x 170mm, 9.9" x 6.7"]

Revised Corrected and Improved by Emanuel Bowen', but what that actually implies for their relative efforts is obscure. The Lancashire map 5F (seen hugely reduced in Fig. 49) is clearly based on the *Large Atlas* map by Bowen, with all the same good and bad features, leaving unclear what Gibson contributed apart from the engraving.

Again as cartouche decorations for Lancashire we have coal and textiles, but here accompanied by livestock. The large blank area below the title around the compass indicator may have been intended for a cathedral view (included on most maps) but never engraved. On a scale reduced to 4½ miles per inch, practically all the details on the *Large Atlas* map are included, as are the characteristic notes, in general similar to those on the earlier map, but expanded in several cases and increased by five additions. The description of the Slave Trade as 'pernicious and inhumane' has been removed from the note on Liverpool, perhaps to placate potential customers there.

The Royal Atlas was not at all a success and the maps from it are very rare. At 45cm x 30cm (18" x 12") and over 2kg [4½ lb], the volume was perhaps not sufficiently reduced in either size or price (£2.10 against the £3.15 for the *Large Atlas*) to tempt buyers away from the bigger one already marketed by all the leading London booksellers. Kitchin had already sold his share in the publication when it was first reprinted in 1778. Nevertheless, *The Royal Atlas* remained on sale until early 1830, like its cousin the *Large Atlas*, and the plates of both were sold for scrap in the same 1825 auction (at 3 kg average for each 'Royal' plate).

Customers for a really small atlas were going for the one by Ellis (5L), as discussed below, and that popularity may have suggested to Bowen that an even smaller version of his maps would have better success. Around January 1767 Emanuel (by then well over 70 years of age) and his son Thomas published the first instalment of what would become *Atlas Anglicanus*, with each monthly part containing three maps based on *The Royal Atlas* at half that size. This was a last ditch attempt to ward off the bailiffs, for despite designing and engraving some very successful publications Emanuel Bowen retained little financial reward from 50 years of toil. That 'Mr. Bowen, reduced by family extravagances, and almost blind through age, had begun to engrave... eighteen penny numbers of three maps each; but dying May 1767, before he had finished above three or four numbers, they were continued by his son', was famously recorded by Richard Gough.[4]

The fifteenth and last instalment came out in July 1768, only four months late despite the death of Emanuel. The maps in the first four issues bear his name alone, except Wiltshire which is by Thomas Bowen, also a skilled engraver with a style indistinguishable from his father (or from Kitchin). Thomas must have been responsible for the subsequent maps, but all carry the names of both Bowens as a pious gesture to the father's memory, like the dignified title in Latin given to the atlas (a very late English example of that scholarly conceit) and the engraved notes within the maps which so characterise Emanuel Bowen's work. Here the notes are fewer and reduced in length, but only because of limitations from the small plate size. Fig. 50 shows Lancashire map 5G from Part II of *Atlas Anglicanus*, where it was published early in 1768 occupying half a Royal sheet of paper at the scale of eight miles per inch. Crowded with almost all the details from *The Large English Atlas*, 5G was neatly engraved by Thomas Bowen in the rococo style of his father. Despite their similar appearance in this book, 5G is half the area of 5F. So for maps 5E, 5F and 5G it is best to compare the actual size samples, rather than the reduced full views.

After achieving all the serial instalments, it seems Thomas Bowen could not finance publication of the finished *Atlas Anglicanus*. It was sold to Thomas Kitchin and published in his name, undated but presumably as soon as part publication was complete, because during the printing run for that first edition he was gradually adding his own imprint to the plates. It is probable that Kitchin had become involved in 1768 as a family commitment rather than as a business opportunity, for he retired in that year and *Atlas Anglicanus* fared no better than *The Royal Atlas*. Despite the higher quality of the Bowen maps, this rather old-fashioned small atlas could not compete with the rival best-seller by Ellis, which was only half the price and promoted in all the best book shops. Thomas Bowen went on to produce many more maps, but died in 1790 as a pauper in the Clerkenwell workhouse.

Thomas Kitchin seems to have been a much better businessman than the Bowens, and certainly prospered by comparison. He was helped by marrying into a wealthy family in 1761, after the death of his first wife Sarah Bowen. He produced several sets of attractive small maps and a set of road strip-maps in his 1767 *Post-Chaise Companion* pocket-book (pirated from Ogilby via John Senex). At the early age of fifty and at the height of his success as engraver and publisher, in 1768 Thomas Kitchin senior retired and was

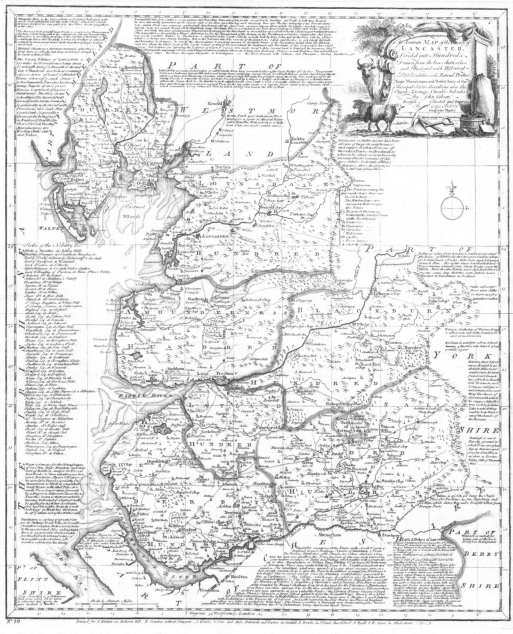

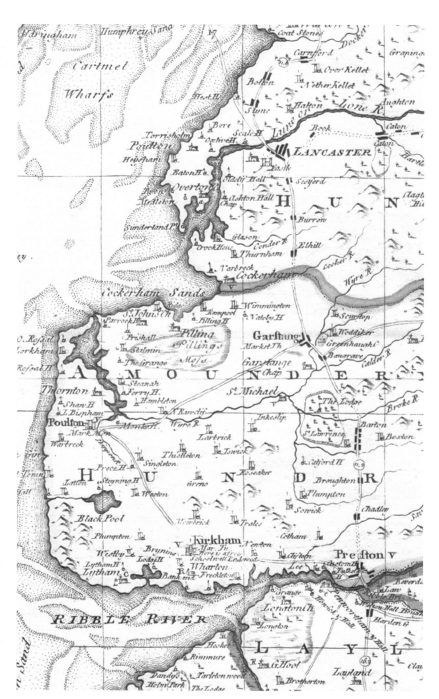

Fig. 49 Map 5F 'An Accurate Map of the County of Lancaster... by John Gibson Revised Corrected and Improved by Eman Bowen...' (1764), from *The Royal English Atlas* by Emanuel Bowen, Thomas Kitchin and Others (T. Kitchin, R. Sayer, *et al.*, London, *c.*1764) [402mm x 476mm, 15.8" x 18.7"]; also a section of that map at actual size [140mm x 170mm, 5.5" x 6.7"]

succeeded by his son Thomas Bowen Kitchin in the Holborn family shop. A second edition of *Atlas Anglicanus* was printed in 1777, but about then the younger Kitchin sold off the business, which had not prospered after his father left. The *Atlas Anglicanus* plates went through various ownerships until they ended up in the hands of those eager collectors of old copper, Robert Sayer and the Bowles family. Carington Bowles revised the plates in 1785 and the maps, now entitled 'Bowles's New Medium Map of ...shire', were on sale in that state until possibly 1830, mainly as loose sheets.

OTHER MAPS BASED ON *THE LARGE ATLAS*

This was a period in which English cartography was being transformed. Large-scale mapping is not discussed here, but we should note that by 1785 almost all of England had been surveyed at the one mile per inch scale. Lancashire was one of the last counties to be surveyed at this large scale and of necessity from 1750 until 1788 maps of Lancashire relied upon the distorted Bowen/Kitchin *Large English Atlas* map as the best version available, as it was for a few other counties for a short period after those maps were published in 1750-60. Thus in this era there are significantly different development histories for the mapping of the individual English counties.

In 1761 Bowen engraved a new quarto map of Lancashire 5H (Fig. 51) in a set originally issued during 1755-62 to illustrate the monthly *General Magazine...* by Benjamin Martin. The complete series was collected as a two volume atlas *The Natural History of England*, but these maps were not reprinted elsewhere later and are rare. Close copies of these Bowen maps were included in a very unusual Dutch version of the Martin magazine series issued in parts from 1757 to 1770 by Pieter Meijer in Amsterdam. An incomplete set of ten county maps at similar size (mainly by Gibson) were published in the monthly magazine *Universal Museum*, including in 1768 a Lancashire map by Thomas Bowen 5J also on Fig. 51. Even though the title states it is 'Drawn from the Best Authorities', for some obscure reason 5J is based on the Kitchin map 5A of 1750 (source in particular of the Ribble estuary north coastline and the scales), rather than a more recent drafting like 5H.

Thomas Kitchin himself made a new complete set of maps (slightly larger than 5H) for Robert Dodsley, the publisher 20 years earlier of the magazine in which the Cowley maps had appeared and the

subsequent atlas containing them. For his second major venture into mapping, Dodsley rather strangely published the complete collected edition first in 1763, a substantial two volume work entitled *England Illustrated*. This was then reissued in twelve separate monthly parts during 1764, reversing the usual sequence of prior instalment publication. Dodsley died during that year and was succeeded by his brother James, who sold *England Illustrated* until about 1781 and also published the maps without text as *Kitchin's English Atlas* in 1765.

The Lancashire map 5K (Fig. 52) shows the good quality of these maps. Market towns with fairs are underlined, and many roads are indicated, but here we see the ultimate degeneration of vertical relief depicted as 'sugarloaf hills', which are scattered across the county like molehills, with no distinction by size or shape to distinguish relative heights, tending to come in rows including a coastal range from Blackpool to Lytham, perhaps exaggerated sand dunes. Of course in the copying sequence nobody has been looking at the *land*, only at the earlier maps. The result is a misleading uniformity, causing an unsuspecting map owner to expect similar terrain in the Fylde and Furness areas. James Dodsley issued a few later editions of the atlas, but unfortunately these Kitchin maps failed to attract good business from the public.

Instead of *Kitchin's English Atlas*, customers bought the new market leader at the same price, *Ellis's English Atlas*, which (as mentioned already) was a best-seller when published near the start of 1766 by the prosperous Robert Sayer and Carington Bowles, who were in a much better position than Dodsley to advertise and market their work. Author Joseph Ellis (often incorrectly named as John Ellis in cartographic literature) was apprentice, son-in-law and heir of Richard Seale. His atlas was on sale until about 1825 through numerous editions, including variants with French titles, and in most popular form was bound in soft red leather to be rolled up and put in a pocket. This success was totally unjust, because the Joseph Ellis maps are plagiarised, extremely close copies of the *England Illustrated* Kitchin maps of 1763, as can be seen in Fig. 52 by comparing the Lancashire maps 5K (Kitchin) with 5L (Ellis). In principle the Parliamentary *Engraving Copyright Act* (8 Geo 2 cap 13) of 1734 had given 14 years copyright protection to engravings, extended to 28 years in 1767, but it was very hard to claim these rights and presumably Dodsley did not have the resources to seek legal redress.

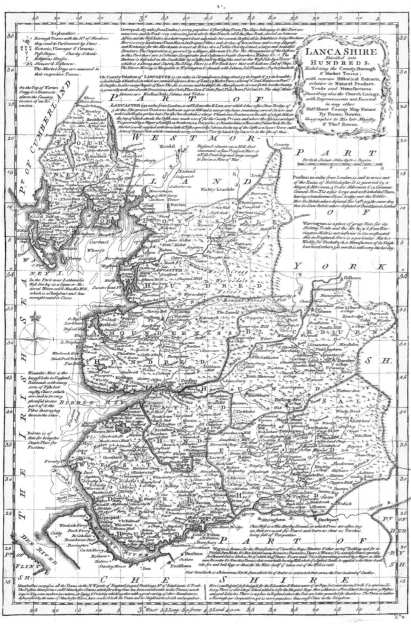

Fig. 50 Map 5G 'Lancashire... with Improvements not Inserted in any other Half Sheet County Map Extant', in *Atlas Anglicanus... by the late Emanuel Bowen,* reduced, drawn and engraved by Thomas Bowen (T. Kitchin, London, 1768) [211mm x 312mm, 8.3" x 12.3"]; also a section of that map at actual size [140mm x 170mm, 5.5" x 6.7"].

The copy by Ellis of the Kitchen map 5K was itself copied very closely at a slightly larger size and lower quality by John Lodge in 1789, as one of a large series of maps by Lodge engraved from 1782 until 1790. Slightly out of chronological sequence this map 5M (Fig. 53) is discussed here with the maps from which it was derived. The Lodge map follows Ellis in misprinting 'Bryam' (now Byrom Hall) near Leigh and omitting the name for Haudley above Blackburn. At the top of all three maps identical 'Remarks' state that underlining indicates the places with fairs, but very few towns are underlined, one being Chipping. The Lodge map was originally printed in the *Political Magazine and Parliamentary, Naval, Military and Literary Journal* issue for February 1789, published by R. Butters and J. Murray, and later reprinted for the *Atlas of Great Britain and Ireland* in the state shown in Fig. 53 where all the imprints indicating the engraver and the original use have been removed. This anonymity was applied to all the maps included in that atlas, which itself was credited to no author.

This John Lodge (1735?-1796) had been apprenticed to Thomas Jefferys in 1750 and produced a large number of very varied maps. His father was also a map engraver named John Lodge, apprenticed to Emanuel Bowen in 1723, but dead before his much more famous son followed him into the trade. A grandson continued the dynasty as the third John Lodge, engraver of maps for Arrowsmith and Laurie & Whittle. That last John Lodge had completed his apprenticeship under William Palmer (1739-1812), who himself was master to a number of celebrated map-makers, including John Cary. The cartographic world was small and professionally interlinked to a very great degree.

STANDARDISATION OF SCALE

The cartographer must choose a map scale large enough to show required detail, but small enough to fit on the page. In practice the size of the page was determined by the quality and budget of the publication, and then map scales differing individually from county to county were chosen to suit this page size. A folio atlas like Speed's *Theatre* shows a large county like Lancashire or Kent at about five statute miles per inch, while small counties are at less than three miles per inch, or grouped together at an intermediate scale, as Cumberland and Westmorland were often paired.

As noted in chapter 3, in all the centuries of English County map publication only a few sets were created with all the maps at the same scale, the first (Figs. 20 and 21) being an extreme case of miniaturisation, the almost useless 'thumb-nail' map series at about sixty statute miles per inch on William Bowes playing cards (2J) of 1590, copied in 1635 by van Langeren (3F) to illustrate distance tables. There would be a final set all at three miles per inch in the splendid Greenwood atlas of 1834, but intermediate in time and scale is *Kitchin's Pocket Atlas* (sic)... *Drawn to one scale. By which the true proportion they severally bear to each other may be easily ascertained...* which was issued in 1769 by Thomas Kitchin. The maps here were deliberately all at a consistent scale of about seven miles per inch (see 5N, Fig. 54).

Technically the experiment by Kitchin was not a success. While the county basis for an English atlas remained in vogue, displaying counties at the same scale was not at all convenient, even if it did aid comparisons. Kitchin's maps vary in size from 290mm x 370mm (11½" x 14½") for Cornwall to 85mm x 105mm (3½" x 4") for Rutland, so the larger maps had to be folded to fit in the atlas, while smaller maps were at two to a page (in nine pairs). It would have been too difficult to adjust each scale separately from a previous county series, and so the maps were derived from an England and Wales map, in this case from Kitchin's own four-sheet general map of England and Wales of 1752, enlarged by about 1.4 as a linear scaling factor and with adjustments to county boundaries.

The mapping details on 5N are almost identical to Kitchin's map 5K of 1764, but Martin Mere is labelled 'now drained', even though on the map it is shown with its islands and in fact had reverted to marsh by the time the map was printed, remaining in that state until 1784. The correct 'Marton Mere' is labelled 'Black Pool' and 'Black Pool Town' is shown separately, as in the *Large English Atlas* and all Kitchin's subsequent maps. This attempt by Kitchin to compete with Ellis was even more unsatisfactory than the first and the great rarity of these maps must indicate a total lack of interest in the concept of scale by the public. Yet in *c.*1778 Carington Bowles (who neglected no opportunity for profit, however slight) published a second edition of the Kitchin maps as *Bowles's Pocket Atlas*, with added titles and plate numbers.

FINAL MAPS BASED ON THE OLD SURVEYS

It was noted above that Alexander Hogg reissued the *London Magazine* maps by Thomas Kitchin (see 5A) from 1787 until 1798 in variously titled works and thus this map was among the last to

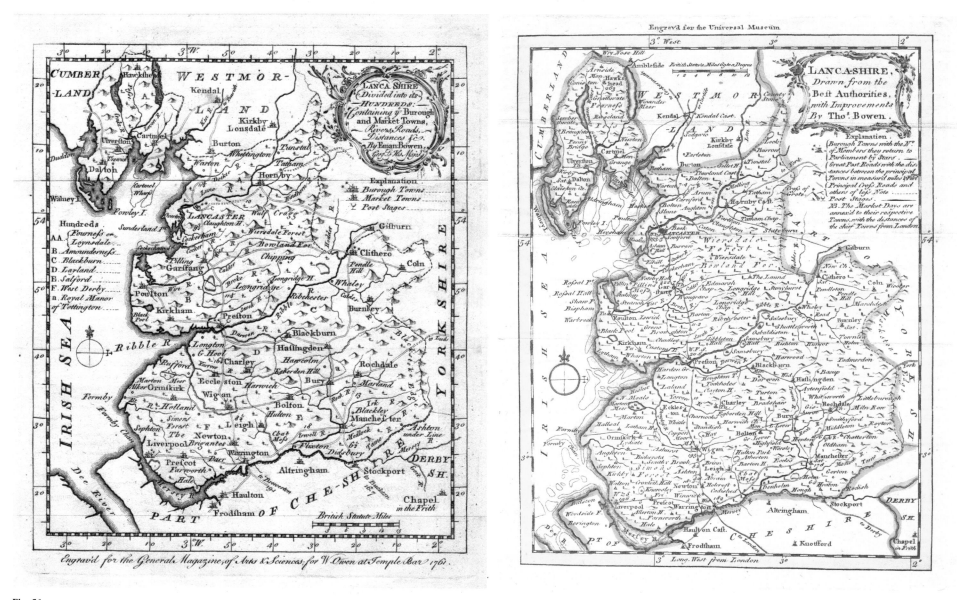

Fig. 51
Left: Map 5H 'Lancashire Divided into its Hundreds...' by Emanuel Bowen, from the *General Magazine of Arts and Sciences* by B. Martin (W. Owen, London, 1761). [154mm x 175mm, 6.1" x 6.9"]
Right: Map 5J 'Lancashire, Drawn from the best Authorities' by Thomas Bowen, in *Universal Museum* (J. Payne, London, 1768). [149mm x 188mm, 5.9" x 7.4"]

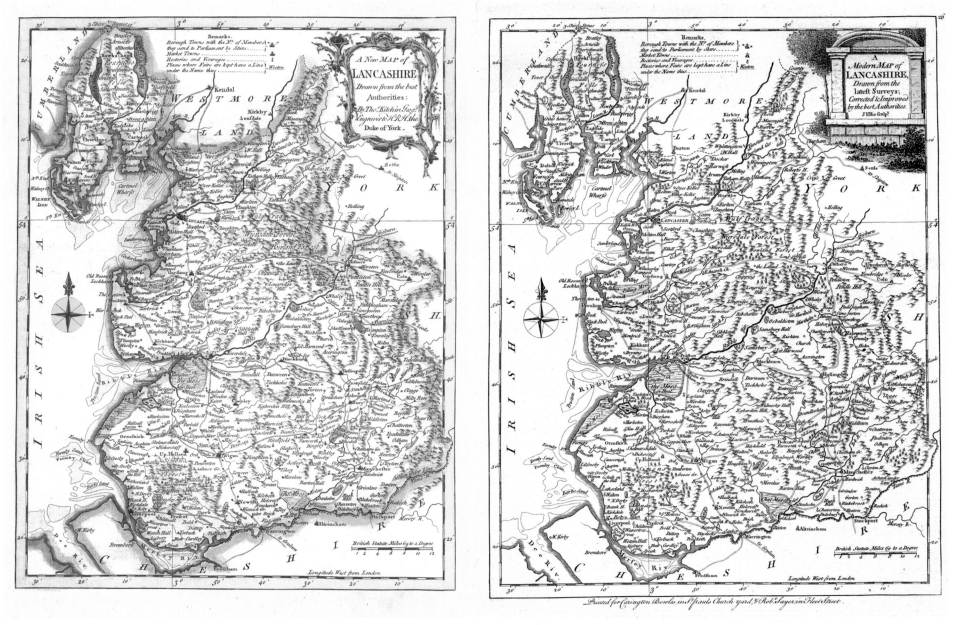

Fig. 52

Left: Map 5K 'A New Map of Lancashire...' by Thomas Kitchin, from *England Illustrated* (R. & J. Dodsley, London, 1764). [182mm x 231mm, 7.2" x 9.1"]

Right: Map 5L 'A Modern Map of Lancashire' (1765) by Joseph Ellis, from *Ellis's English Atlas* (C. Bowles, London, 1768). [180mm x 226mm, 7.1" x 8.9"]

show the distorted Kitchin/Bowen outline at the end of the century (as well as being the first to employ it fifty years earlier in 1750). Hogg also published a set of maps in *Walpoole's New and Complete British Traveller...* of 1784. First issued in 60 weekly parts, this was decorative and cheap to attract the growing mass market among educated craftsmen and shopkeepers. It is likely that the nominal editor George Augustus Walpoole did not exist, as Hogg is infamous for inventing fictitious collaborators.

The maps were based on those by Ellis, with added arms of county towns, and were printed up to four on a page with a common title, imprint and ornamental border. The Lancashire map (5P on Fig. 55) is paired with Lincolnshire and the two maps are usually found split to leave no margin on one side and an incomplete border containing imprint details. Most of the maps were engraved (and probably designed) by Thomas Condor, whose name was added for the second issue in 1794, when the other surrounding details were deleted. Condor had been an apprentice of Thomas Bowen Kitchin. Copies of these maps are relatively common for their age.

The London printer and publisher John Harrison (who should not be confused with the celebrated marine clock maker of the same name) was responsible for a folio atlas containing county maps drawn by John Haywood and engraved by Edward Sudlow at a generous scale of five miles per inch for Lancashire. Here for map 5Q (Fig. 56), we see the last Lancashire plate based on the form used by Bowen and Kitchin for *The Large English Atlas* and engraved in their distorted shape, included here though issued in 1789. The rather bare appearance is partly due to the total absence of decoration (no longer fashionable), but mainly due to persisting lack of knowledge about the topography, as the 'actual survey' conventionally referred to in the map title was by Saxton over 200 years previously. The recently published survey by Yates had not been used, suggesting it was engraved some time earlier than publication, but there are 'Improvements' and in various ways this map does represent a large innovative step forward. Many details from the *Large Atlas* are tidied up and unusual effort has been devoted to the inclusion of new material.

In particular the road system is shown in much more detail than in any previous map, distinguishing turnpike roads from lesser routes and this is the first county atlas map of Lancashire to illustrate the developing canal network by showing the St Helens Canal (1757), the Bridgewater Canal (1773), the section of the

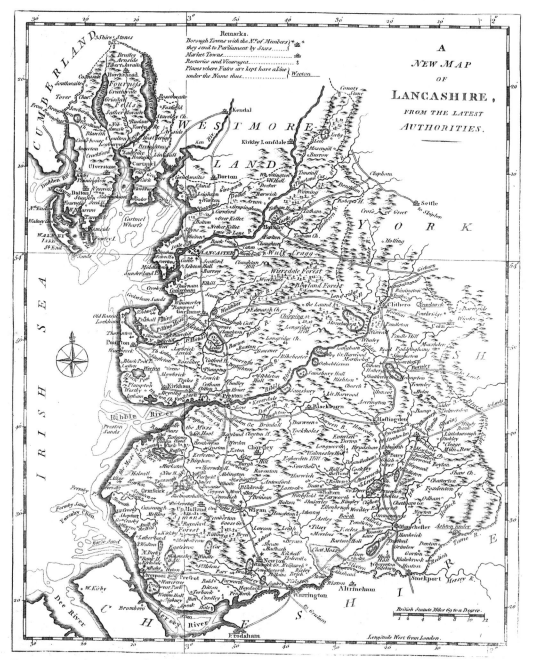

Fig. 53 Map 5M 'A New Map of Lancashire...' by John Lodge (1789), from *The Political Magazine...* (R. Butters & J. Murray, London, 1789), reprinted for an anonymous atlas in 1795. [251mm x 307mm, 9.9" x 12.1"]

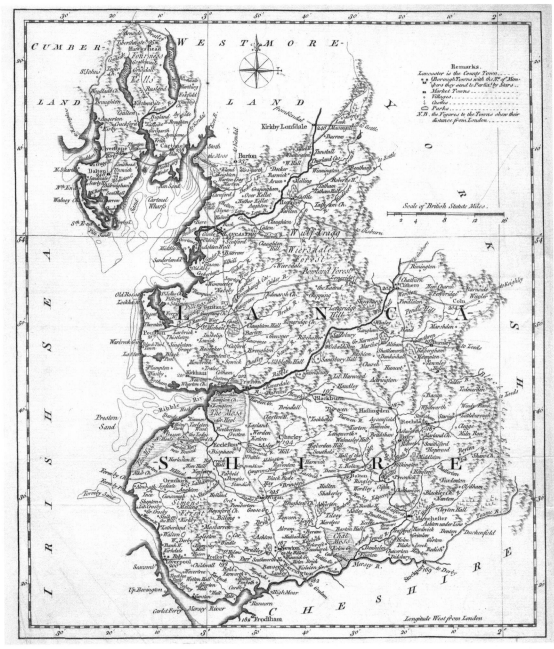

Fig. 54 Map 5N 'Lancashire' by Thomas Kitchin, in *Kitchin's Pocket Atlas of the Counties of South Britain* (T. Kitchin & J. Gapper, London, 1769). [242mm x 278mm, 9.5" x 10.9"]

Liverpool to Leeds Canal completed as far as Wigan (1774) and the Rufford Branch (1781) to the Douglas Navigation. Despite competition from the smaller maps by Cary, the Harrison maps were collected into an atlas in 1791 and reprinted in 1792, reduced in price from £3.15 to £2.10. More surprising is a further reprinting of the Harrison maps unchanged in 1815, although by then they were very outdated indeed. A similar map (not illustrated) was created by William Tunnicliff for *A Topographical Survey of the Counties of Stafford, Chester and Lancaster; containing a new engraved Map of each County...* (London, 1787 and 1789), which also showed some canals.

Finally we note the reappearance of the old John Seller maps (such as 4D) with Saxton as sole source. These had been issued in various works from about 1693 until 1711, and possibly were reprinted again around 1738. Turning up again after a mysteriously long absence from any publication, the Seller plates were used to illustrate a work first issued in monthly parts from 1772 onwards, *The Antiquities of England and Wales* by Francis Grose (1731-1791). The whole set of small county maps was inserted as a supplement at the end of the series in 1787. By then the plates themselves qualified to be considered as antiquities.

The Grose version of the Seller map (in Fig. 57) has a new simpler cartouche with no mention of Seller as the original author, and includes several important towns (Hawkshead, Cartmel, Hornby, Poulton, Clitheroe, Haslingden, Chorley, Newton, Prescot) carelessly omitted ninety years earlier in the first state. There are spelling changes for Liverpool, Ormskirk and Stockport. From variations between editions it is clear that changes were performed in stages during use of the plates.

Grose was a character, much larger than life in all sorts of ways, resembling Sir John Falstaff. Beyond noting that the maps were issued both in the supplement and in an octavo 'new edition' of the whole work which was issued from 1783 in parallel with the original quarto edition before that was completed, the complex history of Grose himself and of the publication of the 'Antiquities' cannot be explored here.[5] The quarto and octavo editions were on sale until about 1815, providing another example of a set of plates having a very long period of use. Here the Elizabethan Saxton map provided the primary mapping source for a final time, extending its influence to a total of 240 years.

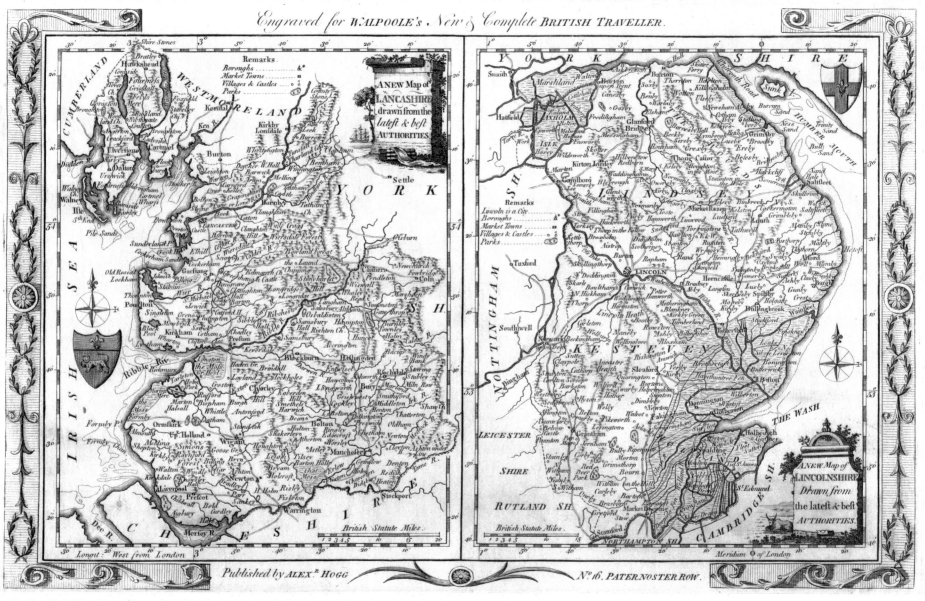

Fig. 55 Map 5P 'A New Map of Lancashire...' (and adjacent Lincolnshire) engraved by Thomas Condor, from *New British Traveller...* (A. Hogg, London, 1784). [Lancashire map 144mm x 178mm, 5.7" x 7.0"]

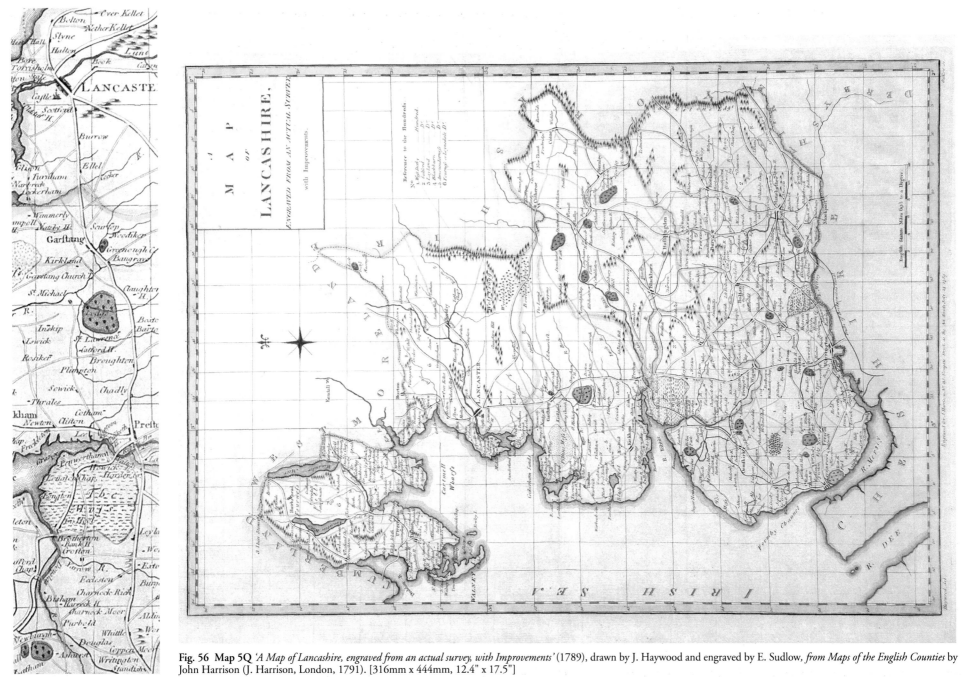

Fig. 56 Map 5Q *'A Map of Lancashire, engraved from an actual survey, with Improvements'* (1789), drawn by J. Haywood and engraved by E. Sudlow, *from Maps of the English Counties* by John Harrison (J. Harrison, London, 1791). [316mm x 444mm, 12.4" x 17.5"]

THE FIRST MODERN MAP OF LANCASHIRE.

As noted above, the preferred county survey scale was one mile per inch, a scale today associated primarily with the ubiquitous twentieth-century Ordnance Survey maps, but their first one-inch survey was not published until 1801 and until 1830 large-scale work was mostly published by private surveyors on their own initiative. Ten English and Welsh counties had been surveyed at the one-inch scale by 1736 and only three more were added by 1760, but a further eleven were published by 1770, and another twelve by 1780. This left only six English counties without a one-inch map, unfortunately including Lancashire. It was early in 1788 when Lancashire mapping belatedly achieved accuracy and detail with the publication of the William Yates map to give Lancashire its first one-inch representation as a revolution in local cartography as great as the political changes in Europe during this era. By 1788 only Wales, Cambridgeshire (1/3" 1690), Sussex (3/4" 1724) and Norfolk (2/3" 1731) had not been surveyed at the one-inch scale.

County mapping activity surged in 1760-80 partly in response to the Society of Arts awarding medals and gratuities for an accurate survey. Overall the Society awarded only thirteen prizes totalling £460 and only four gold medals for outstanding achievement, but William Yates got £100 and a gold medal for his Lancashire map, confirming it was in the very top class. This map 5R (Fig. 58) forms a fitting end to this survey of early maps for our county, with the Cary county atlas derived from such maps as a postscript. A map at the one-inch scale, measuring over 2 metres high (nearly seven feet), cannot be illustrated properly in this book, but the overall view in Fig. 58 and the full size section shown as Fig. 59 does indicate its quality.[6]

A one-inch map for Lancashire was first planned in 1768 by Peter Perez Burdett (1734-1793), a member of the Derby Lunar Society, and the artist who invented aquatinting. Burdett mapped Derbyshire in 1762-7 (with Chapman and Yates) to a standard which won the second award from the Society of Arts. Burdett then moved to Liverpool and began to collect subscriptions for his Lancashire map, but did not obtain enough sponsorship and began to map Cheshire instead. All he had completed for Lancashire was a sketched vignette of the Castle (which eventually did decorate the Yates map) when in 1774 he abruptly fled from his creditors into Germany, where he remained until his death, leaving his wife 'over head and ears in debt' and subscribers in two counties without their promised maps.[7]

William Yates (1738-1802) worked full-time as a customs officer in Liverpool from 1772 until 1796, but cartography must have occupied all his spare time. He had learned this by working in Derbyshire with John Chapman for Peter Burdett. Yates then himself published a map of Staffordshire in 1775 from a survey performed during 1769-75 with Chapman, who also engraved the map. Beginning from 1774 Yates also completed Burdett's mapping of Cheshire, published in 1777, and began mapping Lancashire, again with John Chapman. He also eventually surveyed Warwickshire in 1787-89. All these county maps were of high quality at the one mile per inch scale. It seems that he took no leave from his regular customs employment and although much of his

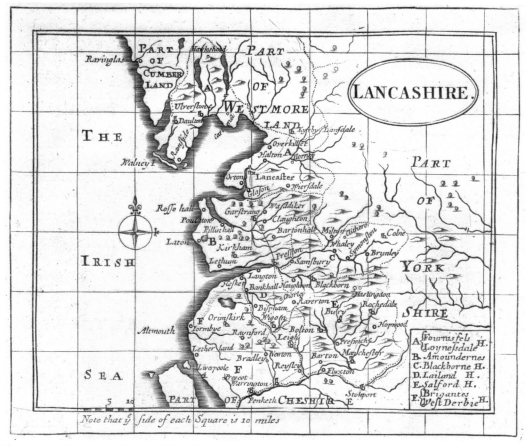

Fig. 57 Map 4D 'Lancashire' (c.1694) by John Seller as reprinted in *The Antiquities of England and Wales* by Francis Grose (S. Hooper, London, 1787). [132mm x 104mm, 5.2" x 4.1"]

cartographic work must have been supervisory rather than in the field, lack of time was surely responsible for some of the delay in converting the survey work into his Lancashire map.[8]

Yates and Chapman planned to complete that survey by 1778 but Chapman died in 1779 before their work in Lancashire was fully complete and the surveying was actually finished in the summer of 1780 by the then young William Green, later a noted Lake District artist. Meanwhile from 1776 the American Revolutionary War was damaging sea trade through Liverpool and it is likely that subscription promises were few. Yates never collected cash in advance (see below) and must have found it hard to finance mapping work on his customs income of about £130 p.a. (after promotion in 1778). It was not until 1786 that Yates delivered final drawings to Thomas Billinge (1741-1816) of Liverpool, who had earlier engraved the Cheshire map for Yates. The date 1786 appears on the Lancashire map, but its actual publication was later.

Billinge made a fine job of engraving the 8 copper plates, each about 500mm x 650mm (20" x 26") and late in 1786 the map was advertised as 'ready for publication' and 'will be delivered to the subscribers in eight large sheets, at one guinea and a half [£1.58 then, about £210 today], or pasted upon canvass (*sic*), and neatly coloured at two pounds and seven shillings [£2.35]; the money to be paid when the work is delivered. That the gentlemen of Lancashire may be assured there was no intention of pocketing a subscription without fulfilling the compact, no money is required till the work is delivered'.[9] Clearly Yates was anticipating a lack of confidence among subscribers (presumably because Burdett indeed had 'pocketed' their previous subscriptions), and repeated almost exactly the unusual promise given to potential subscribers in 1775 when the map was first advertised.[10] However, Yates added, 'That the copy of this expensive, and laborious undertaking may be secured against piratical attempt, the work will not be published until 800 copies are subscribed for'. In reality that number of subscribers was never reached and printing was delayed by more than another year, with Yates providing actual map deliveries starting early in 1788 following publicaton nominally in December 1787.[11]

The map was soundly based on triangulation, using sea-shore base lines from Bootle to Formby and Formby to North Meols while angles for 31 viewpoints were accurately measured to a minute of arc to correct the previous errors in the shape of the county. This is about a hundred times more precise than the best observations

that Saxton probably achieved. A note and diagram on the map show the triangulation details, 'inserted to gratify the curious in Geography; and in some degree to convey an Idea of the Labour and Precision with which...Observations were taken to the most remarkable circumjacent Objects...and the situations of the intermediate parts by the Theodolite and Perambulator'.[12] The improved county outline can be seen in Fig. 46. Kitchin had placed Liverpool at longitude 3°11' west from London, almost exactly the same as Saxton on his general map. Yates got the value correct at 2°54' from London, equal to the modern 2°59' from Greenwich.

Yates included an 'Explanation' table for the varied lettering distinguishing borough towns, market towns, parishes and other places, and a key to symbols for the status of churches, turnpikes (and toll bars) distinguished from minor roads. New inclusions were industrial sites such as mills, coal pits, quarries and mines. However, these were not systematically recorded for all areas, and as the survey was completed before 1780 such details were nearly ten years out-of-date by the time of publication. Yates copied other large-scale county maps by using rather faint crude hachuring to indicate vertical relief, the first time this was done for Lancashire. Overall it is fine work, deserving the Society of Arts award, but not without significant flaws by modern standards. Rather strangely, the map scale is slightly smaller than a strict one statue mile per inch, perhaps at least partly due to paper shrinkage after printing. In two examples directly measured by the author the seven-mile scale bar was 6.78" and 6.85" in length, while Whitaker gives 6.81" as his observation.

The London mapseller William Faden bought the eight map plates from Yates, in all probability when he retired in 1796. Faden reissued the one-inch map of Lancashire in London in 1800 as a second edition with revised landowners and small additions such as canals. In 1816 he published a close copy of the 1800 version reduced to half the original size and scale. Faden's business was sold in 1823 to the notable geographer James Wyld the elder (1790-1836), who had introduced lithography into British mapmaking in 1812 (and was draftsman for the Gregson map 2L described much earlier). James Wyld the younger (1812-1887) inherited the whole concern when his father died and in 1840 he reprinted Faden's reduced copy of the Lancashire map under his own name with no reference to its age or original authorship, adding a triangular distance table and many railways. Wyld's new

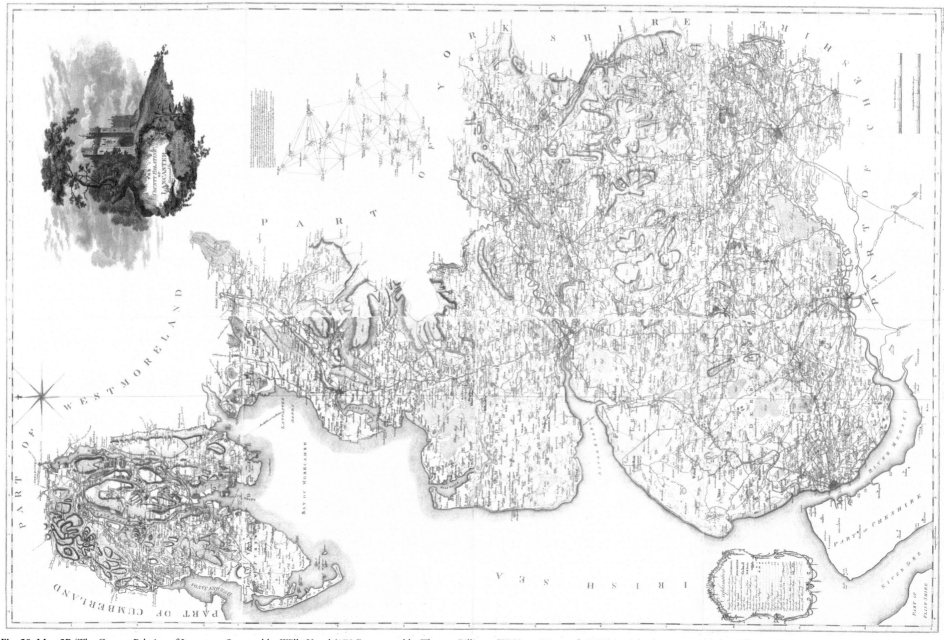

Fig. 58 Map 5R 'The County Palatine of Lancaster, Surveyed by Willm Yates' (1786), engraved by Thomas Billinge, (W. Yates, Liverpool, 1787) in eight sheets, assembled a wall-map. [1.33m x 2.06m, 52.4" x 81.41"]

Fig. 59 Section at full size from **Map 5R** 'The County Palatine of Lancaster, Surveyed by Willm Yates', (W. Yates, Liverpool, 1787). [Part shown is 275mm x 185mm, 10.8" x 7.3"]

title deceptively described it as 'Drawn from an Actual Survey and adjusted by the Trigonometrical Operations carried on under the direction of the Board of Ordnance', although the 'Actual Survey' had been completed 60 years previously by Yates and his excellent trigonometry needed no adjustments.

Wyld the younger was best known as the constructor of the 'Great Globe' on show in Leicester Square from 1851 until 1862. This was over 18m in diameter and displayed a model of the surface of the world on the inside. For his own maps Wyld plagiarised Ordnance Survey maps without scruple, despite becoming notorious (as the MP for Bodmin) for attacking the Ordnance Survey in Parliament over its extravagance with public funds, perhaps hoping the publishing business would be transferred to private map-makers like himself. However, Wyld did have a valid point. The very large expenditure of the Ordnance Survey was derived almost entirely from taxation, and until nearly 1900 the organisation regarded itself as an official information gatherer, rather than as a commercial information publisher.

NEW AND CORRECT, AT LAST

Around 1800 the dominant name in English mapmaking was John Cary (1755-1835), widely regarded as the finest of our native cartographers. His first major work was issued monthly from September 1787 in twelve parts (each containing four quarto maps), building into the *New and Correct English Atlas*, where for once the atlas really deserved its title. A page of information on the county was included with each map in by far the most exact set of county representations yet offered, because for the first time Cary could base nearly all the counties on a large-scale survey. The monthly publication schedule was maintained for six months, but the next four parts appeared over another nine months, the tenth in November 1788. The Lancashire map 5S (Fig. 60) was issued at an unknown date early in 1789 in the eleventh instalment, which also contained maps of Sussex, Cambridgeshire and Norfolk. It cannot be a coincidence that these final four counties (and the Welsh counties in the twelfth part also issued during 1789) were those not yet surveyed at the one mile to the inch scale when Cary began the work. In 1788 the Yates map 5R supplied an up-to-date survey source for Lancashire and there was a 1724 map at three quarters of an inch to the mile scale for Sussex, but of necessity *The Large English Atlas* was used as a basis for Norfolk and

Cambridgeshire (mapped at the one-inch scale only in 1797 and 1821 respectively) and for Wales.[13]

At the foot of his maps Cary gives the standard imprint statement 'Published as the Act directs...' and a date, referring to the 1734 Act of Parliament (8 Geo 2 cap 13) giving a period of publishing copyright. To get the full period of protection most publishers quoted the latest possible date, unlike Cary who had a strange obsession for consistency in his imprint details and to achieve this repeated the publishing date of the first part throughout a complete map series. Thus the dates given on many of his maps and title pages are much earlier than the actual issue itself, misleading many commentators. Like all others in the *New and Correct English Atlas*, the Lancashire map imprint is dated September 1st 1787 (and so it has been included here as a fitting conclusion) and usually the whole atlas is assumed to date from 1787, even though the final parts with Lancashire and the complete volume did not appear until 1789, after the publication of the map by Yates. Via copying of that map almost as soon as it was available, the Lancashire map 5S in Fig. 60 by Cary is the first in a county atlas to show the county as precisely as we expect today, and by including the name 'Bay of Morecambe' from Yates Cary helped to establish that modern usage.

The debt to Yates is nicely confirmed by the way Cary misprints several place-names, such as 'Loulton' for Coulton (in Furness), a Welsh-like 'Llanghton' for Claughton (in the Lune valley), 'Lockerham' for Cockerham (south of Lancaster), 'Lylham' for Lytham (in the Fylde) and 'Flirton' for Flixton (near Chat Moss). All of these errors arise directly from Yates showing 'Parishes which are not Market Towns in Old Print', a form of lettering very hard to read, especially the upper case 'C'. Aside from these forgivable mistakes, Cary shows the county in greatly improved detail and fine accuracy considering the small scale of the map (eight miles per inch). In particular he makes a very fair attempt at showing the main road system and his atlas included road itineraries and an interesting index of postal times and charges from London.[14]

Cary's county maps set new cartographic standards and inspired a new style of mapmaking. He was the first map-maker since 1600 to ignore the Hundreds as no longer of relevance. Although there is no ornamentation, his maps are very attractive to the eye. The *New and Correct English Atlas* was far from cheap (in 1789 the equivalent of £200 today), but rival works were similarly expensive. Uncoloured copies of Cary maps are seldom found and it seems that

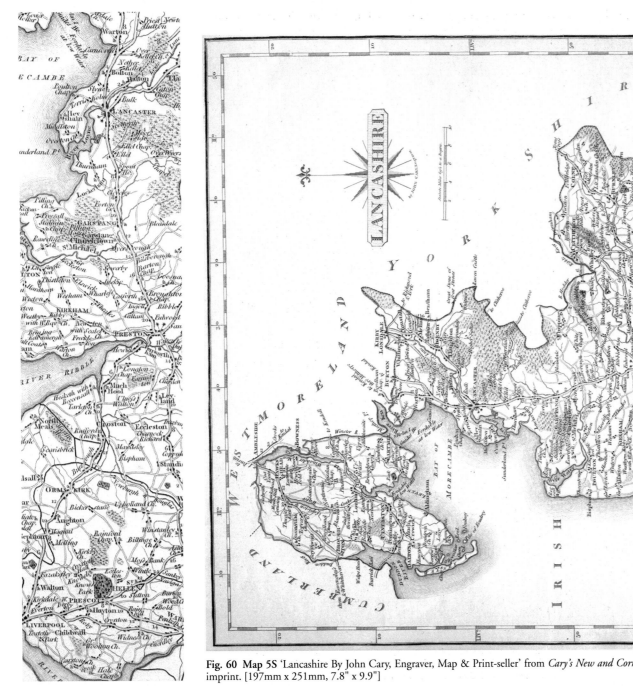

Fig. 60 Map 5S 'Lancashire By John Cary, Engraver, Map & Print-seller' from *Cary's New and Correct English Atlas* (J. Cary, London, 1789), but misleadingly dated 1787 in the imprint. [197mm x 251mm, 7.8" x 9.9"]

most customers opted for the slightly more expensive coloured version.[15] The standard original hand colouring in Fig. 60 is delicate and greatly enhances the maps. It has been suggested that the Ordnance Survey took the style of these early Cary maps as a model for their colouring of one-inch maps from the Third Series onwards a century later, though it seems unlikely that after so many years this convergence of style was a result of deliberate copying. The Cary atlas sold extremely well, both in the original 1789 form and in many later editions. Extensively altered Cary map plates seem to have been used by Gall and Inglis of Edinburgh as the basis for their cycling and road maps until well into the twentieth century.

John Cary and his sons produced many excellent maps during the long period until 1850 when their firm was the most prominent for map production in England, including the first geological map for the country, but their other triumphs fall into the period after that covered in this book and are not described here.

LATER COUNTY MAPPING

During the nineteenth century the depiction of the kingdom continued on the county-by-county basis introduced by Saxon until the one-inch Ordnance Survey sheet maps became the dominant version of national mapping. County atlas publication continued right into the twentieth century. The main cataloguing of Lancashire maps is by Harold Whitaker in *A Descriptive List of the Printed Maps of Lancashire, 1577-1900*, published by the Chetham Society in 1938. In round numbers Whitaker listed 90 issues and reissues of Lancashire maps before 1700 (not including any regional maps like 2A and its clones, also listed), with 120 more by 1788 during the period covered by this book. However, a further 435 are listed for the years from 1789 until 1900 and we must note this is the total of editions and reprints, not related in any way to the actual number of prints in an issue, which also was hugely increasing. New printing technologies made it quicker, easier and cheaper to produce maps, and cartographers responded by expanding the number and range of maps available. Colour printing was introduced, making that available as a standard version for all customers. Maps recorded revolutions in political representation, in transport by canal, on turnpike roads and above all on the railways spreading through the land during the reign of Queen Victoria. Thematic maps for all sorts of purposes were produced, some county based. By the turn of the century county

maps were being adapted with special information for cyclists and later for those strange (and wealthy) new map users, motorists.

So there is a great deal more of the story of Lancashire maps to be told, and it is hoped that a further volume will follow this to conclude the tale.

NOTES

1 According to Bickham (in his preface to *The British Monarchy*), '... by recommending Principles of useful Knowledge with all the Beauties of PENMANSHIP, and Embellishments of PICTURE, the most INCURIOUS and especially YOUNG PERSONS, may be allured to inform their JUDGEMENTS, and to furnish their MEMORIES with such Particulars as must be of Service to them ever after. In a Word, to fit them for the best CONVERSATION, and give them a necessary SUPERIORITY in such COMPANY as have neglected the same Improvements.'

2 The book includes a two-page table on the rates of pay in the Army and Navy, fascinating in the way it indicates the hierarchy and relative 'pecking order' in the services. A fine facsimile of the whole Bickham volume was published by Frank Graham (Northumberland Press, Gateshead, 1967).

3 Advertisement by John Newbery in the *Public Advertiser*, 6 Jan 1762.

4 R. Gough, *British Topography* (Payne & Nichols, London, 1780), vol. I, p.99.

5 For some details see Donald Hodson *County Atlases of the British Isles, Volume III (1764-1789)* (British Library, London, 1997), pp.125-65.

6 Detailed views of a copy of the Yates map may be seen via http://www.lancashire.gov.uk/environment/oldmap/Yates/index.asp

7 J.B. Harley, 'William Yates and Peter Burdett...', *Trans. H. S. Lancs & Ches*, 115 (1963), pp.117-9. The quotation is from Joseph Wright, reported by Bemrose, *Life and Works of Joseph Wright* (Bemrose, London, 1885), pp.77-8.

8 For biographical notes on Yates and analysis of his map see Harley, 'William Yates and Peter Burdett...' (1963), pp.119-31, also introductory text by Harley in *William Yates's Map of Lancashire, 1786* (H. S. Lancs. & Ches., Liverpool, 1968), pp.7-21.

9 *The General Advertiser*, Liverpool, 30 November 1786

10 *The General Advertiser*, Liverpool, 3 March 1775

11 A note at the foot of the plate states it was 'Published as the Act directs', but actual availability to the subscribers was first announced in the *Manchester Mercury*, 4 December 1787

12 Quoted from the note engraved on the map, which gives a full explanation of the triangulation diagram.

13 The publication history of the Cary atlas is given in detail by Hodson in *County Atlases..., Volume III (1764-1789)*, pp.172-84.

14 From entries in the 1809 edition, the mail coach reached Manchester at 11pm on the next day after posting in London, continuing on the following day to Liverpool at 4am, to Preston at 8am and to Lancaster at noon. The cost of a letter to Manchester, Liverpool or Preston (in old pennies) was 10d [about £2.75 today], or 11d [£3 now] for Lancaster.

15 The difference in price was small. As loose sheets the 1789 atlas sold for 24 shillings [£1.20] uncoloured or hand coloured for 30 shillings [£1.50]. Binding cost a further one shilling and six pence [7.5p]. An instalment of four maps cost two shillings plain [£0.10] or two shillings and six pence [£0.125] if coloured. Prices given by Hodson, *County Atlases..., Volume III*, pp.176-9.

APPENDIX 1: TABLES OF MAP DETAILS

MAPS ILLUSTRATED HERE OF LANCASHIRE SHOWN WITHIN A LARGER AREA

Ref./Fig.	Chubb	Whitaker	Shirley	State	Date	Width/mm x Height/mm	Cartographer/ Engraver	Publisher/Notes/Source
- / 3		page iv	page vii		c.1360	1180 x 560	Anonymous	the 'Gough' (Bodleian) MS map of Britain
1C / 4		plate 1	28	1	1540	337 x 247	Münster, S	Basle Edition of Ptolemy *Geographia*, first issue
1A / 1			123	1	1578	383 x 315	Mercator, G	edition of Ptolemy *Geographia*, first issue
2A / 5		plate 3	185	3	1595	448 x 364	Ortelius / Lhuyd	*Theatrum Orbis Terrarum*, from retouched 1573 plate
2B / 6		3	see 180	1	1595	390 x 336	Mercator, G	first issue in *Atlas* appendix; later in Mercator Atlas
2C / 7		10	see 283	1	1609	169 x 124	Hondius, J	version of 2B in *Atlas Minor*, Jansson, Arnhem 1607-37
2C / 7		70	see 476	1	1637	171 x 124	Hondius, J	version of 2B in *Atlas Minor*, London, late English edition
2D / 8	see LV		see 347	1	1616	123 x 83	Bertius, P	version of 2B published by Jodocus Hondius the younger
2E / 8		44	see 401	1	1628	187 x 132	Jansson, J	version of 2B in *Atlas Minor* by Jansson, Amsterdam
2F / 8		52	see 412	1	1630	238 x 170	Hondius, J	version of 2B in *Merc. Atlas* by Cloppenburg, Amsterdam
3N / 30	see CIIa		see Ogilby 1	2	1698	413 x 333	Ogilby, J	road map from *Britannia*, London, reprint of 1675 plate

CHRONOLOGICAL LIST OF THE EARLY PRINTED MAPS OF LANCASHIRE WITH THEIR RECORDED REPRINTS

Ref./Fig.	Chubb	Whitaker	Skelton/Hodson	State	Date	Width/mm x Height/mm	Cartographer/ Engraver	Publisher/Notes/Source
2G / 9	I to VI	1	1	1	1577	456 x 371	Saxton, C	source original 1576 survey; county base map until 1750
	VII	78	27	2	1642		Saxton	in Web edition; new title, date and Stuart royal arms
		114	80	3	1665		Saxton	major changes made by unknown owner; dated 1665
		136		4	1683		Saxton	in first Lea edition; date erased on Lancs. map
		140		5	1689		Saxton	in Lea edition; his name and town symbols added
	VIII	141	110	6	1690		Saxton	in Lea edition; roads added
2H / 11		142	112	7	1693	466 x 378	Saxton	in main Lea edition; new title; Manchester corrected
		143	113	7	1693		Saxton	in Lea atlas (French text)
		164	183	8	1720		Saxton	in Willdey edition; note added in a box
		197	184	9	1749		Saxton	in Jefferys edition; Willdey note removed, leaving box

Ref./Fig.	Chubb	Whitaker	Skelton/Hodson	State	Date	Width/mm x Height/mm	Cartographer/Engraver	Publisher/Notes/Source
2H / 10			185	9	1770	467 x 381	Saxton	in Cluer Dicey loose sheets and probable atlas edition
2J / 21		2	2	1	1590	map 38 x 38	Bowes, W	source Saxton E&W; playing cards
	IX	5	4	1	*c.*1599		van den Keere, P	source Saxton 2G; proof copies, with MS notes *c.*1605
3D / 19	X	30	12	1	1617	120 x 83	van den Keere	in Blaeu edition, Latin title; text abridged Speed *Theatre*
	XI	33	17	2	1620		van den Keere	in George Humble edition, English title
	XII	40	19	2	1627	120 x 83	van den Keere	in George Humble 'miniature Speed'
	XIII	49		2	1630		van den Keere	in George Humble edition
	XIV	86	37	2	1646		van den Keere	in William Humble edition
	XV	106	69	2	1662		van den Keere	in Roger Rea edition
	XVI	115	82,83,86	2	1666-8		van den Keere	in Roger Rea editions (plates retouched)
	XVII	122	93	2	1676		van den Keere	in Bassett & Chiswell edition
		7	3	1	1602		Smith, W (anon)	source Saxton 2G and field work; one proof copy only
2K / 12		107	49	2	1650-65	462 x 355	Smith	for Stent (loose copies only)
			89,91	3	1665-70		Smith	in John Overton atlas
		132	107,111,121	3	1680-1700		Smith	in John Overton atlas editions
2L / 13		370		1	1821	482 x 333	Smith, W (MS)	incorrect version by Gregson for *Portfolio of Fragments*
		588		2	1869		Smith	second lithographic drawing for *Portfolio of Fragments*
		659		2	1888		Smith	as 1869; in *Baines's History*, Croston ed.
	XVIII	11	5	1	1607		Saxton-Hole	source Saxton 2G; from Camden's *Britannia* (Latin text)
3A / 14	XIX	20	6	1	1610	305 x 292	Saxton-Hole	in Camden's *Britannia* (verso blank; English text)
	XX	71	23	2	1637		Saxton-Hole	in Camden's *Britannia* (plate number added)
	XXIII	14		0	1608		Speed proof	incomplete, without sea shading, border etc.
	XXII	21	7	1	1611	493 x 368	Speed, J	sources 2G,2K; in Sudbury & Humble first edition
				2,3	1612		Speed	in Humble reprints with map revisions
	XXIV	27	10	3	1616		Speed	in new Sudbury & Humble edition
	XXIVa	28	11	3	1616		Speed	in Sudbury & Humble edition (Latin text)
		29	14	3?	*c.*1623		Speed	in Sudbury & Humble special edition
	XXV	41	16	4	1627		Speed	in George Humble edition; Speed source of later maps

Ref./Fig.	Chubb	Whitaker	Skelton/Hodson	State	Date	Width/mm x Height/mm	Cartographer/ Engraver	Publisher/Notes/Source
3C / 16		54	18	4	c.1632	495 x 369	Speed	in George Humble edition
		87	36	4	1646		Speed	in William Humble edition
			48,50-52,55,57	4	1650-4		Speed	in William Humble editions
	XXVI	108	81	5	1665		Speed	in Roger Rea edition
	XXVII	123	92	6	1676		Speed	in Bassett & Chiswell edition (with text)
	XXVIII	124		6	1676		Speed	in Bassett & Chiswell edition (sheet issue, no text)
		147	116	6	c.1695		Speed	in Christopher Browne edition
			135	6	c.1713		Speed	in Henry Overton edition
	XXIXa	155	136	7	c.1716		Speed	in Henry Overton edition (crack in plate?)
3C / 17	XXX	157	137	7	c.1720	501 x 371	Speed	in Henry Overton edition (crack in plate)
	XXXI	187	138,143a	7	1743		Speed	in Henry Overton edition (wide crack in worn plate)
	XXXII	239	145	8	c.1760		Speed	in Cluer Dicey edition (final printing)
		633		1	1883		Speed	in Kelly (possible reproduction)
3B / 15	XXXV	36	13	1	1622	305 x 240	Drayton, M	source Saxton 2G; map in Second Book, only 1622 issue
		639		1	1884		Drayton	small photolithograph copy
	XXXVI	669		1	1890		Drayton	copied in Spenser Society Edition
3E / 19	XLI	38	15	1	1626	115 x 82	Bill, J	source van den Keere 3D, text abridged *Britannia*
3F / 20	XLIV	63	20	1	1635	38 x 38	van Langeren, J	source WB card 2J, for small maps on Norden tables
	XLV	67	21	1	1636		van Langeren	unchanged reprint
		68	22	1	1636		van Langeren	London distances added to table
	XLVI	81	25	2	1643		Jenner, T	source Speed E&W map, for larger maps now inserted
3G / 20	XLIX	104	26,62	2	1657	105 x 104	Jenner	in *A Book of the Names...*
	L	109	70	2	1662		Jenner	in *A Book of the Names...*
	LI	117	87,88	3	1668		Jenner	in *A Book of the Names...*
	XLVII?	125		3	1676		Jenner	possible first Garrett edition of above
	LII	130	98,99	3	1677		Jenner	in Garrett edition of above
	XLVIII?	133	101	3	1680		Jenner	in Garrett edition of above
3J / 23		69		1	1636	484 x 361	Jansson, J	source Speed 3C; first state with Poseidon
		72		1	1637		Jansson	in appendix to Mercator Atlas

Ref./Fig.	Chubb	Whitaker	Skelton/Hodson	State	Date	Width/mm x Height/mm	Cartographer/ Engraver	Publisher/Notes/Source
		74		1	1638		Jansson	in appendix to Mercator Atlas
		75		1	1638		Jansson	in appendix to Mercator Atlas
		80		1	1642		Jansson	in appendix to Mercator Atlas
	LXX	89	34	2	1646		Jansson	Jansson Atlas (Latin text); all decoration changed
	LXXI	90	35	2	1646		Jansson	in Jansson Atlas (French text)
	LXXII	92	39	2	1647	486 x 362	Jansson	in Jansson Atlas (French text)
	LXXIII	93	40	2	1647		Jansson	in Jansson Atlas (German text)
	LXXIV	99	46	2	1649		Jansson	in Jansson Atlas (German text)
	LXXV	101	52	2	1652		Jansson	in Jansson Atlas (French text)
3K / 24	LXXVI	102	54	2	1652	486 x 362	Jansson	in Jansson Atlas (Dutch text)
		103	61	2	1656		Jansson	in Jansson Atlas (French text)
	LXXVII	105	66	2	1659		Jansson	in Jansson Atlas (Latin text)
	LXXX	156	130	2	1710		Jansson	in Allard, Amsterdam edition (verso blank)
	LXXIX	137,158	131	3	1714		Jansson	in David Mortier edition, London; many revisions
		159	132,133	3	1715		Jansson	in David Mortier edition, London (French text)
	LXXXI	170	134	3	1724		Jansson	in Joseph Smith edition, London (French text)
	LIX	83	28	1	1645		Blaeu, J	source Speed 3C; in Blaeu Atlas (Latin text)
		84	29	1	1645		Blaeu	in Blaeu Atlas (French text)
		85		1	1645		Blaeu	in Blaeu Atlas (German text)
	LX	88	30-33	1	1646		Blaeu	in Blaeu Atlas (Latin text)
		91	38	1	1647		Blaeu	in Blaeu Atlas (Dutch text)
	LXII	94	42	1	1648		Blaeu	in Blaeu Atlas (Latin text)
		95	43	1	1648		Blaeu	in Blaeu Atlas (French text)
		96	44	1	1648		Blaeu	in Blaeu Atlas (German text)
	LXI	97	45	1	1648		Blaeu	in Blaeu Atlas (Dutch text)
3H / 22		98		1	1648	483 x 375	Blaeu	in Blaeu Atlas (no text)
	LXIII	110	71	1	1662		Blaeu	in Blaeu Atlas (Latin text)
		111		1	1662		Blaeu	in Blaeu Atlas (French text)
	LXIV	112	72	1	1663		Blaeu	in Blaeu Atlas (French text)
	LXV	113	77	1	1664		Blaeu	in Blaeu Atlas (Dutch text)
	LXVI	116	84	1	1667		Blaeu	in Blaeu Atlas (French text)
	LXVII	119	73	1	1672		Blaeu	in Blaeu Atlas (Spanish text)
		679		2	1893	486 x 371	Blaeu	facsimile; Shearer, Stirling

Ref./Fig.	Chubb	Whitaker	Skelton/Hodson	State	Date	Width/mm x Height/mm	Cartographer/ Engraver	Publisher/Notes/Source
3L / 27	XCIX	121	90,100	1	1673	252 x 321	Blome, R	source Speed 3C; the large Blome map
3P / 29		126	94	1	1676	map 56 x 57	Morden, R	source Speed 3C and Ogilby roads; as playing card
		127	94a	1	1676		Morden	in atlas form issued by Morden
3P / 29		129	95	2	1676	map 56 x 57	Morden	with extra names; playing card
3P / 29	CVIII	134	103	2	1680	map 56 x 57	Morden	in Pask atlas
3P / 29	CIX	200	273	2	c.1775	map 56 x 57	Morden	in Turpin atlas
		676		1	1892		Morden	state 1 Lancs., copied as playing card example
3Q / 29		128	96	1	1676	card 55 x 94	Redmayne, W	suit-marks outlined; all stencilled, playing card
		131	97	2	1677		Redmayne	suit-marks engraved; some stencilled; playing card
			146	3	1717		Redmayne	Lenthall reprint with border; playing card
3M / 28	CX	135	104	1	1681	193 x 243	Blome, R	source Speed 3C; the small Blome map
		138	105	1	1685		Blome	unchanged reprint
		144	114	2	1693		Blome	dedication removed, leaving blank area
	CXXXVI	160	139	3	1715		Blome	in Taylor edition; places added in blank area
3M / 28	CXXXVIa	162,163	140	4	1717	193 x 243	Blome	in Taylor edition; roads and distances added
	CXXXVIb	178	141	4	c.1731		Blome	in Bakewell edition; could be 1735
	CXIII	145	117	1	1695	349 x 401	Morden, R	source Saxton-Lea 2H; the large Morden map
	CXIV	161		1	1715		Morden	special collection of maps with MS notes
	CXV	168	169	2	1722	349 x 400	Morden	revised edition; names altered
		180	170	2	c.1730		Morden	no changes
4A / 31	CXVI	209	171	3	1753	345 x 407	Morden	plates retouched, hills in particular
	CXVII	241	172	3	1772		Morden	no changes
	CXVIII	146	115	1	c.1694	130 x 104	Seller, J	source obscure, no clear relations; in *Anglia Contracta*
	CXIX	148	119,120	1	1696-7	131 x 104	Seller	in *History of England*
4D / 34	CXX	150	122	1	1701	131 x 104	Seller	in *Camden's Britannia Abridg'd*
	CXXI	152	124	1	1703		Seller	in *History of England* issues to 1711
			124a	1	1711		Seller	in *Britannia Abridg'd* (remainders)
	CXXII	249	274	2	1784		Seller	in Grose *Antiquities*; title changed and additions
4D / 57			275-280	3	1793	132 x 104	Seller	in various issues of *Antiquities* 1789-1815

Ref./Fig.	Chubb	Whitaker	Skelton/Hodson	State	Date	Width/mm x Height/mm	Cartographer/ Engraver	Publisher/Notes/Source
4B / 32	CXXIV	151	123	1	1701	150 x 194	Morden, R	source Saxton-Lea 2H; the small Morden map
	CXXV	153	125,126	1	1704		Morden	quarto reprint of *New Description and State of...*
	CXXVI	154	127	2	1708		Morden	changes by Moll; scale, compass, etc. for road atlas
4B / 32	CXXVII	165	128	2	1720	147 x 194	Morden	reprint of state 2 in *Magna Britannia*
	CXXVIII	181	129	2	1739		Morden	remaindered 1720 edition issues
4C / 33				1	1719		Nutt & Morphew	source 3G; distances table with 4B in magazine issue
				2?	1720	148 x 186	Nutt & Morphew	distances table published with 4B; atlas edition
3R / 29			147	1	1717	56 x 57	Lenthall, J	close copy of Morden playing card state 2; no border
			147	2	c.1717		Lenthall	second playing card edition with decorated border
4E / 35	CXLVII	166	149-151	1	1720	107 x 117	Bowen, E	source Morden 4B 1708; in road atlas *Britannia Depicta*
	CXLVIII	167	152	1	1721		Bowen	county maps stable, but roads being revised
	CXLIX	169	153	1	1723		Bowen	editions differ in minor ways
	CL	171	155	1	1724		Bowen	editions differ in minor ways
	CLI	175	156	1	1730		Bowen	editions differ in minor ways
	CLII	176	157	1	1731		Bowen	editions differ in minor ways
	CLIIa	177	158	1	1734		Bowen	edition recorded by Fordham, but dubious
	CLIII	179	159	1	1736		Bowen	editions differ in minor ways
	CLIIIa	198	160	1	1749		Bowen	editions differ in minor ways
	CLIV	204	161	1	1751		Bowen	editions differ in minor ways
	CLIVa	210	162	1	1753		Bowen	editions differ in minor ways
	CLV	215	163	1	1759		Bowen	some revisions to plates
	CLVI	222	164	1	1764		Bowen	many revisions to plates
4F / 36	CLX	172	173	1,2	1724	180 x 243	Moll, H	source Morden 4A state 1; in *New Description...*
	CLXI	173	174	2	1725		Moll	maps only; now numbered (46 for Lancs.)
		174	175	2	1733		Moll	in weekly issues of *New Description...* remainders
	CLXII	182	176	2	1739		Moll	maps only
		194	177	3	1747	179 x 243	Moll	numbering (now 23) changed to alphabetical
	CLXIII	211	178	4	1753		Moll	plates cut down and revised
	CLXX	184	188	1	1741		Badeslade, T	source Moll 4F; in *Chorographia Britanniae*

Ref./Fig.	Chubb	Whitaker	Skelton/Hodson	State	Date	Width/mm x Height/mm	Cartographer/ Engraver	Publisher/Notes/Source
	CLXXI	185	189	2	1742	99 x 139	Badeslade	state 2; many additions
	CLXXII	186,188	190	3	1742		Badeslade	state 3; more additions and new imprint
	CLXXV-VI	190	191	3	1745		Badeslade	unchanged, with imprint date 1742
4G / 38	CLXXIII-IV	195	192,193	3	c.1746-9	101 x 140	Badeslade	unchanged, with imprint date 1742
4H / 39	CLXXXI	189	194	1	1744	116 x 169	Cowley, J	source Morden 4B 1708
	CLXXXIII	191	195,196	1	1745		Cowley	in *A New Set of Pocket Mapps*
	CLXXXV	193	197	1	1746		Rocque, J	source Moll 4F; in *The English Traveller*
	CCVII	212	198-200	2	1753		Rocque	revisions done by Rocque for his *Small British Atlas*
	CCVIII	219	201	3	1762		Rocque	page number (19) added for state 3
	CCIX	223	202	3	1764		Rocque	unchanged reprint
4J / 40	CCXXXVI	237	203	2	1769	154 x 194	Rocque	page number removed; in *England Displayed*
4K / 40	CLXXXIV	192	204	1	1746	152 x 189	Simpson, S	close copy of 'Rocque' map 4J in state 1
4L / 41	CXC	201	205	1	1748	161 x 136	Hutchinson, T	source Morden 4A; a.k.a. Osborne/Wale
	CLXXXIX	196	206	1	1756		Hutchinson	edition dates revised by Hodson via analysis of owners
	CXCII	199	209	1	1749		Kitchin & Jefferys	source Badeslade & Toms 4G in state 3
4M / 42	CXCIII	205	210	1	1751	122 x 111	Kitchin & Jefferys	in *Small English Atlas*; late issues numbered as plate 23
		244	211	2	1775		Kitchin & Jefferys	state 2, separated, revised with extra roads etc.
			212	2	1776		Kitchin & Jefferys	in Sayer and Bennett edition *English Atlas*
	CXCIV	255	213	2	c.1787		Kitchin & Jefferys	in Sayer edition *Small English Atlas*
	CCLIX	261	214	2	1787		Kitchin & Jefferys	in Sayer edition *English Atlas*
			215,216	2	1794-6		Kitchin & Jefferys	in Laurie & Whittle editions of *English Atlas*
5A / 43	CLXXXVII	202	229	1	1750	150 x 191	Kitchin, T	source Kitchin's E&W map revised from all new sources
		203		1	1750		Exshaw/Kitchin	re-engraved in Dublin (Hodson *C.A. vol. II*, pp.175-9)
		259	281	2	1786		Kitchin	Grose/Hogg state 2 without imprint
		286	282-284	2	1798	151 x 192	Kitchin	in various editions of Grose *Antiquities*
5B / 43	CLXXXVIII	206	253	1	1751	171 x 182	Bowen, E	source Kitchin 5A; in *Universal Magazine*

Ref./Fig.	Chubb	Whitaker	Skelton/Hodson	State	Date	Width/mm x Height/mm	Cartographer/ Engraver	Publisher/Notes/Source
5E/47,48	CXCV	208		1	1752	506 x 665	Bowen, E	sourced as 5A; *Large English Atlas*, Hinton sheet issue
		213		2	1753		Bowen	further loose sheet issues, imprint now Tinney
	CXCVI	217	221	3	1760		Bowen	first entire *Large English Atlas* edition, new imprint
		221	222,223	4	1763	510 x 666	Bowen	plate number 19 added; Tinney removed from imprint
	CXCVII	225	224	5	1765		Bowen	plate number now 21; J.Bowles & Sayer edition
		229	225	6	*c.*1767		Bowen	in C. Bowles editions; available dissected
	CXCVIII	262	226	7	*c.*1775		Bowen	in Sayer editions
	CXCIX	251,253	227	8	*c.*1780	509 x 668	Bowen	in Wilkinson editions
	CC	245	228	9	*c.*1785		Bowen	in Sayer editions
		277	228	10	1795-1825		Bowen	in Bowles & Carver / Laurie & Whittle editions
5C / 44	CLXXVIII	214	217	1	1754	142 x 221	Bickham, G	source almost entirely in Bickham's imagination
	CLXXX	285	218	2	1796		Bickham	cut down state 2; Laurie & Whittle edition
	CCXIII	216	219	1	1759		Gibson, J	source Kitchin 5A; in John Newbery editions
5D / 45	CCXIV	240,250	220	1	*c.*1780	56 x 104	Gibson	in Thomas Carnan editions
5H / 51	CCXV	218	230	1	1761	154 x 175	Bowen, E	source 5E; in *General Magazine / Natural History*
5F / 49	CCXVIII	220	233	1	1764	402 x 476	Bowen, E	source Bowen 5E; in *Royal English Atlas*
			234	2	1778		Bowen	in Carington Bowles edition
	CCXIXa	252	235	3	1778		Bowen	in Sayer & Bennett edition
	CCXIX	246	236	4	1780		Bowen	in Wilkinson edition
		278	237	5	*c.*1828		Bowen	in R. Martin issue of remainders
	CCXXIV	224	231	1	1763		Kitchin, T	source Bowen 5E; in Dodsley *England Illustrated* atlas
5K / 52		224		1	1764	182 x 231	Kitchin	Dodsley *England Illustrated* magazine
	CCXXXVIII	232	232	1	1765		Kitchin	*Kitchin's English Atlas* without text
			238	1	1765		Ellis, J	close copy of Kitchin 5K; first edition in small run
	CCXXVII	226-228	239-243	1	1766		Ellis	in *Ellis's English Atlas*; variations on title page, etc.
5L / 52	CCXXVIII	233-235	244,245	1	1768	180 x 226	Ellis	in *Ellis's English Atlas*; variations of printers, etc.
	CCXXIX	242	246	1	1773		Ellis	in Sayer & Bennett edition
	CCXXX	247	247	1	1777		Ellis	in Sayer & Bennett edition
			248-252	1	1780-1800		Ellis	in Bowles & Carver / Laurie & Whittle editions

Ref./Fig.	Chubb	Whitaker	Skelton/Hodson	State	Date	Width/mm x Height/mm	Cartographer/ Engraver	Publisher/Notes/Source
5G / 50	CCXXXII	231	254	1	1767	211 x 312	Bowen, E & T	source Bowen/Gibson 5F; in *Atlas Anglicanus*
	CCXXXIII	248	255	2	1777		Bowen	Kitchin imprint added to map
	CCLV	257	256	3	1785		Bowen	in *Bowles's New Medium English Atlas*
			260	1	1767		Meijer, P	copy of Bowen 5H for Dutch version of *Natural History*
5J / 51	CCXXI	236		1	1768	149 x 188	Bowen, T	source 5A; in *Universal Museum* (Hodson *C.A. vol. III*, p200)
5N / 54	CCXXXV	238	258	1	1769	242 x 278	Kitchin, T	source Kitchin 4 sheet map; in *Kitchin's Pocket Atlass*
		258	259	2	1785		Kitchin	in *Bowles's Pocket Atlas*
5P / 55	CCLI	254	269	1	1784	144 x 178	Condor/Hogg	source Ellis 5L; with Leicestershire in *New British Traveller*
	CCLII	279	270-272	2	1794		Condor/Hogg	state 2; border erased; Condor cited
		264		1	1787	310 x 370	Tunnicliff, W	source Bowen 5E?; in *Topographical Survey...*
		265		1	1789		Tunnicliff	unchanged reprint
5R/58,59		260		1	1788	1320 x 2040	Yates, W	original Yates one inch survey, 1776-1780
		288		2	1800		Yates	state 2; Faden issue
5Q / 56		268		1	1789	316 x 444	Harrison, J	source Bowen 5E sheet from *Large English Atlas*; sheet issue
	CCXCI	271		1	1791		Harrison	in atlas edition of *Maps of the English Counties*
	CCXCII	274		1	1792		Harrison	in second edition of *Maps of the English Counties*
				1?	1815		Harrison	in *General and County Atlas* (cited by Beresiner, p113)
	CCXLIX	269		1	1789		Lodge, J	source Ellis 5L; in *Political Magazine...*
5M / 53	CCL	282		2	1795	251 x 307	Lodge	in atlas issue with imprint erased
5S / 60	CCLX	263	285	1	1789	197 x 251	Cary, J	source Yates 5R; in *New and Correct English Atlas*
	CCLXI-XX	e.g. 313	286				Cary	many later reprints
1B / 2		417		1	1831	207 x 349	Walker, J & C	1086 map in *Baines's History*, Vol 1

APPENDIX 2: THE 'FAMILY TREE' OF ALL LANCASHIRE MAPS WHICH DESCEND FROM THE SAXTON SURVEY

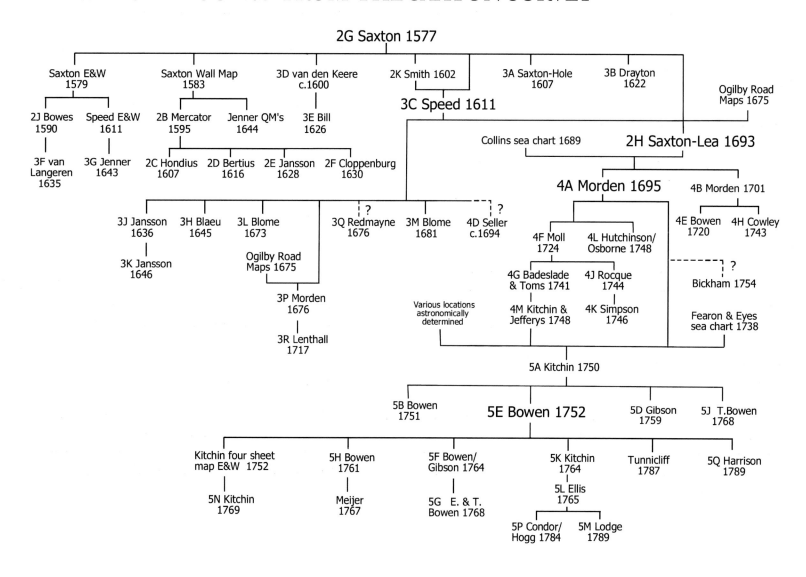

APPENDIX 3: SCALES FOR LANCASHIRE MAPS

Apparently scales were chosen to fit the page (except by Yates) or via direct copying from an earlier map. Values directly measured from the scale engraved on the map are in bold font. The other numbers are calculated equivalents (assuming a customary mile of 2400 yards) and are approximate.

Statute miles per inch	Customary miles per inch	km per cm	Proportional scale	Lancashire Map Examples
54.5	**40**	34.6	1 : 3,456,000	Bowes, 1590; van Langeren, 1635
36.8	27	23.3	1 : 2,333,000	Morden, 1676
32	23.5	20.3	1 : 2,028,000	Gibson, 1759
31.4	**23**	19.9	1 : 1,987,000	Jenner, 1643
20.5	**15**	13.0	1 : 1,296,000	Seller, 1695
19	13.9	12.0	1 : 1,204,000	Kitchin and Jefferys, 1749
17.7	**13**	11.2	1 : 1,123,000	E. Bowen, 1720
16.4	**12**	10.4	1 : 1,037,000	Badeslade and Toms, 1741
10.9	**8.0**	6.91	1 : 691,200	Morden, 1701
8.7	6.38	5.51	1 : 551,200	Kitchin, 1764; Ellis, 1766
8.73	**6.4**	5.53	1 : 553,000	Blome, 1681
8.3	6.09	5.26	1 : 525,900	E. & T. Bowen, 1767
8.0	5.87	5.07	1 : 506,900	Cary, 1789
7.3	5.35	4.63	1 : 462,500	Kitchin, 1769
6.55	**4.8**	4.15	1 : 414,700	Saxton-Hole, 1607; Blome, 1673
5.45	**4.0**	3.46	1 : 345,600	Speed, 1612; Jansson, 1636; Blaeu, 1645
5.32	**3.9**	3.37	1 : 337,000	Saxton, 1577; Morden, 1695
4.8	3.52	3.04	1 : 304,100	Harrison, 1789
4.6	3.37	2.91	1 : 291,500	E. Bowen (and J. Gibson), 1762
4.23	**3.1**	2.68	1 : 267,800	W. Smith, 1602
3.3	2.42	2.09	1 : 209,100	E. Bowen, 1752
1.027 (mean)	0.753	0.6507	1 : 65,070	Yates, 1787
1.00	0.733	0.6336	1 : 63,360	Standard large scale used in future

PICTURE CREDITS

Fig. 17, Chris Abram; Fig. 19 (foot), Fig. 21, Fig. 29 (a), (b) and (f), Fig. 44 (Bickham original), Philip Burden; Fig. 29 (e), Brian Kentish; Fig. 58, Fig. 59, Bill Shannon. The remaining figures, including illustrations on the cover and title page, are derived from the author's personal collection.

BIBLIOGRAPHY

GENERAL REFERENCE WORKS FOR BACKGROUND AND RESEARCH

Andrews, J.H., *Maps in those Days* (Four Courts Press, Dublin, 2009).

Beresiner, Yasha, *British County Maps* (Antique Collectors' Club, Woodbridge, 1983).

Berggren, J.L. & Jones, A., *Ptolemy's Geography* (Princeton University Press, Oxford, 2000).

Booth, John, *Looking at Old Maps* (Cambridge House Books, Westbury, 1979).

Chubb, Thomas, *The Printed Maps in the Atlases of Great Britain and Ireland* (Homeland Association, London, 1927).

Delano-Smith, C. & Kain, R., *English Maps – a History* (British Library, London, 1999).

Goss, John, *The Mapmakers Art* (Studio Editions, London, 1993).

Hindle, P., *Maps for Historians* (Philimore, Stroud, 1998).

Hodson, Donald, *County Atlases of the British Isles*, in follow-up to R.A. Skelton
  vol. I (1703-1742) (Tewin Press, Welwyn, 1984).
  vol. II (1743-1763) (Tewin Press, Welwyn, 1984).
  vol. III (1764-1789) (The British Library, London, 1997).

King, Geoffrey, *Miniature Antique Maps*, 2nd ed. (Tooley Adams, Oxford, 2003).

Moreland, C. & Bannister, D., *Antique Maps – a Collector's Guide* (Phaidon/Christies, Oxford, 1989).

Shirley, R., *Early Printed Maps of the British Isles 1477-1650* (Antique Atlas, East Grinstead, 1991).

Shirley, R., *Printed Maps of the British Isles 1650-1750* (Map Collector Publications, Tring, 1988).

Skelton, R. A., *County Atlases of the British Isles 1579-1703* (Carta Press, London, 1970).

Smith, D., *Antique Maps of the British Isles* (Batsford, London, 1982).

Smith, D., *Victorian Maps of the British Isles* (Batsford, London, 1985).

Tooley, R.V., *Tooley's Dictionary of Mapmakers (*Map Collector Publications, Tring, 1979) and *Supplement* (Map Collector Publications, Tring, 1985).

Tooley, R.V., *Tooley's Dictionary of Mapmakers – Revised Edition*, 4 Volumes (Map Collector Publications, Tring; A-D 1999, E-J 2001, K-P 2003, Q-Z 2004).

Woodward, D. (ed.), *Five Centuries of Map Printing* (University of Chicago Press, London, 1975).

Worms, L., & Baynton-Williams, A., *British Map Engravers* (Rare Book Society, London, 2011).

ON LANCASHIRE AND ITS MAPS

Bagley, J.J., *A History of Lancashire with Maps and Pictures* (Darwen Finleyson, London, 1961).

Bagley, J.J. & Hodgkiss, A.G., *Lancashire: a History of the County Palatine in Early Maps* (Neil Richardson, Manchester, 1985).

Harrison, William, 'Early Maps of Lancashire and their Makers', *Trans. Lancs.& Ches. Antiquarian Society*, XXV (1907), pp.1-31.

Whitaker, Harold, *Maps of Lancashire 1577-1900* (Manchester University Press and the Chetham Society, Manchester, 1938).

ON THE MAPS OF ADJACENT COUNTIES

Curwen, J.F., *Printed Maps of Cumberland and Westmorland*, CWAAS NS XVIII (1918).

Higham, J., *Antique County Maps of Cumberland* (Bookcase, Carlisle, 1997).

Rawnsley, A., *Antique Maps of Yorkshire*, 3rd ed. (M.T. Rigg, Leeds, 1983).

Whitaker, Harold, *Maps of Yorkshire and its Ridings 1577-1900*, Yorks. Arch. Soc. Record Series LXXXVI (1933)

OTHER WORKS REFERENCED IN THE TEXT

Andrews, J.H., 'A Saxton Miscellany', *Imago Mundi*, vol. 65, 1 (January 2013), pp.87-96.

Bendall, Sarah, 'Draft Town Maps for John Speed's Theatre of the Empire of Great Britain', *Imago Mundi*, 54 (2002), pp.30-45.

Bendall, Sarah, 'Speed, John (1551/2–1629)', *Oxford Dictionary of National Biography* (Oxford University Press, Oxford, 2004); online edn, Jan 2008 [http://www.oxforddnb.com/view/article/26093].

Bickham, George, *The British Monarchy...*, facsimile edition (Frank Graham, Gateshead, 1967).

Burton, William, *Description of Leicestershire*, 2nd ed. (Whittingham, Lynn, 1777).

Cary, John, *New and Correct English Atlas*, revised edition (Cary, London, 1809).

Chesterton, G.K. & Bentley, E.C., *Biography for Beginners* (T.W. Laurie, London, 1905).

Edvinsson, Rodney, *Foreign exchange rates in Sweden 1658-1803*, Stockholm Papers in Economic History, No. 8 (Stockholm University, Stockholm, 2009).

Evans, I.M. & Lawrence, H., *Christopher Saxton: Elizabethan Map-maker* (Wakefield Historical Publications, London, 1979).

Fordham, Sir Herbert G., *John Cary, Engraver, Map, Chart and Print-Seller and Globe Maker, 1754 to 1835, a Bibliography* (Cambridge University Press, Cambridge, 1925).

Goss, John, *Blaeu's The Grand Atlas of the 17th Century World* (Studio Editions, London, 1990).

Gough, Richard, *British Topography*, vol. I (Payne & Nichols, London, 1780).

Granger, James, *A Biographical History of England...* (T. Davies, London, 1779).

Gregson, Matthew, *Portfolio of Fragments relative to the History and Antiquities of the County Palatine and Duchy of Lancaster* 2nd ed. (Gregson, Liverpool, 1824) and 3rd ed. (Routledge, London 1869).

Harley, J.B., 'William Yates and Peter Burdett...', *Trans. H.S. Lancs. & Ches.* 115 (1963), pp.107-31.

Harley, J.B., *William Yates's Map of Lancashire, 1786* (H.S. Lancs. & Ches., Leeds, 1968).

Heawood, Edward, 'Some Early County Maps', *The Geographical Journal*, 68 (October 1926), pp.325-37.

Hewitt, Rachel, *Map of a Nation* (Granta, London 2010).

Hind, Arthur, *Engraving in England in the Sixteenth & Seventeenth Centuries, vol. II* (Cambridge University Press, Cambridge, 1955).

Horsley, J., *Britannia Romana*, Book III (John Osborn & Thomas Longman, London, 1732).

Jackson, A., Jonkers, A.R.T. & Walker, M.R., 'Four centuries of Geomagnetic Secular Variation from Historical Records', *Phil. Trans. R. Soc. Lond. A*, vol. 358, no.1768 (2000), pp.957-90.

Koeman, Cornelis, *Atlantes Neerlandici,* vol. II (Theatrum Orbis Terrarum, Amsterdam, 1969).

Leigh, C., *The Natural History of Lancashire, Cheshire and the Peak in Derbyshire* (Leigh, Oxford, 1700).

Manley, Gordon, 'Saxton's Survey of Northern England', *The Geographical Journal*, 83 (April 1934), pp.308-16.

Mann, S. & Kingsley, D., *Playing Cards Depicting Maps of the British Isles...*, Map Collectors Series 9, No 87 (The Map Collectors Circle, London, 1972).

O'Donoghue, J., Goulding, L. & Allen, G., *Consumer Price Inflation Since 1750*, Economics Trends 604 (Office for National Statistics, London, 2004).

Osley, A.S., *Mercator* (Faber & Faber, London, 1969).

Ravenhill, W., 'As to its position in respect to the Heavens', *Imago Mundi*, 28, part 2 (1976), pp.79-93.

Ravenhill, W., *Christopher Saxton's 16ᵗʰ Century Maps* (Chatsworth Library, Shrewsbury, 1992).

Richeson, A.W., *English Land Measuring to 1800* (Cambridge MA, MIT Press, 1966).

Shannon, William D.,'From Morikambe to Morecambe: Antiquarians, Periploi and Eischuseis', *CWAAS*, Third Series, 12 (2012), pp.37-54.

Shannon, W. & Winstanley, M., 'Lord Burghley's Map of Lancashire Revisited, *c.* 1576-1590', *Imago Mundi*, 59, part 1 (2007), pp.24 - 42.

Skelton, R.A., *Saxton's Survey of England and Wales* (Nico Israel, Amsterdam, 1974), a reprint of the 1583 wall-map with detailed notes on Saxton, etc.

Speed, John, *The Theatre of the Empire of Great Britaine* (Sudbury & Humble, London 1612).

van den Broecke, M.P.R., *Ortelius Atlas Maps* (HES, Tuurdijk, 1996).

van der Krogt, Peter, introduction in *Blaeu Atlas Maior* (Taschen, Cologne, 2005).

Van Eerde, K.S., *John Ogilby and the Taste of His Times* (Dawson, Folkstone, 1976).

Whitaker, J., *History of Manchester*, vol. 1, 2nd ed. (J. Murray, London, 1773).

Winterbotham, Diana, 'John Speed's Map of Lancashire', *CNWRS Regional Bulletin*, 9 (1995), pp.65-8.

INDEX OF ATLASES, BOOKS AND MAGAZINES WITH MAPS

WORLD ATLASES (NATIONAL AND REGIONAL MAPS) (WITH PUBLISHER/S OF FIRST EDITION)

Atlas... (Mercator)	8, 10, 13, 32; Fig. 6; Map 2B
Atlas... (Mercator-Hondius)	8, 10, 33, 35, 45, 47
Atlas Minimus (Newbery)	68
Atlas Minor (Hondius, Jansson)	10, 13, 28, 30; Figs. 7, 8; Maps 2C, 2E
Atlas Minor (Bertius)	13, 30; Fig. 8; Map 2D
Atlas Minor (Cloppenburg)	13; Fig. 8; Map 2F
English Atlas (Blome)	38
English Pilot (Seller)	52-53
Ptolemy's Geographia (Mercator, Münster)	1, 3, 4, 6, 8, 10; Figs. 1, 4; Maps 1A, 1C
Purchas His Pilgrimes (Purchas)	10; Fig. 7; Map 2C
Theatrum Orbis Terrarum (Ortelius)	v, 8, 10, 14, 22, 49, 91; Fig. 5; Map 2A
World Described (Moll)	55

COUNTY MAP ATLASES (WITH PUBLISHER/S OF FIRST EDITION)

Agreeable Historian (Walker)	59, 61, 64; Fig. 40; Map 4K
Anglia Contracta (Seller)	49, 53, 55; Fig. 34; Map 4D
Antiquities of England (Grose)	78, 81, 82; Figs. 43, 57; Maps 5A, 4D
Atlas Anglicanus (Kitchin)	74, 76; Fig. 50; Map 5G
Atlas Major (Blaeu)	33, 38, 46
Atlas Novus (Blaeu)	10, 33, 35, 38; Figs. 22, 25, 26; Map 3H
Atlas of Great Britain and Ireland (unknown)	78; Fig. 53; Map 5M
Bowles's New Medium English Atlas (C. Bowles)	76; Fig. 50; Map 5G
Bowles's Pocket Atlas (C. Bowles)	78; Fig. 54; Map 5N
Britannia (Blome)	6, 39, 46, 47, 69; Fig. 27; Map 3L
Britannia (Camden) 1607 (Bishop & Norton)	iii, 23, 26, 39, 47, 54; Fig. 14; Map 3A
Britannia (Camden) 1695 (Swale & Churchill)	6, 23, 39, 47, 49, 50, 55; Fig. 31; Map 4A

Britannia (Camden) 1789 (Payne & Robinson) — 23

Britannia (Camden) abridged (Bertius) — 13, 30; Fig. 8; Map 2D

Britannia (Camden) abridged (Blaeu) — 30, 31; Fig. 19; 3D

Britannia (Camden) abridged (Bill) — 31, 35, 49, 53; Fig. 19; Map 3E

Britannia (Camden) abridged (Seller) — 53, 63; Fig. 34; Map 4D

Chorographia Britanniae (Toms) — 57, 61, 62, 63; Fig. 38; Map 4G

Ellis's English Atlas (Sayer & C. Bowles) — 74, 76, 78, 81; Fig. 52; Map 5L

England Displayed (Adlard & Browne) — 59, 61, 62, 64; Fig. 40; Map 4J

England Exactly Described (Taylor) — 39, 42; Fig. 28; Map 3M

England Illustrated (Kitchin) — iii, 76; Fig. 52; Map 5K

English Atlas (Kitchin & Jefferys) — 61-63; Fig. 42; Map 4M

English Traveller (Read) — 58, 61, 62, 64; Fig. 40; Map 4J

Fifty-six New and Acurate Maps (Nicholson *et al.*) — 50; Fig. 32; Map 4B

General Magazine of Arts and Sciences (Martin) — 76; Fig. 51; Map 5H

Geographia Magnae Britanniae (Osborne) — 6, 61, 64; Fig. 41; 4L

Geography of England (R. Dodsley) — 57-8, 76; Fig. 39; Map 4H

History of England (Seller) — 49, 53, 55; Fig. 34; Map 4D

Kitchin's English Atlas (J. Dodsley) — 76; Fig. 52; Map 5K

Kitchin's Pocket Atlass (Kitchin) — 78; Fig. 54; Map 5N

Large English Atlas (Hinton, Tinney *et al.*) — 46, 63, 64, 66, 68-71, 76, 78, 81, 89; Figs. 47, 48; Map 5E

London Magazine (Baldwin) — 63, 64, 66, 69, 70, 76, 78, 81; Fig. 43; Map 5A

Magna Britannia et Hibernia (Nutt, Morphew & Cox) — 50, 52; Figs. 32, 33; Maps 4B, 4C

Maps of the English Counties (Harrison) — 81-82; Fig. 56; Map 5Q

Miniature *Speed* (G. Humble) — 30-31; Fig. 19; Map 3D

Natural History of England (Martin) — 76; Fig. 51; Map 5H

New and Accurate Maps of... (J. Gibson) — 68; Fig. 45; Map 5D

New and Complete British Traveller (Hogg) — 81; Fig. 55; Map 5P

New and Correct English Atlas (Cary) — 64, 89-91; Fig. 60; Map 5S

New description and State of England (Morden) — 49, 50, 54; Fig. 32; Map 4B

New description of England and Wales (Moll) — 49, 55, 57, 59; Fig. 36; Map 4F

New Sett of Pocket Mapps (R. Dodsley) — 57-8, 76; Fig. 39; Map 4H

Novus Atlas... (Jansson) — 8, 26, 33, 35, 38, 47; Figs. 23, 24, 25, 26; Maps 3J, 3K

Overton *Atlases* (J. & H. Overton) — 16, 20; Fig. 12; Map 2K

Pocket Book (Morden & Pask) — 45; Fig. 29c; Map 3P

Political Magazine (Butters & Murray) — 78; Fig. 53; Map 5M

Poly-Olbion (Mariott *et al.*) — 23, 25, 66; Fig. 15; Map 3B

Portfolio of Fragments ... (Gregson)   20, 86; Fig. 13; Map 2L

Post-Chaise Companion (Kitchin)   74

Public Register or Weekly Magazine (R. Dodsley)   57-8, 76; Fig. 39; Map 4H

Royal English Atlas (Kitchin, Sayer, Bowles *et al.*)   68, 71-74; Fig. 49; Map 5F

Shires of England (Saxton later reprints)   14, 16, 46, 47, 50, 69; Figs. 10, 11; Map 2H

Small British Atlas (Rocque)   58, 59, 61, 62, 64; Fig. 40; Map 4J

Small English Atlas (Kitchin & Jefferys)   61-63; Fig. 42; Map 4M

Speed's Maps Epitomised (Blome)   42; Fig. 28; Map 3M

Theatre of the Empire of Great Britaine (Speed)   iii, v, 16, 20, 25-29, 30, 35, 39, 46, 47, 78; Figs. 16, 17, 18, 25, 26, 37; Map 3C

Universal Magazine (Hinton)   64, 66, 69, 70; Fig. 43; Map 5B

Universal Museum (Payne)   66, 76; Fig. 51; Map 5J

INDEX OF PEOPLE

Aa, Pieter van der (1659-1733) 38, 46

Arrowsmith, Aaron (1750-1823) 78

Badeslade, Thomas (?-1745) 57, 61, 62, 63; Fig. 38; Map 4G

Bakewell, Thomas (1704?-1749) 42

Baldwin, Richard Junior (1724-1770) 64, 66; Fig. 43; Map 5A

Basset, Thomas (1637?-1699) 28

Bennett, John (?-1787) 62, 76; Figs. 42, 49, 50, 52; Maps 4M, 5F, 5G, 5L

Bertius, Petrus (1565-1629), 13, 30; Fig. 8; Map 2D

Bickham, George Junior (1704?-1771) 66, 68, 91; Fig. 44; Map 5C

Bickham, George Senior (1684-1758) 66, 91

Bill, John (1576-1630) 31, 35, 49, 53, 55; Fig. 19; Map 3E

Billinge, Thomas (1741-1816) 86; Fig. 58; Map 5R

Blaeu, Johan (1596-1673) 3H v, 13, 26, 30, 33, 35, 38, 46, 47; Figs. 22, 25, 26; Map 3H

Blaeu, Willem (1571-1638) 3D 10, 13, 30, 31, 33, 53; Fig. 19; Map 3D

Blome, Richard (1635-1705) 6, 38, 39, 42, 46, 47, 69; Fig. 27, 28; Maps 3L, 3M

Bowen, Emanuel (1693-1767) 20, 53-55, 57, 58, 62, 63, 64, 66, 68-71, 74, 76, 78, 81; Figs. 35, 43, 47, 48, 49, 51; Maps 4E, 5B, 5E, 5F, 5H

Bowen, Thomas (1733?-1790) 66, 71, 74, 76; Figs. 50, 51; Maps 5G, 5J

Bowes, William (fl. 1590-1605) 32, 42-43, 45, 78; Fig. 21; Map 2J

Bowles, Carington (1724-1793) 54, 71, 76, 78; Figs. 47, 48, 49, 50, 52, 54; Maps 5E 5F, 5G, 5L, 5N

Bowles, Henry Carington (1763-1830) 54; Figs. 47, 48, 49, 50, 52, 54; Maps 5E 5F, 5G, 5L, 5N

Bowles, John (1701-1779) 54, 62, 70-71; Figs. 36, 42, 47, 48, 49; Maps 4F, 4M, 5E, 5F

Bowles, Thomas (1688-1767) 54, 62, 70-71; Figs. 36, 42, 47, 48; Maps 4F, 4M, 5E

Braun, George (1541-1622) 66

Burdett, Peter Perez (1734-1793) 85, 86, 91

Burghley, Lord - see Cecil, William

Burton, William (1575-1645) 16, 22

Butters, R. (fl.1782-1803) 78; Fig. 53; Map 5M

Camden, William (1551-1623) iii, 6, 23, 39, 47-50, 55; Figs. 14, 31; Maps 3A, 4A

- as source for later copying

Cary, John (1755-1835)

Catherine of Braganza (1638-1705)

Cecil, William, Lord Burghley (1520-1598)

Chapman, John (?-1779)

Chandler, Richard (c.1713-1744)

Charles II (1630-1685)

Chiswell, Richard (1640-1711)

Chubb, Thomas (fl.1911-1928)

Cloppenburg, Jan Evertsz (15898-1636)

Collins, Captain Greenvile (?-1694)

Condor, Thomas (c.1750-1831)

Cowley, John (?-c.1744)

Cowley, John Lodge FRS (1719-1787)

De La Hire, Philippe (1640-1718)

Derby, 9th Earl of (William Stanley) (1655-1702)

Dicey, Cluer (1714-1775)

Dodsley, James (1724-1797)

Dodsley, Robert (1704-1764)

Doppelmayr, Johann (1677-1750)

Drayton, Michael (1563-1631)

Elizabeth I (1533-1603)

Ellis, Joseph (c.1834-1802)

Exshaw, John (c.1712-1776)

Exshaw, Sarah (fl. 1748-1757)

Eyes, John (?-1773)

Faden, William (1749-1836)

Fearon, Samuel (fl. 1735-1766)

Fleetwood, Thomas (c.1660-1717)

Fordham, Sir Herbert G. (1854-1929)

Gall, James (1784-1872)

George I (1660-1727)

Gibson, Edmund (1669-1748)

Gibson, John (1724?-1773)

Gough, Richard (1725-1809)

Granger, James (1723-1776)

13, 26, 30, 31, 33, 39, 47, 53, 54, 63; Figs. 19, 34; Maps 3D, 3E, 4D

23, 63, 64, 78, 82, 85, 89-91; Fig. 60; Map 5S

43, 45

4, 7, 13, 20, 22

85, 86

52

28, 43

28

55, Appendix 1

13; Fig. 8; Map 2F

47, 53, 70

81; Fig. 55; Map 5P

57-58, 76; Fig. 39; Map 4H

58

69

42

16, 28

iii, 76; Fig. 52; Map 5K

iii, 57-58, 76; Figs. 39, 52; Maps 4H, 5K

70

23, 25, 66; Fig. 15; Map 3B

13

74, 76, 78, 81; Fig. 52; Map 5L

66

66

70

62, 86

70

55

47, 63

91

51

6, 39, 47, 49, 50, 55, 63; Fig. 31; Map 4A

68, 71, 74, 76; Figs. 45, 49; Maps 5D, 5F

4, 6, 7, 38, 46, 74, 91; Fig. 3

45

Green, William (1760-1823) — 86

Gregson, Matthew (1749-1824) — 20

Greville, Sir Fulke (1554-1628) — 25

Grose, Francis (1731-1791) — 82; Fig. 57; Map 4D

Harrison, John, printer (fl. 1784-1815) — 26, 81, 82; Fig. 56; Map 5Q

Haywood, John (fl. 1781-1791) — 81; Fig. 56; Map 5Q

Heawood, Edward (1865-1949) — 16, 22

Hinton, John (1716-1781) — 64-66, 69, 70; Figs. 43, 47, 48; Maps 5B, 5E

Hogenberg, Frans (1535-1590) — 8, 14

Hogenberg, Remigius (1536-1588?) — 14, 23, 35, 66; Fig. 9; Map 2G

Hogg, Alexander (1752-1809) — 64, 78, 81; Figs. 43, 55; Maps 5A, 5P

Hole, William (?-1624) — 23, 25; Figs. 14, 15; Maps 3A, 3B

Holland, Philemon (1552-1637) — iii

Hollar, Wenceslaus (1607-1677) — 32, 39

Homann, Johann Baptist (1663-1724) — 70

Hondius, Henry (1597-1651) — 10, 33, 45; Fig. 7; Map 2C

Hondius, Jodocus I, the elder (1563-1612) — iv, 8, 13, 16, 20, 26, 30, 33, 35; Figs. 7, 12, 16, 17; Maps 2C, 2K, 3C

Hondius, Jodocus II, the younger (1594-1629) — 8, 12, 33; Fig. 8; Map 2F

Horsley, John (1686–1732) — 3, 7

Humble, George (1572-1640) — v, 16, 20, 26, 28, 30-31; Fig. 16; Map 3C

Humble, Sir William (1611-1686) — 28

Hutchinson, Thomas (c.1706-c.1755) — 61; Fig. 41; Map 4L

Inglis, Robert (1820?-1887) — 91

Jansson, Jan I, the elder (fl. 1597-1629) — Fig. 7; Map 2C

Jansson, Jan II, the younger (1588-1664) — iv, 8, 10, 13, 26, 33, 35, 38, 45, 47, 53; Figs. 8, 23, 24, 25, 26; Maps 2E, 3J, 3K

Jefferys, Thomas (1719-1771) — 16, 61-63, 78; Figs. 10, 42; Maps 2H, 4M

Jefferys, Thomas the younger (1755-?) — 62

Jenner, Thomas (c.1600-1673) — 16, 32, 52; Fig. 20; Map 3G

Keere (Kaerius), Pieter van den (1571-1646) — 30-31; Figs. 8, 19; Maps 2F, 3D

Kip, William (?-1618) — 23

Kitchin, Thomas (1719-1784) — 61-63, 64, 66, 68-71, 74, 76, 78, 81, 86; Figs. 42, 43, 50, 52, 54; Maps 4M, 5A, 5G, 5K, 5N

Kitchin, Thomas Bowen (c.1740-1781) — 76

Langeren, Jacob van (fl.1635-1656) — 32, 42, 78; Fig. 20; Map 3F

Laurie, Robert (1755-1836) — 62, 68, 78

Lea, Philip (c.1660-1700) — 16, 47, 50, 54; Figs. 10, 11, 18; Map 2H

Leigh, Charles (1662–1701) — 63

Lenthall, John (1683-1733)   45; Fig. 29; Map 3R

Lhuyd, Humphrey (1527-1568)   8, 14, 49; Fig. 5; Map 2A

Lodge, John I (1708?-c.1750)   78

Lodge, John II (1735?-1796)   78; Fig. 53; Map 5M

Lodge, John III (1771-1823?)   78

Marshall, Joseph (fl. c.1750)   52

Martin, Benjamin (1705-1782)   76; Fig. 51; Map 5H

Meijer, Pieter (fl. c.1755-1770)   76

Mercator, Gerardus (1512-1594)   3, 8, 10, 13, 16, 22, 26, 32, 33, 49, 66; Figs. 1, 6; Maps 1A, 2B

Moll, Herman (1654-1732)   49, 50, 55-57, 58, 59, 61, 63, 70; Figs. 32, 36; Maps 4B, 4F

Morden, Robert (c.1640-1703)   6, 28, 43, 45, 47-50, 50-52, 54, 55, 58, 61, 69; Figs. 25, 29, 30, 31 , 32; Maps 3P, 3R, 3N, 4A, 4B

Mount, Richard (1654-1722)   53

Münster, Sebastian (1489-1552)   6, 10; Fig. 4; Map 1C

Murray, John (1745-1793)   78; Fig. 53; Map 5M

Newbery, John (1713-1767)   68; Fig. 45; Map 5D

Norden, John (1547?-1625)   22, 23, 32, 52; Figs. 20, 33; Maps 3G, 4C

Norton, John (1557?-1612)   31; Fig. 14; Map 3A

Ogilby, John (1600-76)   16, 23, 43, 45, 46, 47, 53, 54, 55, 64, 69, 70; Fig. 30; Map 3N

Ortelius, Abraham (1527-1598)   v, 8, 10, 14, 22, 23, 30, 33, 49; Fig. 5; Map 2A

Osborne, Thomas (fl. 1740-1750)   61; Fig. 41; Map 4L

Overton, Henry (1676?-1751)   28; Fig. 17; Map 3C

Overton, John (1640-1713)   16, 20; Fig. 12; Map 2K

Owen, John (fl. 1720)   54, 63; Fig. 35; Map 4E

Page, Thomas (c.1680-1733)   53

Palmer, Richard (?-1689)   42; Fig. 28; Map 3M

Palmer, William (1739-1812)   78

Pask, Joseph (fl. 1680-1700)   45; Fig. 29c; Map 3P

Paris, Matthew (?-1259)   43

Pepys, Samuel (1633-1703)   28, 30, 46, 47

Petrus Kaerius – see Keere, Pieter van den

Plantin, Christopher (1514-1589)   33; Fig. 5; Map 2A

Ptolemy, Claudius (c.90-c.150)   1, 3, 4, 6, 8, 10, 53; Figs. 1, 4; Maps 1A, 1C

Rea, Roger I (1606-1665) & Roger II (1637-1677)   28; Figs. 16, 19; Maps 3C, 3D

Read, Thomas (fl. 1743-1753)   58, 59, 61; Fig. 40; Map 4J

Redmayne, William (fl. c.1676)   45; Fig. 29; Map 3Q

Rocque, John (1704-1762)   58-59, 61, 62, 64; Fig. 40; Map 4J

Rocque, Mary Ann (fl. 1762-1773)   59; Fig. 40; Map 4J

Rudd, John (c.1498-1579)   13

Sanson, Nicholas (1600-1667)   38

Saxton, Christopher, (1543?-1610?)   6, 13-16, 22, 26, 28, 30, 31, 35, 43, 47, 64, 69, 70, 81, 86

  - county atlas maps   13, 23, 25, 30, 31, 42, 49, 64, 82

  - Lancashire (early states)   iv, 13, 14, 20, 26, 28, 30, 35, 53, 55, 61; Figs. 9, 10, 18, 26; Map 2G

  - Lancashire (Saxton-Lea states)   16, 22, 47, 50, 54, 69, 71; Figs. 10, 11, 18; Map 2H

  - 'Anglia' map   16, 32, 42

  - wall-map of 1583   10, 13, 15, 31, 32, 86

Sayer, Robert (1725?-1794)   62, 76; Figs. 42, 47, 48, 49, 50, 52; Maps 4M, 5E, 5F, 5G, 5L

Schenk, Pieter (1645-1715)   38

Seale, Richard (1703-1762)   66, 70, 76

Seckford, Thomas (c.1515-1588)   13

Seller, John (1630-1697)   49, 52, 53, 55, 70, 82; Figs. 34, 57; Map 4D

Senex, John (1678-1740)   74

Simons, Mathew (?-1654)   32; Fig. 20; Map 3F

Simpson, Samuel (pseudonym?)   59, 61, 64; Fig. 40; Map 4K

Simpson, Samuel (1711-88), Mayor of Leicester   61

Skelton, Raleigh A. (Peter) (1906-1970)   iv, 13, 22, 63, Appendix 1

Smith, William (1550-1618)   6, 16, 20, 22, 25, 26, 47, 61, 69, 70; Fig. 12; Map 2K

Speed, John (1563-1631)   iii, iv, v, 6, 16, 20, 25-28, 30, 32, 33, 38, 39, 45, 55, 78

  - Lancashire Map   iv, 4, 16, 26, 28, 30, 33-36, 38, 39, 46, 47; Figs. 16, 17, 18, 37; Map 3C

  - as source for later copying   10, 13, 16, 26, 28, 33-36, 39, 42, 55, 62; Figs. 25, 26

Stent, Peter (1613?-1665)   16, 20; Fig. 12; Map 2K

Sudbury, John (?-1621)   v, 16, 28; Fig. 14; Map 3A

Sudlow, Edward (fl. 1784-1793)   81; Fig. 56; Map 5Q

Swale, Abel (fl. 1665-1699)   43; Figs. 30, 31; Maps 3N, 4A

Swift, Jonathan (1667-1745)   55

Taylor, Thomas (?-1726)   42; Fig.28; Map 3M

Tinney, John (1706-1761)   42; Figs. 47, 48; Map 5E

Toms, William Henry (c.1701-1761)   57, 61, 62, 63; Fig. 38; Map 4G

Tooley, Ronald V. (1898-1986)   16, 22, 55

Towneley, Richard FRS (1629-1707)   70

Turpin, Homan (fl. c.1760-1790)   45; Fig. 29d; Map 3P

Valck, Gerard (1650?-1726)   38

van den Keere - see Keere, Pieter van den

van Langeren - see Langeren, Jacob van

Vitellius, Regnerus (1559-1620)   30; Fig. 19; Map 3D

Vrients, Jan Baptiste (1552-1612)   8, 10

Wale, Samuel (1721-1786)   61; Fig. 41; Map 4L

Walker, John (1787-1873) & Charles (1799?-1872)   3; Fig. 2; Map 1B

Walker, Robert (fl. c.1740-1750)   59, 61; Fig. 40; Map 4K

Walpoole, George Augustus (pseudonym?)   81

Ward, Caesar (1710-1759)   52; Figs. 32, 33; Maps 4B, 4C

Web, William (fl. 1628-1655)   14; Fig. 10; Map 2H

Whitaker, John (1735-1808)   3,7

Whittle, James (1757-1818)   62, 68, 78

Wilkinson, Robert (1752?-1825)   62; Figs. 47, 48; Map 5E

Willdey, George (1676-1737)   16, 46; Fig. 10; Map 2H

Wyld, James the elder (1790-1836)   20, 22, 86; Fig. 13; Map 2L

Wyld, James the younger (1812-1887)   22, 86, 89; Fig. 13; Map 2L

Yates, William (1738-1802)   64, 81, 85-89, 91; Figs. 58, 59; Map 5R

GENERAL INDEX

Abram	20, 61
Advance subscriptions	43, 53, 85, 86
Amsterdam	v, 10, 14, 16, 26, 30, 33, 38, 47, 76
Anonymous series - see Smith, William	
Antiquities	55, 57, 63, 64, 82
Antwerp	8, 23, 33
Arnside	55; Fig. 37
Astronomical observations	49, 64, 69, 70
Atlantic Ocean	49, 53
Authorship and labelling of maps	6
Bankruptcy, insolvency	28, 52, 59, 62, 74, 85
Base lines (for surveying)	86
Bird's-eye views	66, 68
Blackburn	3, 26, 61, 78
Blackpool	66, 76, 78
Bolton	28, 35
Bowland	10, 25
British Library	7, 20, 22, 43
Bury	52, 58
Cambridgeshire	47, 85, 89
Canals	81-82, 86, 91
Capital investment	20, 26, 46
Carnforth	30, 35, 61
Cartmel	6, 49, 82
Cartouche	7, 10, 23, 35, 42, 53, 69, 74, 82
Chat Moss	35, 89
Cheshire	16, 26, 35, 45, 63, 68, 85, 86
Children, maps for	45, 66, 68
Civil War, English	14, 32, 43

Clitheroe 6, 50, 52, 82

Coal iii, 69, 74, 86

Coastal shading 10, 57, 61, 63, 70

Coastline form 4, 6, 10, 31, 35, 64, 66, 69, 70, 76

Colouring by hand and printing 6, 8, 10, 23, 25, 28, 33, 57, 80, 91

Compass rose (and true north indicator) 23, 26, 35, 43, 50, 63, 74

Computed miles - see Customary miles

Copper plates, engraving 4, 6, 7, 8, 26, 30, 32, 33, 35, 45, 86

  - plate cost and value 7, 26, 45, 46, 50

  - plate ownership 8, 10, 14, 16, 28, 33, 38, 52, 62, 64, 66, 76

  - plate numbers 23, 55, 78

  - plate mark 7, 61

  - plate wear and cracking 7, 10, 16, 28, 39, 49, 55, 59, 61

  - plate stretching 28

  - plate scrapping 52, 62, 71, 74

  - printing rate 6-7, 26-28

Copper-plate writing 8

Copyright protection and privilege 16, 26, 76, 89

Cornwall 49, 69, 78

Costs and prices of atlases and maps iv, v, 8, 13, 28, 33, 39, 43, 45, 50, 64, 66, 70, 91

County and hundred boundaries/size 3, 4, 16, 42, 55, 57, 70, 78

County towns 26, 45, 81

Cumberland 13, 14, 30, 31, 45, 78

Customary miles (long) 14, 32, 42, 43, 50, 52, 53, 54, 55, 61, 63, Appendix 3

Declination, magnetic - see Variation

Distance scale (or bar) - see Scale bar

Distance tables 32, 52, 78, 86

Distances from London 32, 43, 45, 49, 52, 53, 58, 69, 86

Distortion of Lancashire outline 55, 61, 64, 66, 69, 70, 76, 81

Domesday Book 3, 30

Dublin 66, 70

Edge calibrations 10, 26, 31, 49, 61, 66, 70, 76

English Civil War 14, 32, 43

English miles 50, 61, 63, 66

English national mapping 13, 43, 69, 70, 91

Engraving and costs - see Copper plates

Fictitious coastline	31, 35
Fires at map shops	v, 33, 35, 38, 46, 59
Florin	iv, v, 8, 33, 46
Form lines (sea boundary) - see Coastal shading	
French cartography	69, 70
Furness	1, 4, 26, 76, 89
Garstang	14, 43, 55
Germany	4, 16, 55, 85
Globes	6, 8, 33, 89
Gold medals - see Society of Arts awards	
Gough (Bodleian) Map	4, 6, 7
Greenwich	31, 50, 53, 69, 70, 86
Great Fire of London, 1666	16, 28, 43
Greenwood atlas	78
Grid lines	53
Gulliver's Travels	55
Hachuring	59, 86
Heraldry	10, 13, 14, 16, 33, 39, 42, 52, 54, 61, 81
Hornby	35, 61, 82
Hundreds	3, 4, 16, 20, 26, 55, 89
Ichnographic view	43, 46, 67
Industrial features	70, 86
Ingleborough	14, 26
Ireland	30, 33, 47, 66, 78
Isle of Man	10, 13
Kendal	4, 20, 43
Kent (Ken) Sands	3, 49
Lake District	14, 68, 86
Lancaster	v, 3, 4, 6, 14, 26, 35, 43, 45, 50, 53, 55, 61, 70, 89, 91
- Lancaster Duchy	1, 3, 13, 26
- Lancaster Sands	3, 49
- Lancaster, plan of town	14, 26, 28
Landscape format	39, 47
Landscape-view prints	66-68
Large-scale county surveys	53, 62, 68, 76, 85, 86, 89
Latin, use of	6, 8, 13, 23, 30, 47, 53, 63, 74

Latitude and longitude calibrations   10, 26, 31, 49, 50, 61, 64, 70

Latitude and longitude values   1, 3, 31, 49, 53, 55, 66, 69, 70, 86

Lithography   20, 22, 86

Liverpool   1, 4, 20, 49, 50, 55, 69, 70, 71, 74, 82, 85, 86, 91

Local time   49

Location symbols   10, 14, 35

Long miles - see Customary miles

Longitude origin - see Prime meridian

Lonsdale   1, 3, 69

Lune valley and estuary   35, 70, 89

Lytham   76, 89

Magnetic compass   13, 49

Magnetic north   13, 14, 20, 23, 26, 35, 43, 45, 49, 50, 61

Manchester   1, 14, 28, 30, 43, 49, 50, 57, 58, 91

Manor houses   iii, 14, 45

Manuscripts   1, 4, 6, 10, 16, 20, 43

Mappa Mundi   6, 23

Marine charts - see Sea charts

Market towns   14, 16, 76, 86, 89

Martin (or Marton) Mere   55, 59, 71, 78

Measured miles - see Statute miles

Mercator's projection   10

Merchant Taylors' Company   25, 45

Mersey   1, 4, 10, 68

Milestones   43

Monthly part publication   50, 64, 70, 74, 76, 82, 89

Morecambe Bay   3, 4, 7, 26, 49, 89

Mosses   iii, 14, 35, 89

National mapping - see English national mapping

Newton   50, 54, 61, 82

Norfolk   85, 89

Nuremberg   16, 70

One-inch scale   43, 64, 69, 70, 85, 89

Ordnance Survey   62, 85, 89, 91

Orientation of map   1, 4, 6, 13, 20, 23, 26, 31, 32, 43, 45, 47, 49, 53, 55, 57, 61, 69

Over-sands routes   1, 4, 32

Oxford and Oxfordshire	6, 47, 70
Paper sheet size	iv, 1, 28, 69, 71, 74, 86
Parishes and churches	6, 14, 45, 57, 86, 89
Parks	14, 28, 35
Parliamentary representation	16, 50, 54, 55, 57, 59, 61, 86
Pendle Hill	14, 26
Peutinger Table	43
Place-names	4, 7, 10, 28, 35, 42, 43, 49, 50, 53, 55, 62, 68, 89
Plane table plotting	8, 13, 22
Plates - see Copper plates	
Playing card maps	16, 32, 42-45, 46, 47, 68, 78
Pocket-size atlas	33, 45, 57, 58, 71, 74, 76, 78
Portrait format	39, 47
Postal times and charges	89, 91
Poulton-le-Fylde	55, 82
Preston	4, 14, 50, 52, 55, 61, 62, 91
Prime meridian	3, 10, 31, 48, 53, 69, 70
Quartermaster's Map	16, 20, 33, 71
Railway Time	50
Revolving a book	6, 39, 47
Rhumb lines (loxodromes)	35
Ribble	3, 49, 66, 70, 76
Rivers	4, 10, 14, 20, 25, 28, 30, 35, 47, 53, 55, 70, 82, 89
Roads and road mapping	1, 14, 16, 22, 23, 28, 32, 42, 43-45, 46, 47, 50, 53-55, 57, 58, 59, 61, 63, 64, 68, 69, 71, 74, 76, 81, 86, 89, 91
Printing press	4, 7, 26, 28, 33
Sandbanks and marine surveys	47, 70, 78
Scale of mapping	iv, 1, 6, 14, 20, 23, 26, 31, 39, 43, 53, 54, 61, 63, 64, 68, 69, 70, 74, 76, 78, 81, 85, 89
Scale bar	23, 26, 35, 50, 59, 61, 63, 66
Scenographic view	45, 67
Scotland	v, 4, 30, 33, 47, 58
Scrap copper - see Copper plate scrapping	
Sea charts	3, 28, 33, 35, 47, 52-52, 70
Septentrio	20, 26
Sea-shading	6, 10, 26
Slave trade	71, 74

Society of Arts awards	64, 85, 86
St Paul's Cathedral	49, 53, 58
Staffordshire	46, 47, 85
States (successive for plates)	7, 10, 14, 16, 20, 22, 28, 30, 35, 42, 45, 49, 50, 53, 55, 57, 59, 61, 62, 64, 68, 71, 76, 78, 82
Status symbol	8, 33
Statute miles	1, 6, 14, 20, 23, 43, 50, 53, 54, 57, 59, 61, 63, 66, 69, 78, 86, Appendix 3
Strip-maps	43, 54, 74
Sugar-loaf hills	1, 14, 26
Surveyors	6, 13, 23, 43, 57, 58, 62, 64, 70, 85, 86
Sussex	49, 85, 89
Taxation	43, 52, 57, 89
Textiles	70, 74
Thumbnail maps	32, 78
Thurland	35, 52
Towneley	70
Triangulation	8, 22, 64, 86, 91
True north	6, 20, 31, 43, 49, 50, 53, 55, 71
True north indicator - see Compass rose	
Turnpike roads	47, 81, 86, 91
Variation, magnetic (declination)	35, 43, 49, 50, 61
Wales	4, 6, 8, 13, 16, 26, 30, 32, 42, 43, 45, 55, 64, 69, 70, 71, 78, 82, 85, 89
Warrington	4, 20, 43, 70
Warwickshire	45, 85
Way-Wizer (Wheel Dimensurator)	43
Weekly part publication	57, 58, 59, 61, 64, 81
Westmorland	4, 13, 14, 23, 30, 35, 55, 62, 78
Whitaker map list (1938)	7, 13, 14, 22, 86, 91, Appendix 1; Fig. 3
Wigan	20, 50, 70, 82
Wiltshire	58, 74
Windermere	14, 55
Wirral, the	31, 35, 61
Woodcut	4, 6, 7
Worcestershire	50, 61
York and Yorkshire	3, 4, 13, 26, 35, 43, 45, 50, 52, 55, 62